THE MEANING OF CULTURE

THE MEANING OF

CULTURE

By

JOHN **COWPER POWYS**

VILLAGE PRESS

Printed by Villiers Publications Ltd
Ingestre Road, London NW5

CONTENTS

PREFACE

It is perhaps unwise to attempt any single dogmatic definition of culture; but by approaching the subject first from one angle and then from another it seems as though in a gradual process of elimination and selection a general attitude of mind to this complicated subject may emerge, which being at once more fluid and more comprehensive than any rigid statement, may bring the problem into regions of concrete experience such as would be impossible of attainment even by the most carefully worded theory.

One rather felicitous definition runs as follows—"Culture is what is left over after you have forgotten all you have definitely set out to learn"—and in this sally you get at least a useful warning against associating culture too closely with the academic paraphernalia of education.

INTRODUCTION

In any tentative excursion of this kind, covering so vast a field of human experience, it were certainly advisable at the very start to indicate some of the more obvious limitations of the writer who attempts such a task; for then, at least, the reader will be spared the irritation of growing more and more vexed with the author for not undertaking a task upon which he never dreamed of entering. Let the reader understand then, that the present writer looks at his subject rather from a philosophical and literary point of view than from a scientific or an aesthetic one. Science indeed he does not presume to touch upon at all; and in the matter of the major arts he deals, by reason of quite personal limitations, very little with music and not much more with architecture or sculpture. But in a more subtle direction than that of such definite omissions—and one would have to be a modern Goethe or Leonardo Da Vinci to deal adequately with such a wide chart of human life— the present writer is conscious of certain constitutional prejudices and predilections, which, useful enough in their places as *aperçus* and *points d'appui,* should nevertheless be brought at once into full prominence, so that the reader may know in advance along what general manner of way he is likely to be led, and thus be spared the trouble of girding himself for the journey, if, so to speak, he prefers to travel by rail or by boat, rather than on foot!

The most serious of such confessions of bias in the author of this book is undoubtedly the simplest and the most pardonable—he is an Englishman. Now it is surely undeniable that every great race among our human tribes contributes, when it is a question of cultural qualities, certain very definite gifts to the general stock of human sensations and ideas. And with the possession and bestowal of these gifts, each great race has to confess itself cursed by creative Nature with the defects of its quality. The philosophic originality of the German temper, for instance, is balanced by that lack of critical finesse which is so obvious in many of their most powerful writers and artists. The critical reasonableness of French psychology, on the other hand, seems to reach too quickly—so at least it seems to one's alien taste and foreign exigencies—a certain marbly barrier, a smooth impenetrable wall. The smouldering craters of the Unconscious, for instance, those dark mysterious mine-shafts into the under-side of the cosmos seem to be screwed down, in French literature, under a hermetically, sealed lid; so that the abyss does not heave up its contents amid these analytical niceties and nuances.

The passionate religiosity and desperate psychological clairvoyance of the Russian genius, its strange masochism, its confessional emotionalism, carry for an Anglo-Saxon nature an atmosphere too heady, too excessive, too pitiful and at the same time too cruel. The extraordinary nimbleness and receptivity, also, of the American mind, its indiscriminate cosmopolitanism, its irreverent humour, strike a foreigner with the same kind of shock produced by the poetry of Walt Whitman.

And just as with these other nations there is as much to perplex and bewilder a stranger as to interest him in the racial characteristics, so also with the peculiar gifts of the English temperament. This very English attempt, then, at a definition of culture, covering only about three hundred pages, would no doubt strike the German mind as too concrete, practical, cursory, pragmatical; lacking in that metaphysical depth and philosophical weight which the gravity of the subject demands.

On the other hand, to the average American mind this book might, only too easily, seem pompous, heavy, incoherent, solemn; lacking in the airy touch and playful facetiousness that such a work demands. To the French critical sense, again, a volume of this sort would seem totally devoid of that logical smoothness, that architectural unity, that polished reasonableness, which alone according to their view give value to any human effort. The book in fact must be regarded as a typically English contribution to the study of culture, and this, to the attentive reader, will account for the number of circumstantial concrete instances it contains and for the absence from it of any definite philosophical or aesthetic theorizing. It will also doubtless account for its very inadequate treatment of music, and its rather wilful and eccentric attitude to many of the great modern European ideas. It will also account for the more valuable portions of the book; namely its detailed treatment of the part played in any worthy, personal culture by one's inherent character and by one's habitual attitude to Nature.

The general gist of the book is an attempt to isolate the mysterious human creation known by the name of culture from other equally important, and perhaps more important, achievements of the human mind. In this attempt emphasis is laid upon the special conditions of our modern life, at once ameliorated so greatly and menaced so profoundly by our industrial system.

The mental confusion and moral bewilderment of our age shows itself as much in the intensity of religious revivals as in the general decline of religious faith. What is aimed at here is to find in the instinctive and rationalized habits of human culture itself a sort of working substitute for the simpler religious faith of the past, for its heroic synthesis of so many human activities and emotions; something, in fact, that shall at once awaken us to the magic of life, so overlaid and vulgarized by modern conditions, and calm us and steady us in our intelligent enjoyment of it.

The earlier portion of this book will be devoted to an analysis of the true nature of what we call culture; the later portion to the application of culture to the struggle for existence; how, for example, it reacts upon life, how it is affected by practical necessities, how it overcomes, or is overcome by, various obstacles and enemies, what it would do to the general temper of human society if it were to prevail and what its relation is to the various movements for ameliorating the condition of man, which exist independently of culture.

The line taken in all this is a positive rather than a negative one. The writer feels that it is much easier to give way to bitter onslaughts upon stupidity and obscurantism than to build up, fragment by fragment, a new emotional and mental synthesis; using the sounder stones and bricks and beams that have weathered the storms of the great war and integrating the whole intellectual and sensuous structure around what remains surest and firmest in the consciousness of the individual.

PART I
ANALYSIS OF CULTURE

CHAPTER I

CULTURE AND PHILOSOPHY

The long personal pilgrimage of culture begins with the formulation of one's own philosophy and ends, if I am not mistaken, with an attempt to express this philosophy in such a form and to such a purpose that it may definitely influence, even if only to an infinitesimal degree, the life of the nation to which we belong. Between these two extremes we have to examine as warily as we may, what culture actually is; and then, again, what it will cost us, in concentration and organized effort, to practise it amid the pell-mell of life.

In considering those obscure motions of the mind, wherein our individual consciousness, ceasing to be content with blind responses to its environment, begins to look before and after, it is important to remember that behind all the great controversial names, such as "will," "behaviour," "soul," "First Cause," "the One, the Many," "universe," "multiverse," "good and evil," "substance," "essence," "immortality," there lies some actual feeling or sensation or experience; which, under a quite different name, or perhaps under no name at all, *must still exist,* when the logical fashion of the hour, refusing to use such traditional expressions, has moved on and away.

In attempting to deal with the living emotions, with those nameless subjective feelings which underly such historic words, it seems wiser to direct the introspective mind towards each particular feeling rather by means of the older symbols than by means of the newer ones, just because these traditional names—"will," "souls," "universe," "nature," "ego," and so forth—have by long use on the highroads of human intercourse acquired such a rich, thick, emotional connotation that, however mythological they may be, they are more suggestive of what lies behind all words than the newer, more logical terms, coined by clever modern thinkers, so puzzlingly obscure except to the initiated, and of necessity so abstract and thin.

The art of self-culture begins with a deeper awareness, borne in upon us either by some sharp emotional shock or little by little like an insidious rarefied air, of the marvel of our being alive at all; alive in a world as startling and mysterious, as lovely and horrible, as the one we live in. Self-culture without some kind of integrated habitual manner of thinking is apt to fail us just when it is wanted most. To be a cultured person is to be a person with some kind of original philosophy. And thus the difficult problem arises—how is this philosophy to be developed?

It is clear that there must be a will to philosophize at the very start. This implies a desire to focus such *imaginative reason* as we possess upon the mystery of life. The subtle and imperceptible stages, however, by which this will to think condenses and hardens into a will to live according to one's thought are not always easy to articulate.

Our innermost self, as we grow more and more conscious of it, surprises us again and again by new explosions of feeling drawn from emotional, nervous, and even chemical reactions; but for all its surreptitious dependence on these impulses, its inner report upon its own nature is that it is a clear, hard, enclosed, secretive nucleus with a detached and independent existence of its own. Our reliance upon this introspective report may easily be shaken by logical argument; but it is not often that any argument, however plausible, disposes of the *feeling* of this interior identity, of the *feeling* of this integral "I am I," underlying the stream of our impressions. The truth is that every man and every woman has, consciously or unconsciously, some sort of patched-up, thrown-together philosophy of life, a concretion of accumulated reactions gathered round this nucleus of personality. What, however, denotes the cultured person is the conscious banking up of this philosophy of his own, its protection from disintegrating elements, the guiding of its channel-bed through jungles of brutality and stupidity.

The more culture a man has, the more austerely—though naturally with many ironic reserves—does he abide by his own taste. It is ever the mark of the parvenu in education to chafe and fret till his opinions correspond to the last word of modish sophistication. Culture, however, like aristocracy, goes its own way and does not bother about justifying itself. Why should it justify itself? Thus, in real culture, scope is allowed for the most extreme idiosyncrasies of philosophical opinion. Half-educated people permit their personal vision to be interfered with, to be smoothed out and flattened out, by a slavish respect for modern science or by a conventional respect for traditional religion. The cultured person takes both these dogmatic authorities with a considerable pinch of salt. Science is not everything—nor is religion! The last word is with a certain free poetic humanism that uses both science and religion for its own purposes and is not dominated by either. An educated person can glibly describe what he wishes you to regard as his last ready-made philosophy. A cultured person often finds it very difficult to explain what his philosophy is; but when he does manage to articulate it you feel that this is what he has secretly and profoundly lived by for many a long year. For in a cultured person's life intellectual snobbishness has ceased to exist. He is not interested in the question whether his attitude is "intellectual" according to the current fashion or not. He might even be guilty of a certain malicious satisfaction when it appears so completely out of fashion as to seem naive and simple to the point of imbecility. Real culture has almost always a certain tendency to combine infinite subtlety with a kind of childish naïveté. Thus to the smartly clever it must often appear both affected and foolish. What a perpetual stumbling-block, for instance, is the cultured person's innate predilection for combining extreme opposites in his thought and his taste! His philosophical opinions will be found as a rule, judged by the standards of the merely educated, to be at once startlingly revolutionary and startlingly reactionary. Thus Mr. Wells, valuable and sincere thinker though he is, will never quite satisfy a cultured taste because he is neither revolutionary enough nor reactionary enough. One always feels that a merely educated man holds his philosophical views as if they were so many pennies in his pocket. They are separate from his life. Whereas with a cultured man there is no gap or lacuna between his opinions and his life. Both are dominated by the same organic, inevitable fatality. They are *what he is*.

It is often an astonishment to the erudite philistine how ignorant a really cultured individual can prove to be. The truth is that a man's ignorance is as much a part of the instinctive art of his life as any learning he may acquire.

Both are the expression of his psychic fatality; both are calculated, both habitual.

By what tenuous and filmy degrees the first outlines of a man's original philosophy precipitate themselves on the retina of his vision, like frost-marks upon a window, hardly the man himself can determine. As when a new light falls unexpectedly upon familiar things, he suddenly becomes aware of a certain pattern, a certain tone, a certain peculiar emphasis in his life's scenery which seems to satisfy at once both his good and his evil eye. What he sees seems ordered and beautiful in a particular way, disordered and repulsive in a particular way. He has now his own optimism, his own pessimism. The world lends itself to his interpreting imagination; lends itself to his penetrating malice.

That this personal philosophy already exists before it is brought into conscious articulation cannot be doubted; nor can it be doubted that a thousand floating straws of human speculation, caught at random on wandering airs from the great philosophical systems, have helped to give it form, or at least to make its form visible to its possessor. It is indeed the countless broken shells and the thin black line of the sea's windrow that outline for us the tide's water-mark. When a man is destined to become what we have agreed to name "cultured" it is not long before the tide-mark of his philosophy is outlined for us by his stray and casual words. His philosophy? Call it his life-vision or his life-illusion; for these are fundamentally the same thing. Slowly, as life tightens the knot of our inner being, our outer leaves, like those of a floating water-plant, expand in the sunshine and in the rain of pure chance; but we still are aware of the single stalk under the surface, of the single root that gives meaning to all.

Since we are men and women, however, there soon arrives a moment when our philosophy loses its plant-like passivity. Grown now into a conscious system of thought it draws from the flowing saps and vegetative essences of its organic sub-life an active integral consciousness which feeds upon the spectacle of the world. It projects sensitized antennae, this consciousness; it thrusts forth a moth-like tongue. It selects, refuses, advances and recoils before what confronts it. And yet the further it explores . . . and that is the whole secret of the mysterious process . . . the more does its awareness of its buried life become vivid and paramount. It is perhaps the most important moment of all in the secret growth of our philosophy when we first discover the unbelievable power of the imaginative will in giving a heightened value to our days.

One has to be crafty enough not to be led astray by any trick of verbal logic, however cogent, which questions the efficacy of this imaginative will. Even if our rational view of it were erroneous there would seem to remain something which corresponds to the *interior feeling* that we have; and that, after all, is tantamount to the same thing.

To philosophize with the real wisdom of the serpent and the real harmlessness of the dove it is not necessary to exhaust one's brain upon riddles which are likely enough eternally insoluble. What is necessary, is to experiment with ordinary life; to adjust one's appreciative and analytical powers to all the natural human sensations which are evoked by the recurrences of the seasons, by birth and death, by good and evil, by all those little diurnal happenings which make up our life upon earth.

Too well one knows how the pure reflections of these essences can be destroyed . . . as when a stone is flung into smooth water . . . by any violent gesture or drastic action. Too well one knows how they can be destroyed by the fret and fever of the world. To isolate them, as they form and re-form in the calm-flowing stream of the deeper reality, to contemplate them, to assimilate them, as they pass, this is the true philosophical art.

The disciples of the ancient Greek philosophers were better taught to cope with the chaos of reality than are most of our educated people. A cultured man is not one who turns from a disorganized feverish day to a nightly orgy with Hegel or Bergson. He is rather one for whom the diurnal magic-mirror, whether its fleeting images catch the sun or sink into shadow, offers a vision of the world that becomes steadily more and more his own. To philosophize is not to *read* philosophy; it is to *feel* philosophy. The raw spikes and jagged edges, the sour-tasting dust and wind-blown débris of superficial real life have to be deliberately comprehended, or at least deliberately evaded, before the more secret rhythms, the more recondite patterns of Nature, her humours, her tragedies, her poetry, take shape in the mind. None can call himself a philosopher whose own days are not made more intense and dramatic by his philosophizing. Even if his vision of things be bitter and grim, his world is made more interesting by his pondering upon it, not more commonplace or tedious. This heightened continuity, when a person's days are charged with conscious impressions, is always being banked up by accumulated memories. These the conscious psyche reduces to what one might call a secondary world. For by selecting, refining, sifting and analysing these memories and by assimilating them to her own fatality of intellect, she half-creates and half-discovers a particular universe that is entirely her own. This is the

highest pitch of the art of philosophizing: when the ego
has so adapted itself to the mystery it contemplates and has
so slyly adapted that mystery to itself, that it is no longer
possible for it to suffer the raking, scraping, scooping, and
harrowing misery which maladjustment to the chaos of
superficial reality produces in human nerves.

For although this slowly evolved vision of things, which
is a man's very own, is concerned with what might be called
"life in itself," apart from practical affairs, it must be
remembered that this life in itself is not passively re-
flected, but is something that has been half-created, as well
as half-discovered, by the creative mind. Thus it is impossible to eliminate what is popularly known as the will
from any ultimate philosophizing. But it must be noted
that in this region where philosophy is a part of the psyche's
very life, such will is not used in the sense of a will to
believe but in the sense of a will to select and a will to
reject.

The particular continuity of our deepest life . . . its
accumulative weight of gathered impressions . . . is constantly being made more formidable in the face of the
brutality and the rawness of things by this exercise of our
will. Our receptivity flows with an ever-increasing mo-
mentum along the channel that the will has obstinately
dug to receive it.

Our philosophy does not, when it is formulated after
this fashion, test its truth by our power over others or
over material events. It tests its truth by a certain secret
and stoical exultation known only to ourselves. Such a philosophy could be practised in fact by a person dying of
cancer; or by a madman, in his few lucid moments, in a

barred room. What philosophy can do for a deep organic personal culture is concerned with *contemplation,* with the attitude adopted by the psyche to its environment, and not with any sort of external happening.

Having granted then that the true way of philosophizing is to use our will upon the images, static or fleeting, which surround us; until by the help of memory and habit we acquire the art of moulding the chaos of superficial reality into what we can deliberately concentrate upon or deliberately forget, the natural question arises, what is our attitude likely to be towards the last residual mystery we can imagine, the mystery behind all these fleeting impressions and floating images, behind the universe itself?

Unless the psyche within us—and this is not impossible—be its own God, its own Eternal, its own Absolute, there must be some object, knowable or unknowable, which remains its ultimate cause, substratum, or demiurgic begetter; something that is, in fact, responsible for there being a universe at all or a consciousness to contemplate that universe. Even if the consciousness were its own God and a secret-sharer, beyond conception, in the magic that builds the world, it would still be aware, however extravagant its pride, of levels of creative energy totally beyond its reach. Such levels would represent the ultimate mystery I am referring to, this remote "Unmoved First-mover." Whether this unknown be regarded as one or many, as conscious or unconscious, the psyche retains a place for it among her normal feelings that it alone can fill.

And it would appear that in the lovely-ghastly world, which, in the fatality of our nature, we are all of us half-creating and half-discovering, it is a grim relief and a stoical comfort to concentrate our mind upon this *unknown,* the fountain, whether consciously or unconsciously, of all responsibility.

It would indeed seem that all deep culture must supply itself with some constantly recurrent substitute for what traditionally is known as prayer; and, for the philosophic mind, nothing can serve this purpose but a lonely, wordless, one-sided dialogue with the mystery of mysteries. When one further enquires, in this dim region of intellectual being, what kind of emotions they will be with which this naked and stripped consciousness contemplates this ultimate, the answer is: with intense gratitude and intense defiance! Thus alone, in this way and in no other way, can the feelings excited by the subjective-objective spectacle of life, in all its appalling contrasts, find their apogee of satisfaction.

We are aware of aspects of our world which are too hideous to dwell upon, which can only be borne, so to speak, by being daily forgotten. Under the burden of having to forget these cosmogonic atrocities, the naked and lonely psyche satisfies her nature by a secret protest. In the solitariness of her dialogue with the Infinite she hesitates not "to return to It its ticket." On the other hand *to what else,* finally and instinctively, can the ego look, when in the sudden overbrimming of its cup of happiness, it desires to offer up its unutterable thanks? Thus the dilemma of the self's secret dialogue with that which lies behind its world must remain forever unresolved; divided between the horn of its everlasting gratitude and the horn of its everlasting defiance.

But it matters not so much what the emotional content may be of the psyche's dialogue with the final mystery; what matters is that in the depths of a person's culture there should be some sort of grim, stark, bed-rock philosophizing. It is this basic grimness and starkness that gives to any worthy culture the iron it needs, the formidableness it needs, if it is going to remain undazzled by the brutally glittering surface, undeafened by the brazen voices.

That tender compromise called resignation is only an eloquent name for the dying down, the wearing thin, of the vital impulse in us. It is just here that it would seem of the utmost importance, for occidental minds, to shake off the sad, self-satisfied metaphysic of the Orient where such weary resignation, patronizingly contemptuous of what it regards as the mad illusions of youth, prides itself on its irrefutable wisdom. Far nearer to Nature's secret would seem to be an attempt to get the two spontaneous reactions, of gratitude to Life and of defiance of Life, fused in some way in our solitary contemplations. Thus a return would be initiated to that Homeric simplicity of response, where what is called philosophy cannot be separated from what is called poetry; where the instinctive life-impulse, brimming up from the fathomless reservoirs of Nature, is not poisoned at its source by the tricky perversities of logic; and where finally that stoical imagination which springs from the deepest levels of our being utters the last word.

It is most salutary for our personal culture when, in these "dialogues with mystery," we are compelled to recognize the one-sided and unsatisfactory nature of every rational explanation of the world-riddle. It is just here that the uncultured but educated man finds himself irritated, bewildered, nonplussed, by the sophisticated childishness which exists in the heart of true culture. For it would appear that no scepticism has gone far enough till it has reached the point where almost any magical interpretation of the universe seems truer than almost any scientific one. The permanent mental attitude which the sensitive intelligence derives from philosophy is an attitude that combines extreme reverence with limitless scepticism; and the result of this is that the temper of true culture will be found to be much more akin to the immemorial superstitions of the human race than to the dogmatic arrogance of the last mechanistic theory.

To sum up the argument once more: since the conscious development of our awareness of existence is the very essence of culture, it is necessary to acquire the habit of falling back in our thoughts upon the basic human situation. This situation must be realized in such a way as to be utterly unshakable by any kind of rational doubt. To assure ourselves that no doubt can touch it and that when we sink down upon it we are at the unassailable heart of things, it is necessary to clear our mind of every preconception, whether philosophical or religious. Thus in our lonely communion with the cause of our being there will be no place for optimism or for pessimism. Our personality will simply strip itself bare and will commune with this ultimate power in a concentrated, if one-sided, dialogue. It will feel both gratitude and indignation; not only for itself but for all other sentiencies that are aware of happiness and of unhappiness. Such will be its natural feelings; and such feelings would be the same whether it had lived through a thousand incarnations and were destined for as many more, or whether it had been brought to birth out of non-existence and were destined at death to return whence it came. The next rung, so to speak, in the philosophical ladder, is the recognition by the psyche of its own depths and its own powers. It passes in fact from its colloquy with the mysterious first cause to a searching conversation with itself. Isolated in its inviolable solitude it finds within itself potencies of will and degrees of magnetic force such as it cannot measure or fathom.

Among these forces is the power to regulate thought by the use of thought; in other words, to choose what thoughts shall be indulged in and what shall be dismissed. The discovery that the mind *can* regulate its thoughts, fostering some and dismissing others, is one of the most important stages in the art of self-culture. It is astonishing to note how little this art is practised among us Westerners. Indeed where our art of culture ought to begin is by taking those concentrated habits of mind which the Orient devotes to mysticism and applying them to the rational and imaginative life.

Nowhere is real culture more easily distinguishable from pedantry and philistinism than in its attitude to the great metaphysical systems. The pedant's point of view is the strictly explanatory one. What in every least detail were the opinions of Aristotle, of Hegel, of Spinoza? As to the living application of these doctrines to his own stream of consciousness—that is another matter. The typical philistine, on the contrary, labours under the illusion that all these early systems are steps forward in a steady line of progress. Philosophy, to the philistine, is an evolutionary process, watched over by some sort of brisk dynamic Providence, and culminating in the supreme insight of modern thought. This is far worse than any scholarly pedantry; and it is unfortunate for the simpler intellects of our generation that so many clever expositors of modern ideas take such banalities for granted.

What then, when we resolve to advance with a wary

step in this delicate affair, is the wiser and more fruitful way of approach? Is it not to treat each one of these great philosophic systems as if it were contemporary with ourselves? Is it not to recognize them as all equally true; but, like poetry and painting, representing this truth through endless variations of imaginative reason?

It is not very difficult for a malicious psychologist to track down the emotional self-scourging, the furtive cruelty, the secret pride, the serpentine will to power, in these philosophical systems. But what vistas of mystical sensation, what luminous mental landscapes, what avenues of planetary reverie are opened up when one follows these voyagers through the void!

The sort of continuous life-awareness that I have been endeavouring to disentangle from the more vivid shocks of experience is surely the best background for a genuine use of these massive systems of thought. How provocative, for example, is the great difficult Platonic doctrine of the "Ideas," those mysterious godlike Entities that overshadow "the Good, the True and the Beautiful" with hints, glimpses and overtones of some unutterable Absolute. What an escape from the endless teasing antinomies of life offers itself in the magic *Triads* of Hegel; wherein we suddenly discover that the very fatality of our own thought processes, the contemplation of contemplation, *is* the Absolute; and the teeming concretions of Nature *only the same thing* on its spiral way to fulfilling the divine circle!

None of these great philosophical visions are adequately appropriated to our use until our aesthetic sense and our imaginative power have laid hold upon them. They are not a part of our culture till we have enjoyed them like bodily feelings, until they have associated themselves with what we daily see and touch of earth and air and sky and the chance groupings of people and things, under the fluctuating lights and shadows of intermittent recognition. What a planetary sensation, for example, dark, rank and sweet as a hidden vice, flows through our nerves when we first apprehend the formidable conception of Schopenhauer's "Absolute Will," driving us forward on its heaving universal tide, until we escape its obsession by pure aesthetic contemplation or by a purer renunciation! What a world-drama of spiritual tension summons us to shake the dust of the market-place from our feet as we vision the ice-cold heights touched by the "eternal noon" of Nietzche's Zarathustra! How exciting, in their sly, caressing feminine-feline logic, are the iridescent arguments by which Bergson leads us to substitute for Reason itself some incredible process of intuitive under-life!

All these visions of the unsolved mystery are equally true. They resemble the pictures of the great artists. We see life under their spell as Velasquez sees it under his, and then as El Greco sees it, or Rembrandt or Picasso. The mind of him who is bent upon making a living use of philosophy soon discovers how unwise it is to see the world through any other windows save those which he has polished and stained for himself. But the colours in these windows of his can be most cunningly mingled; a little green from Plato, a little yellow from Hegel, a little scarlet from Nietzsche. And when we stand back a few paces from our philosophic aperture or pass it with a hurried glance, how beautifully such colours fuse and blend—merging soon enough, however, into that dominant life-tint of our own deepest intellectual fatality!

The value of philosophy to any organic culture is that

it thickens and enriches our universe of vision. Incidentally a little metaphysical reading saves us, as nothing else can, from that slavish adherence to popular scientific catchwords which is so barbarous a fault in many clever moderns. It is not so much that we come to accept any definite theory of the universe from our metaphysical studies. It is that we acquire a shrewd inkling of the amount of attic salt with which all fashionable scientific theories should be liberally sprinkled. We learn how not to be swept off our feet by any new logic of a Russell or a Whitehead, by any new generalization of psychoanalyst or behaviourist. In fact the great gift of metaphysical reading is that it gives a person the feeling that there is some truth in every vision, all truth in none.

We learn further, as our culture brings our philosophy into closer and closer touch with life, that the truth of each great system lies in its general atmosphere rather than in any unanswerable train of argument. No man, however learned, can be called a cultured man while there remains an unbridged gap between his reading and his life. It is for this reason that the deliberate tone of character evoked by the old stoics is a nobler and truer philosophic temper than any rationalized realism or idealism such as leaves the will undisciplined and the imagination undeveloped.

A philosophy of one's own, grown tough and flexible amid the shocks of the world, is a far more important achievement than the ability to expound the precise differences between the great philosophic schools of thought. It is for this reason that the writers of what might be called applied philosophy—such as Plato, Montaigne, Goethe, Wordsworth, Emerson, Pater, Proust—are far more valuable to one's individual growth than Hume or Kant or

Spencer or Whitehead. The chief advantage of a wide reading in philosophy is that it gives one both the scepticism to stand up against every dogmatic claim and the imagination to treat with reverence and humility every original hint and illuminating suggestion.

CHAPTER II

CULTURE AND LITERATURE

The reading of books can become a drug, a vice, an obsession; something that weakens the very roots of a person's resistance to the miseries of life, something that corrodes his power of getting things under control. Where, however, our reading is assimilated by our whole inner nature and orientated towards our own secret cultural purpose, literature gives us more "iron," more penetration, more philosophy, more character.

The person who uses literature to the best effect is he whose private vision of things has been so integrated and clarified that it is as if he were himself a writer. For although this mythologizing of one's own identity and its projection upon reality can exist without our having written a single word, it is this way of life and this way alone that makes the essence of every writer's imaginative world.

There are book-lovers, of course, who are so bookish as to find every sort of reality detestable; unless it can be given a sort of literary twist, or can be made to remind them, in some detail or other, of a favourite author. Most of us, however, in the cross-currents of existence, have gathered up a more or less original response to things, a response which, on the imaginative plane, corresponds to the created worlds of the great writers. It is when we sit down to enjoy a stimulating book that this interior response of ours is allowed to sink into temporary passivity. We are, for the nonce, hypnotized by this alien mind. While we read our world is Balzac's world, not ours; Henry James' world, not ours; Herman Melville's world, not ours. But when, on the contrary, we plunge once more into the stream of life, although now and again we are tempted to think— "How like Henry James!—How like Dickens!"—what really has happened is that our private response has been made more intensely itself than it was before. It has not suddenly ceased to be itself and become the response of Goethe or Emerson or Hardy. It has become itself twice over; and this has happened to it because of its assimilation of these great writers' moods into its own mood.

The question as to how far each one of these various transmutations of reality represents an essence that really and truly exists, like a Platonic Idea "Eternal in the heavens," is still an open question. Certainly the thrill one gets from a sudden flash of insight in a great writer seems to be connected with a certain faith that this insight which has pleased us so much represents an authentic objective discovery.

For example, it seems hard to believe that the curious excitement which is stirred up in us by the careful, hesitant, intensely conscious receptivity of Miss Dorothy Richardson, her revelations of the minute changes that forever take place, none exactly repeating another, among the material surfaces of inanimate things and among the intangible surfaces of human minds, is not caused by a feeling that we are getting into touch with something more permanent in the world than one individual's emotions.

But whether our separate visions of things are eternally and fatally subjective, or whether they approximate, first in one way and then in another, to some hidden reality that exists, independently of us all, as if it lay mirrored in the mind of an Eternal Being, the fact remains that to have consciously cultivated a definite attitude in ourselves with regard to life is the best way to get a heightened awareness of how the air tastes, so to speak, in these diverse "foreign" minds.

To realize the advantage that a person who loves books has over one who cares nothing for them, consider the contents of two separate human heads whirling through a New York subway tunnel. Both these heads are covered with conventional hats. Both are staring helplessly at the subway advertisements. Both are swaying to and fro with a dense crowd of other human heads. Both are preserving an expression of democratic patience. But there the resemblance ends. The un-bookish head, likely enough endowed by Nature with a whimsical philosophy all its own, has probably been so debauched by its daily reading of newspapers and magazines that its only humour consists in a pathetically standardized facetiousness. Such facetiousness is no doubt at this very moment playing grimly enough over very practical problems. The angry or the sarcastic words of our gentleman's employer . . . the worry about his unpaid doctor or furious landlord . . . his wretched quarrel over God knows what, with his difficult sweetheart . . . such matters, gone over and over again in this harassed mind, throw their fretful patterns over the pictures of soap and tooth-paste and toilet-powder. On the other hand his thoughts may be complacent and self-satisfied; his curiosity piqued by some recent scandalous incident, may be pleasantly provoked to humorous ponderings. It is quite possible to live a busy, entertaining, and eminently respectable life, independent altogether of literature; but in such a case it will probably be concrete objects, realistic situations, external shocks rather than any kind of fanciful dreaming that will fill a person's head.

But what about that other human skull? If one could visualize mental impressions one would be able to observe, floating in and out of this opaque, bony structure, how many airy clouds of fanciful craziness! *This* human head would doubtless in any case dream its dreams; but now, in its present pendulous position, when the charm of its own vision of things shrinks and wilts under reality at its worst, now is the moment when the imaginative worlds created by great geniuses, long ago dead, may, if the mental will is strong enough, come to that poor head's rescue. Under more normal conditions these imaginary "worlds" would serve, when our book-lover was reminded of them, to rouse him to mould reality after his own secret pattern. But now, driven inwards, driven back upon itself, his mind struggles to fling the magic of these real-unreal worlds, like a sorcerer's hypnosis, over this whirling panorama of the raw and the crude. From Charles Lamb's "Essays," for example, why should he not be snatching something that might hover ironically and with a rich mellowness between himself and those violent tooth-pastes, between himself and those rows of monotonous grey hats and black boots? Then there would arise in that Manhattan tunnel a friendly assemblage of old-word humours, a fragrance, as it were, of old folios, old wainscotted hall-ways, old gardens and purlieus of old college courts!

But more relevant perhaps to the nature of the motley spectacle before him might there not float and eddy round such a head quite a different host of airy sprites . . . the grotesque-sentimental population of Dickens' reckless fancy? Weeping, chuckling, leering, grimacing, *this* cloud of lively hobgoblins might bear a resemblance to our traveler's strap-supported neighbours. Hardly a photographic resemblance; a cerebral phantasmagoria rather, wherein a chance-tossed crowd of preoccupied New Yorkers is transformed into fairy-story ogres and angels!

But it is not only when in contact with the great outer world that a person's saturation with literature thickens by a phalanx of portentous witnesses his vision of the familiar. Alone in one's room of a late evening, bending over the fire, with the night-sounds of the city or the night-silences of the country flowing through one's absent-mindedness, how deeply does one's inkling of the nature of life's wild dream-stuff respond to the gestures of Dostoievsky's fatality-masks! Let them beckon to us, these living figures, from amid their red coals! They are more than characters in fiction, these people of Dostoievsky. They are apocalyptic prophecies of psychic ecstasies, only to be revealed when some use-and-wont shutter of the human mind swings back in some pentecostal wind! Furtively at this moment can we follow the steps of Stavrogin as he stumbles through the mud to drink tea from Kirilov's samovar or to endure the furious incoherence of Shatov as that strange man makes of the God he cannot believe in the very *raison d'être* of his desperate life. It will be ourselves and not Ivan Karamazov who will *know,* in a terrible under-knowledge deep down below all consciousness, that when we went off on our little business trip at our petulant father's bidding we deliberately planned the old man's abominable end! Nor will that ghastly dialogue between the prince and Natasia Philippovna's mad lover draw itself out through the long sultry

hours over the girl's silent body witho⌐
there, in those caverns of red coals, o⌐
we, our very selves, will be watching a⌐
and sharing in its monstrous terror. And h⌐
while from the wretched tales of contemporary b⌐
there only rises within us a wretched nausea of outrageu
nerves, or, at best, a simple human pity and indignation,
there should mount up from these Dostoievsky tragedies a
strange quivering beauty, that beyond all and in spite of
all, seems to avenge and to absolve the human race? Is it
that in the great moments of these heart-piercing novels
we touch the fringe of some unguessed-at Absolute of feeling, which, in "the dark backward and abysm" of human
suffering, hints at unspeakable consolation? Or is it simply
that art itself, creating a reality beyond reality, turns with
its demiurgic finger the intolerably pitiful into the symboli-
cally tragic?

A person certainly does not realize all in a moment the
influence that literature exerts over human minds, the
power it has of transferring to one's real experience that
mythical heightening which it diffuses through its imaginary world. It is indeed only after we have saturated ourselves in these things, only after we have read these books
over and over again, that the charm begins properly to
work. But delayed though it may be, the moment will come
at last when we find ourselves better able to cope with our
own misadventures because of what we have caught, let
us suppose, from the heroic fantasies of the author of Don
Quixote, or from the sly humours of the author of Tristram Shandy.

One of the most invaluable clues to that difficult casuistry
that keeps the integrity of the ego intact amid the rough-

-tumble of life can be derived from the writings of
Henry James. But neither does the spacious aroma of this
high secret reveal itself at the first encounter; too diffused
is it in the provocations of plot, too involved in the com-
plications of character. By degrees, however, as we read—
say "The Golden Bowl"—for the second or third time, it
dawns upon us that these punctilious and roundabout approaches to the quintessence of life, these wavering and reluctant moth-hoverings about the problems of good and
evil, have a definitely significant worth in one's personal ad-
judication of human values, as one goes through the world;
a worth, that, although implicated here with the cunning
craftsmanship of a rich aesthetic creation, is in reality a
redoubtable asset to the armoury of one's own private life-
weapons.

But it is by no means only from ostensibly "creative"
works that a person can strengthen in himself that mysterious intellectual magnetism that enlarges the circumference
of his ego. No writer conveys more subtle mastery, for
instance, of the habit of imaginative concentration than
does Walter Pater, even when working in the sphere of in-
terpretative criticism. To many devotees of what might be
called the "Aesthetic à la Mode" Pater's famous methods
of style and treatment seem antiquated and even affected;
but to anyone who has made that first grand cultural plunge
which implies the reduction to a *spiritual contemporaneousness* of all past methods, the stimulus afforded by this noble
and meticulous fastidiousness is second to none.

No one, for example, is more alive to the essential art
of forgetting than Walter Pater. To treat all the litter and
débris of the commonplace as though it did not exist is one
of the deep secrets of his imaginative device in the handling

of existence. One learns from him too that while there are certain shocking and ghastly possibilities—that of spiritual annihilation for example, or the grim chances of a sudden violent death—which can be treated with tragic exultation, there are other horrors in the world which if they are dwelt upon long and closely mean a risk of sheer madness. But the essence of Pater's genius and the mental trick from which the richest profit can be wrung is his way of associating the spiritual vision of his artists and philosophers with the thousand and one little physical aspects of their material environment. No one is more of an adept than he in indicating the manner in which the various inanimate objects which touch the sensibility of exceptional minds affect the symbols of their thought. External objects of all kinds, landscapes, houses, gardens, furniture, the fabrics of dress, the qualities of food and drink, hot and cold airs, moist and dry airs, the stuff of the soil, the feeling of masonry, the way the light falls, the way the darkness flows— all these things, as he introduces them in his slow, careful, reticent, economic way, yield up their recondite essences and grow little by little to be incorporated and embodied in the shapes and contours of the particular thought for which he is seeking the precise formula.

More cognizant of course than Pater of the especial problems thrust upon us by modern life, Marcel Proust, too, is a writer from whose tricks of sensibility, quite apart from the convoluted fascination of his dramatis personae, much illumination can be transferred to our own wayfaring. Awareness! And again and again *awareness!* For one does surely come at last to recognize that it requires as much effort, as much stoical austerity, to shake off those heavy vapours of use-and-wont which betray us into taking the passing moments for granted, as to devote ourselves to some great ideal cause.

A most poignant test of one's aptitude for such cultured intensity of outlook may be found in one's attitude to the writings of James Joyce. Liberated once for all from the snobbishness of assuming that what is new is better than what is old, we have a perfect right to wash our hands of James Joyce if he only outrages us, or on the other hand to exploit his genius to the limit if he suits our humour. What, of course, we have not the right to do is to denounce him roundly as an enemy of all decency. But it will indeed only be a certain type of cultured person—the type who is driven by a strange demonic urge to wallow savagely in the rank ooze of the great river-bed of modern life; in its slang, its psychological catchwords, its mechanical toys, its circus-manias, its furious alternations between Atheism and Catholicism, its brutal eroticism—who will be able to snatch from Joyce's ferocious philology, from his excrement-obsession, from his sublime scavenging, the oil which is required for the feeding of the sacred flame.

It is very noticeable that in the overtones and undertones of great prose, whether it be fiction or otherwise, the profounder racial attributes are untranslatable. Not only are they untranslatable—just as is the rarest poetry—but they tend to pass unrecognized by all except those who have the same blood in their veins. This seems to be especially true of the work of Thomas Hardy. Without some measure of an English strain in one's being, it is doubtful how far even the most Nature-loving mind can do full justice to the taut, tense, uncompromising artistry of this great craftsman. But if once such grey, sombre, incisive handling—all form, scant colour—adapting and adjusting itself to the contours of reality like the blade of a plough to the unevennesses of a flinty pasture, has conveyed its stark integrity to your vision, then, whenever you set out for a walk through any countryside that has the least English quality, you will find that all your impressions of the way, the white road crossing the hill-top, the noon-drowsed grasses on the high banks making arabesques of filmy patterns against the sky, the motionless branches of the Scotch firs carrying like tattered gipsy rags the mental burdens of so many forgotten wayfarers, can arrange themselves into forms of such intense significance that they write their runes, as if with a remorseless engraver's tool, upon the brain that once yields up to them.

To turn, however, from earth-symbols to ocean-symbols. In one's passage through the world it is impossible to escape noticing how vibrant a response is roused in one nature, and again *not* in another nature, by certain scenes, certain episodes, certain pregnant atmospheres. Such a scene, hitting one onlooker to the heart while it is utterly disregarded by another, might well happen to be the unlading of a ship at a darkening water-front or at the crowded foreign docks of some big mercantile city. How easily all this might pass you by, completely unrecognized, if you had not been a reader of Joseph Conrad. But, if you have been, it will prove not only the laborious stevedores at the gangway, not only the anxious Captain Anthony on the bridge, not only the caustic, nervous group of petty officers, not only the pleasure-drugged bewildered seamen who will excite your interest. Your eyes will wander presently into the interior of some little chandler's shop in the street nearby, caught by the tar-smelling cavernous darkness, by the coils of rope, by the polished poop-lanterns, by the mysterious nautical instruments, and behold! that stooping figure, so youthful and yet so fatally isolated from normal life, just now engrossed with that elderly skipper—why, it is Lord Jim himself, poised for a season again like some desperate migratory bird, before making another reckless flight!

That is the whole thing. A mind that is totally uncultured gets its own especial thrills, no doubt, from a raw direct contact with unmitigated experience; but the cultured mind approaches everything through an imagination already charged with the passionate responses of the great artists; so that what it sees is a fragment of Nature double-dyed, so to speak, a reach, a stretch, of time's whirling tide, that carries upon its chance-tossed eddies the pattern of something at once transitory and eternal.

What any intensely conscious personal culture is always seeking from literature is an enhancement of its own peculiar vision. With this as its secret purpose it is extraordinary how various, how far-fetched are the Fortunate Isles from the shores of which it brings its cargoes home to port. A cultured reader's bookshelves present indeed a very different appearance from those of a specializing student or from those of a collector of first editions. These accumulate their books for some purpose alien to their diurnal impressions from the life-stream. The cultured man reads in order that this life-stream may itself take on a peculiar tinge, the reflection in those waters of his mind's assimilations. And thus side by side in such a person's bookshelves very strange companions will look out together upon the world. Since it is the essence of life that concerns him—how life really looks from the point of view of such as have pressed through to the living sap—we may expect to find a book like Goethe's "Conversations with Eckermann" sedately reposing between Montaigne's "Essays" and some volume from the last surprising installments of Miss Dorothy Richardson's "Pilgrimage."

The rank sweet-natured egoism of Montaigne—that earthy sunburnt "physicalness," whereby the shameless bodily senses are accepted on their own terms, not as ends in themselves but as Nature's unbetraying milestones on the great toll-pike of reality—does not fall so out of place when it finds itself cheek by jowl with such a book as Miss Richardson's "Interim" or "Revolving Lights." From the famous "Essays" one learns the trick of a sturdy, masculine *profanity of detachment*. From Miss Richardson one learns the exact feminine counterpart of this. In both it is a case of "born fresh every day!" Yes, from both these writers, when one descends to the bedrock, underlying their honey-sweet thrills, we learn that a rich, relaxed, ecstatic happiness is something that has to be fought for afresh every day—fought for by convoluted mental tricks, fought for by lying back on certain forms of sensuality, fought for by remorselessly beating away those "ideal" treacheries wherein the insane spirit of man seeks to murder Nature.

Miss Richardson's heroine might easily, like Montaigne, have caused herself to be awaked before dawn, so that she might taste the full sensation of going back to sleep, in that little attic of hers in Tansley Street, to the tune of St. Pancras' bells! Just as we gradually gather up from Montaigne a not easily definable attitude—and yet it is an attitude—to the spectacle of life; so from the history of Miss Richardson's young lady—and one comes to know the wisely selfish Miriam as well as one knows one's own family—a hardly less important secret steals by subtle degrees into one's intelligence. For just as Montaigne makes of relaxed and most natural sensualities a series of clues that lead us to the edge of the subtlest human pieties; so, from the proud secretive raptures of Miriam over her roofs, her walls, her carpets—their very dust a sacred mystery!—over her abstemious sunlit breakfasts, over her wet lamplit pavements, her bells of St. Pancras, her barrel-organ tunes, her first lilac-buds, her southwest winds, we can derive a solitary, sub-human sense of life that is of the deepest value to our awareness of the under-tides of our own being. What one derives indeed from the reveries and soliloquies of this heroine of Dorothy Richardson, who is in a sense the best-known character in modern fiction, is a formula of culture totally independent of success, of fame, of money (beyond bare necessity), of religion, of friendship, and of every sort of scientific knowledge! It is a formula that leaves the psyche free to give herself up at every fortunate escape into quiescence, to all those impalpable outflowings, lovely and evasive as odours on the air, which our senses receive, like the projected eidola of Epicurus, from the inanimate presences about us.

There is one particular prose-work the spiritual reaction to which, with its imaginative after-taste, is so penetrating and peculiar that it would be a pity not to call attention to it just here. This is Doughty's "Arabia Deserta." The singularity of this extraordinary book is that from its pages one is able to arrive at a personal conception of what such a primeval existence, lived in a majestic closeness to Nature, dignified by the laws of immemorial ritual, touched by a tragic and tender courtesy in that cosmogonic desolation, really feels like. Certainly in "Arabia Deserta" what I have in mind as the essence of culture is justified as a legitimate purpose for the whole of life. These

Bedouin Arabs of Doughty's explorings, although greedy, selfish, tricky, treacherous and lecherous, have—throughout their gesture-ornamented life—a rich rare human dignity that nothing seems able to diminish or abrogate.

In catching the life-heightening accents from the life of these people one realizes what a deep part is really played in any adequate culture by what Lord Chesterfield calls *"les manières, les agrémens, les graces."* In "Arabia Deserta" this aristocratic good-breeding is associated with the barest necessities of existence, with the bedrock ritual, so to say, of the "bread and salt" of life. These *manières, agrémens,* and *graces* become here the poetic *ascesis* of an existence pruned of everything but the naked essentials. Human emotions are banked up here till they are stripped of all irrelevancies, fripperies, frivolities. One has the feeling that one is isolated between these blinding sandstorms and these burning rocks till the naked soul is left completely alone with Allah, the All-merciful, the All-compassionate. The style of Doughty is so saturated with the vocabulary of the old great English writers that to appreciate "Arabia Deserta" at all is a good proof that one has advanced a certain distance in one's pilgrimage of literary culture. An even greater proof than what one gets from Doughty, however—indeed a convincing proof that one's aesthetic sophistication is an authentic thing—would be one's appreciation of the incommunicable quality of style in Sir Thomas Browne's "Hydriotaphia" or "Urn-Burial." The recognition of the particular kind of eloquence that has the power, in the midstream of its gigantic imagery, to reveal a humorous awareness of its own extravagance is a recognition that an unbookish person would rarely have the wit to feel; any more than he would be able to catch the myste-

rious echoes that follow these great reverberating paragraphs, like the very feet of the "hungry generations"
themselves, treading down the memory of the perpetuity of
mortality.

It is a memorable moment in one's intellectual life when
one realizes that it is not learning for learning's sake, or
knowledge for the sake of knowledge that is the object of
our secret struggle with inertia and futility. It is simply
that we may enjoy the most exciting sensations that life
offers; and enjoy them over the longest possible extension of
time. Among such sensations one of the most thrilling is
that vague feeling of old countryside romance which emanates from certain far-off highways and certain remote
villages. Standing upon some old stone bridge where the
moss grows green and untouched on the curve of the dark
arches above the water, one often feels that there is a silent
unspeakable secret hovering about such places that no
writer has ever really caught. Perhaps these are things that
cannot be caught; but, if they ever are, it will be by a mind
that has made of such memories a rich, dim background, a
background full of supernatural power that has the strength
to push back, if not to obliterate, the crude pressure of
modern preoccupations. Such a mind was that of Emily
Brontë. Even if your nature finds something monstrous and
shocking about the physical brutalities in "Wuthering
Heights"—the cruelties of Heathcliff to Isabella and to his
own son—it yet remains that around that desperate love-
affair there have been gathered such impressions of rain and
storm, of flying rooks and of tossing clouds crossing distorted moons, of drenched moor-lanes full of last year's
piled-up beech-leaves, that the drift of romance across one's
mind, as one reads, absorbs everything else. "Wuthering

Heights" is indeed a terrific emanation—the breaking out of an electric storm—from that obscure reservoir of unexpressed yearnings that most hearts conceal under a thousand decorous masks. To lose the power of imaginative sympathy with their dark thunderous ways were to subside upon a sort of death-in-life! From such a death-in-life Emily Brontë exultantly releases us, as if she were herself one of those strange mythic figures in William Blake's pictures.

The place occupied in the older times by poetry seems in our own day to be occupied by imaginative prose. The rôle of culture among modern minds must imply, therefore, an attempt to turn all the critical searchlights we can summon upon contemporary writings, choosing what stimulates us and avoiding what disintegrates and confuses us. The desirable effect upon one's mind of imaginative literature is not to strengthen one's memory or enlarge one's learning, or to inspire one to gather together a collection of passages from "great authors"; it is to encourage one to learn the art of becoming a "great author" oneself; not in the sense of composing a single line, but in the sense of sufficiently detaching oneself from the chaotic spectacle of reality so as to catch on the wing that fleeting loveliness of which no genius has the monopoly and which only the stirred depths of one's own deepest nature can prevail upon to pause in its eternal flight.

The difference between an educated mind and a cultured mind is that the former tends to use, in a quite literal sense, the great achievements of the past as academic standards by which to measure the achievements of the present; whereas the latter assimilates, spontaneously and freely, what best suits its own individual mental fatality, in both past and present. The educated mind is proud to be able to register any pleasure at all in reading Montaigne, let us say, or "The Anatomy of Melancholy"; whereas the cultured mind nourishes its own original sensibility—of which every person has at least the rudiments—upon those various imaginative, humorous, spiritual, analytical moods, which tally best with its inherent bent, apart altogether from where they may be found.

Thus, while an educated mind might love to display its pedantry by berating Anderson, Hemingway, the Sitwells, Aldous Huxley, T. S. Eliot, Dr. Williams, E. E. Cummings, Dos Passos, Joyce, Wyndham Lewis, from the viewpoint of the old writers, and while a clever modern mind might, in its prejudice and ignorance, eulogize these contemporaries while it relegated to oblivion the masterpieces of a thousand years, the kind of mind I am attempting to outline possesses enough naturalness and enough sophistication to extract the quintessence of both "old" and "new" and to recognize that *there is much more resemblance between old and new* than either the old-fashioned pedant or the modernistic fanatic would in their one-track notions dream as possible.

As a matter of fact what is called "Literature" plays a much larger part in the creation of those impalpable "worlds," in which we all live, than one always recognizes. A chaotic flood of impressions rolls in upon us, amorphous and mountain-high, and what is it that selects from this meaningless mass? What is it that gives this tidal wave of sensations any kind of intelligible significance? Nothing but tradition! And how is tradition expressed? In words! Generally in words that are so heavily encrusted with images and feelings that we forget that after all they are only words! Let no one try to maintain that words are too remote from reality to possess this power. They cannot be remote from reality when they create reality. The individual universes of impression and feeling in which we all live are as a matter of fact penetrated to the core by literary catch-words. The blunt, brutal, downright realism, so popular at the moment, is not one bit more close to Nature than the sentimental rhetoric or the dignified reticence of those habits of behaviour and expression from which it is a violent reaction. Reality is a thousand times more subtle and complicated, more labyrinthine in its retreats and evasions, than the dream-world of the most recondite idealist. It is also a thousand times more stark and bleak than the crudities of the most ferocious realists. It is both these, because it is the Protean offspring of the psychic embraces of every sensibility that exists with the original plastic life-stuff.

Literature being a congeries of organized word-patterns, every unit of which swirls up, bidden, unbidden, from unconscious race-traditions and half-conscious personal impressions, it must itself act and react upon each individual experience. We are tempted to treat as pure direct perception what is actually a series of mirror-pictures, whereof the images are created and sustained by the subtle auras of words. Persons who are proud of being well-educated but who are in reality totally uncultured are always inclined to separate what they call "literature" from what they call "life." The former they endeavour to enjoy in itself, as a sensation apart from the rest, an escape, a distraction, an anodyne; while the latter is simply taken for granted as the element they swim about in.

What they mean when they talk of "life" is something that belongs to the pressure of the practical world; something that has to be dealt with by the help of a series of resolute human gestures; gestures which have been consecrated by age-long habits of conventional behaviour as the proper response to such a world.

But there is, in reality, no such thing as this practical "life," opposed to literature and free from any tinge of literature.

The essence of literature hovers round us all the time. Whether we are writers, whether we are readers, or unable so much as to read or write a word, it flows forth continually from certain chance groupings of palpable, visible things. It emanates from shapes, forms, sounds, odours, events, situations. The atmosphere which encircles our planet is like those air-regions described by Rabelais through which the vessel of Pantagruel sailed. It is positively thick and sultry with the as-yet-unembodied essences of words.

Quite apart from writing or reading there is always going on a magical inter-vibration, a creative movement, between race-made words and individual impressions. We all move to and fro in a fluctuating mist of pseudo-verbal, pseudo-sensory images. These images are nothing less than the protoplasmic world-stuff of every kind of literature. Men of genius give shape to these floating nebulae, to these hovering simulacra, until some palpable organic form swings free in space. What has been once snatched out of the "casing air" now moves through that air on its own orbit. Limbo is thus ravished; new "worlds" are created; and upon the ambiguous coasts between mind and matter the wave-curve of beauty is petrified in mid-descent.

It is the cultured mind rather than the educated that senses this constant interpenetration between the "auras" of intelligible words and the "auras" of what we call "inanimate" things. The literary mind and the un-literary mind look at the same crowded platforms from the windows of the same subway express. The essence of literature is there, for all the vulgarity and the garishness, and both types of mind respond to it. It is only that the literary mind is aware of what it responds to while the other takes it for granted.

So also with what one observes in the crowded streets. The sensation of "blueness," for example, as it is glimpsed between the tall buildings, ceases for both types of mind to be a mere sensation because of all the quasi-literary traditions that hang about one single word. The word "sky," the word "cloud," the word "grass," the words "autumn leaves"—these apparently arbitrary syllables—carry with them so cumulative a weight of human association that they fling a complicated atmosphere about the simple sensations of "blue" or "green" or "white" or "red."

One of the most interesting features of modern literature is its trick of exploiting the crudest forms of slang, the most brutal aspects of megalopolitan amusements, the most unromantic developments of mechanistic science, to startling imaginative effect. This only confirms our view that the "protoplasm," so to speak, of the finest literature floats and drifts, as the wind blows, round the unlikeliest places. But the more cultured, in the sense here advocated, a human mind may be, the more serpentine will be its power of adjusting itself both to the ivory towers of the old-fashioned aesthetic responses and to the circus-tent sawdust of the new.

What we call "literary taste" changes like all other mortal fashions. Just at present we are living in a curious transition between an age of pseudo-scientific realism and an age of pseudo-scientific classicism. The essential cravings of the human heart, however, being what they are, it is impossible to believe that the shifting of the psychic compass-needle between the north-north-west of Theodore Dreiser's naturalistic objectivity and the south-south-east of Paul Valéry's depersonalized precision will be more than a passing phase.

All good literature is spread out, like a Platonic over-world of ideal forms, just a little above the "real world" in which we spend our material being; and it will not be long ere those elements, at present slighted, of romance and sentiment are summoned back to earth from their temporary exile by the magnetic lodestones of new imaginative adventurers.

CHAPTER III

CULTURE AND POETRY

Poetry, considered as an art, is the expression of a certain aspect of life, which for the moment I must content myself by defining simply as *the poetical element*. The deliberate heightening of one's life by the aid of this mysterious and fluctuating quality in things seems to be an inevitable impulse in the mentality of any nature worthy of the title "cultured." But what precisely *is* this quality? What *is* this floating element in life that the human race by an overtone of universal agreement has come to name the poetical? We can at least narrow down its field by indicating what it is not. It is not the ideal. It is not the beautiful. It is not the artistic. It is not the noble. It is not the moral. So much at least we can say. But, approaching the thing itself more closely, can we not, by means of concrete examples, arrive at some notion of what constitutes its essence? I will proceed to point out—and not blindly or simply at random—the sort of objects, that, without reluctance, most men and women would agree to call by this name. As I enumerate things of this kind, the reader will, I believe, find little to quarrel with in my feeling that they have something—though it is not easy to say what—in common between them all. But whatever this evasive essence of the poetical element may be, it is from this, from this floating and fluctuating quality, shared by so many things, that the written art of poetry draws its selected material.

Loaves of bread . . . honey in the honeycomb . . .
summer hay-stacks and spring withy-beds . . . the flames
of candles . . . the flight of birds . . . the darting of
shoals of fish . . . the shadows of clouds . . . the rising
and sinking of the sun . . . old buildings, old rituals, old
mythologies . . . the annual procession of the seasons . . .
weeds and shells at the ocean's edge, wet pebbles and the
thin black windrow . . . rain on roofs . . . thunder on
horizons . . . murmuring of brooks, sweetness of grass
. . . sadness of stirred leaves . . . the deep symbolic
meaning of such objects as a plough, a sword, a grindstone,
a windmill, a boat, a cradle, a coffin . . . the friendliness
of wind-tossed smoke, arising from hearth or chimney . . .
the forlornness of swaying reed-tops above lonely salt-
marshes . . . the warmth of sun-scented leaf-mould, the
udders of cattle, the horns of goats, the spouting of whales
. . . frost marks in ditch-mud . . . vapour-circles round
misty moons . . . rivers and highways that carry old legends, old memories, old tragic transactions into the unborn
future—all these things, and the emanations proceeding
from these things, possess some mysterious quality in common; and it would seem that this quality cannot be named
by any other name than that of *the poetical element* in life.

But a difficulty arises at this point that must be dealt
with before we can accept this element as the only proper
subject of the art of poetry. The difficulty I refer to springs
from the fact that apart from this *poetical* element there
is also—and it is a totally different thing—the element of
the beautiful. The ultimate secret of existence, as far as
we have come to approach it, reveals itself to our minds in
a threefold way. It reveals itself as the true, as the good,
and as the beautiful. What we call beauty therefore, is, in

its inherent nature, one of the mysterious manifestations of what our older philosophers call the absolute. Now it seems as if the whole subject of the nature of poetry is clarified and simplified by separating the purely poetical altogether from the purely beautiful. For when such a separation begins to formulate itself in one's mind, a new and very interesting light begins to fall upon the nature of this particular element which we have been pursuing. By realizing how completely different a world of impressions is occupied by the beautiful, we find this other world, that of the poetical, shrinking back and narrowing itself down into much more definite limitations. And do we not now in comparison with this mystery of the beautiful, begin to detect certain very definite characteristics of the purely poetical? It seems that we do; and it seems also as though the chief of these were the presence of something emotionally anthropomorphic, something traditional, customary, ritualistic, something adhering to our race's inherited sentiments, hopes, loves, fears, feelings of bodily ease, feelings of romantic un-ease.

To realize this difference between beauty and poetry one need only visualize for a moment the illuminated body of some swiftly moving aeroplane, an aeroplane engaged in advertising, let us suppose, some toilet-necessity or some new brand of cigarettes, upon a city sky. Such a spectacle might easily be conceived as a genuine revelation, in the spheres of form and colour, of beauty considered as a non-human absolute. But with that peculiar quality in things I am trying to indicate as belonging to the essence of poetry such a spectacle would have nothing to do. In fact it would exercise a destructive influence upon the natural poetry of the particular night or twilight when such an occurrence took place.

This is no extreme case, no unusual case. In modern life, where machinery and inventions have so often a strange and startling beauty of their own, a beauty which beyond refutation springs from the same absolute as all other ideal forms, there must constantly arise in our minds a disturbing conflict. On one side there appears this untraditional ideal beauty, which can be equally exploited by the inspirations of art and by the laws of mechanics, and on the other side there is the familiar atmosphere of the historic poetry in things which is hostile both to the new and to the mechanical. The chosen material both of modern mechanics and of modern aesthetics is bound to appear to the spirit of poetry as something alien and troubling; a discord, a menace. The reason for this is to be found in the fact that any manifestation of beauty may be completely unsympathetic to traditional emotion, feeling, sentiment; whereas it is of the very essence of poetry to remain saturated with all the historic human reactions, with every sort of old-world sentiment. Poetry is in fact a thing so totally different, in both its substance and its entelechy, from beauty that the two revelations appeal to different types of mind. We must remember that an object can be beautiful without being in the least poetical; just as it can be poetical without being in the least beautiful. Poetry is composed of a certain traditional body of feelings about life; a body which has gathered by slow adhesions into a presence of values, nuances, discriminations to which must conform what every nation and every age may add as an indigenous quota of its own.

Poetry is thus something profoundly and emotionally humanized; and since time alone can humanize inanimate objects, the mere fact of being very old can make ugly objects poetical; while the mere fact of being very new can make beautiful objects unpoetical. To select what might be regarded as absurd examples but which really are significant—a torpedo-shaped racing motor-car is beautiful but not poetical, whereas a bare "wishing-bone" is poetical because of fairy-story association but absolutely unbeautiful.

It is, as may be believed, this basic difference between the beautiful and the poetical that underlies many temperamental hostilities in every age. From some of these clashes of temperament our personal culture may be most subtly deepened and intensified. From others it may issue forth maimed, bewildered, side-tracked. It is of course the discovery of one's own secret intellectual fatality that alone can decide whether it is wiser for the individual mind to concentrate on the poetical or on the beautiful. And though we may be eclectic enough to cultivate both, it will save us from much interior confusion if we can come to realize with full mental clarity towards which of these two great orientations we are congenitally urged. Each of them calls forth certain spiritual powers, but these powers are not the same. It would seem as though the imaginative emotion has deeper and freer play in dealing with the poetical; while the imaginative reason is able to assert itself to greater advantage in regard to the beautiful.

Throwing aside any fatalistic resignation to the particular epoch in which we happen to be born, it would seem as though there existed in the individual mind a power to make its own secret choice in these things, whether that choice jumps with the spirit of the age or directly contradicts it. The mind that is thrilled by stupendously high buildings, by the amazing flight of aeroplanes, by the incredible swiftness of great liners, more than by rocks and grass and

trees, is a mind that loves beauty more than poetry. There
are even certain landscapes upon the earth that one instinctively recognizes as appealing to the beauty-loving mind
rather than to the poetical mind. Such landscapes have non-
human, non-historical, chemic-cosmogonic character and
their power over the mind is not a matter of literary suggestion but a direct impact of form and colour arranged in
non-human patterns.

Would it seem a too narrow doctrine if we were to take
for granted that the art of poetry will be most *sui generis*,
most entirely *itself*, when it expresses in words the purely
poetic view of life? From the viewpoint of this doctrine, if
we do accept it, most modern poetry falls short of the
earlier kind. If any characteristic more than another stamps
as modern the poetical experiments of our day it is the invasion of the peculiar terrain of the art of poetry by the
more purely aesthestic values of the arts of painting and
music. Poetry hovers over everything that has been a background to human life, over everything that has been a
permanent accessory, a daily tool, long enough for a certain
organic identification to have grown up between the diurnal
usages of our race and this or that fragment of material
substance. Thus it is not surprising that the most deeply
satisfying poetry, and that which stirs the imagination most
strongly, is the poetry of old times wherein this animism or
vitalization of the inanimate is most marked. Homer is thus
greater than Aeschylus, Aeschylus than Dante, Dante than
Milton, Milton than Matthew Arnold, Matthew Arnold
than W. B. Yeats!

This particular sliding-scale of values must of course be
taken loosely; for it would be protested by many cultured
people that Shakespeare was more appealing than Homer,

Goethe than Dante, Keats than Virgil, Walt Whitman than Milton. But it does seem approximately true that from a bird's-eye vision of the procession of poetry the earlier masters are more poetical, more definitely creators of a poetical atmosphere than the later ones.

But though this historic lapse and lamentable subsidence of high human feeling, this gradual sinking down of poetic values from the simplicities of Homer to the sophistries of our contemporaries, cannot be gainsaid, there are epochs in English poetry that possess a magic of their own unlike anything else in the world. Such for example are those honey-breathing purlieus of enchantment, those green vistas and richly receding margins of romance, that we enjoy in the poetry of Keats or in the poetry of Walter de la Mare. Such too are the rambling ways we follow, in so many anonymous ballads, across moor and fen, by mountain and sea-shore. Wherever the wild-tossed branches of the tree of life creak in the wind, be it on lonely cattle-drove or on lamp-lit street, the roaming falcon of poetry hovers, swoops and dips.

It would seem as if the most natural and fruitful impulse in the growth of a sensitive mind, as far as poetry is concerned, is to plunge into a temporary obsession for one poet's style and one poet's vision, one after another. Anthologies have their place; but real culture loves better to saturate itself, first with one type of imagination, and then with a different one. A mind preoccupied with Blake, let us say, must needs perceive no single grey thistle on the roadway, no single red geranium in a window-box, but these objects become strange symbolic portals to a whole world of mystical impressions. After the same manner a mind hypnotized by the sensibility of Coleridge will catch the fantastic motions of "one last leaf," shivering against a winter sky, so intimately close that it will come to partake of the very essence of that leaf's planetary feeling.

Nor will such a mind be in the least limited, in its spiritual-sensuous wanderings, by the clamorous assertiveness of any modern fashion of artistic expression. It would seem as if one of the most unforgettable intimations that ever comes to us in our intellectual life comes when we first recognize with a thrilling rush of liberating scepticism that all the great poetic epochs are—from the viewpoint of personal culture—equal and contemporaneous. A magical liberation dawns for us the moment we recognize that we have a perfect right to throw ourselves with complete sceptical detachment from modern science into the mythopoetic mood of any early poet whose temper of vision hits our peculiar humour or fancy. Thus it can happen that any green glade of rustic woodland can give place to some Spenserian rider, dreamlike and glittering, under the dark boughs. Thus it can happen that any dawn-touched strip of sandy shore can reveal shell-bright sea-gods and glaucous-eyed maidens, as in an Idyll of Theocritus. Thus a solitary bird's nest full of snow can bring all the poignance of Villon's mood, all the fantasy of Verlaine's imagination, rushing over us in one memory-charged beat of the heart.

The eclectic transformations of any real poetic culture are boundless, just because all the ages are made equal and contemporary to the sceptical mind. Thus the hot, shrill ecstasy of the lark's music can be at the same moment glamorous with the pantheistic thrill of Shelley's vision, desperate with that wild protest against modern sterility such as we get in T. S. Eliot's "Waste Land," and sweet and

mellow to the sick heart as the love-litany of a slow-moving
Sonnet of Shakespeare.

All equally present, in their pressure upon any real culture, are the reactions to life of the very earliest poets
whereof there is record. Thus it is entirely possible to give
oneself up without reserve to Homer's vision of the world,
even in the midst of the most mechanized modern metropolis; possible actually to live, here and now, according to
Homer. And what would this living according to Homer
really mean?

It is, of course, hard to sum up in a few paragraphs
the drift of an entire system of imaginative life; but,
roughly expressed, what it would seem to mean is a quite
definite characteristic of selecting from the flux of life
certain "first and last things" and of concentrating upon
these things held up, as it were, in purged and stripped relief, against the chaotic background of the unessential.

A word of crucial warning would not be out of place
just here. If one happens to be ignorant of Greek the only
wise thing to do is to read Homer in the simplest prose
translation one can possibly obtain. Reading him in this way
it will not be long before we grow conscious that we are
imbibing a quite definite manner of regarding earth, water,
air, clouds, blue space, the sun and the moon, trees, animals
and human beings. We shall come to see all these things
under a certain purged and rarified atmosphere. We shall
come to see them from the vantage-ground of a certain
stoical exultation, a mood neither spiritual nor sensual, but
simplified, concentrated and profoundly poetic.

It is not enough to admire this image or that metaphor or
to enjoy the swing and roll of the words or the dignity of
the story. No one has a right to say he enjoys Homer until

his actual reaction to sun and moon and earth and sea, and to the significant groupings of people and things, has been liberated by the Homeric open secret.

And now there arises a very interesting point. No one can be blamed for being temperamentally attracted to certain remote epochs of poetry, and on the other hand bitterly hostile to others. Working upon us all the while in the darker regions of our nature—in defiance of the power over us of the particular age into which we are born—is always a furtive predilection for some historic era against all the others. One may indeed suspect, too, that the blind antipathy, amounting to a savage maliciousness, that we feel for a certain past time, is due to the fact that the psyche within us is a lost child of that age's spiritual opposite and cultural antagonist.

Certain ages are certainly more exacting towards their lovers than others and more difficult to appropriate and adjust in an eclectic system of culture. Such are the Middle Ages. The modern temperaments whose pulses of existence beat in the mediaeval way are bound to experience many shocking outrages to their nerves in the attempt to adjust themselves to the life of a modern city. But what a heavenly escape for such people, what an anodyne for all their sorrows, when they first stumble upon Dante! Not Dante himself, when he first encounters Virgil, experiences a more reassuring ecstasy of safety and peace.

The best way to appreciate Dante is to lay hold upon an edition where, as in Dent's "Temple Classics," a literal prose translation is placed opposite the text. Incidentally we must submit that it is well worth it—however unscholarly we are—to learn at least enough Greek and Latin and

Italian to be able to read these old poets aloud, if it be only to ourselves.

And when it comes to reading the "Inferno," wise indeed will the reader be who reads for imaginative and emotional pleasure and not as a student. One has to be a student in youth in order to get the clue to culture. But the perpetual student is seldom a cultivated person. Slide lightly, therefore, over the historical allusions. Dodge the theological problems. Fight shy of such abominable passages as reveal a vein of unmistakable sadism in the great poet. But with these exceptions there are things that one can well read in the "Inferno" over and over again, till rarer passages, memorized by love and repetition, come to be like chain-armour for our human spirit against the insolent intrusions of the vulgar present. Then it will prove true how possible it is, by a kind of empathy or nerve-transference, to share a great poet's most intimate life-illusion. For your feelings will actually grow Dantesque in their concentration so that as you drag your legs in weariness along your river-side or stare at the water-flies in the ditch by the tow-path, or tilt your head back to gaze at the flying swallows, you will actually come to share that curious realistic awareness of the stark physiognomy of life which it is this poet's especial gift to express.

It seems sometimes as if it were very rare to find a person who reads Shakespeare for his poetry alone. And yet this, surely, is the one thing needful. The saturation of ourselves with this Shakespearean poetry, with this peculiar style, will be found to imply, just as in the case of Homer and Dante, a gradual approximation of our own personal vision of life to that of the poet. For Shakespeare's religion of life lurks in every word of this style of his and dyes it in woof and grain, through and through. It is the fragrance of dairy-field cowslips mingled with the wild salt airs from the tossing sea, that gives to the dewy pastures of Shakespeare's poetry a spiritual philosophy of their own, by which a person could wisely live, and beget or conceive children, and deal with the affairs of the world.

It is often possible, in reading an original but un-self-critical poet like Wordsworth, to disregard his conscious and intended teaching, and to appropriate his unconscious art of life. Incidentally and between the lines, one can draw from Wordsworth himself a most subtle and liberating art of living entirely by physical sensation; not so much by the sensations of gross sensuality as by those more delicate sensations which seem to come and go upon the wind, and which may be summed up in Wordsworth's own line, "the pleasure which there is in life itself."

In this whole matter of the secret enrichment of life by the use of poetry it surely must be allowed that there is much more satisfaction to be got from feeling the stream of life after the manner, say, of William Blake or of Matthew Arnold, than from merely enjoying the rounded perfection of some particular lyric or sonnet whose especial fantasy may delight us.

To return therefore to the definition of the subject with which this chapter began, I hope I have convinced my reader that the difference between what we call beauty, this revelation of a non-human absolute, and what we call poetry, this revelation of an accumulated human tradition of certain primitive reactions to life, is something that indicates a wide gulf between what one's culture draws from the aesthetic and what it draws from the poetical.

One can easily visualize, for example, some Japanese picture of an aeroplane, or an airship, or a war-ship, or an iron girder, or a locomotive, or a factory-chimney, or an automobile, that might express the very quintessence of this mysterious Beauty, and yet remain totally unpoetical; remain shocking and outraging, in fact, to the poetic in us.

But compare with this the peculiar atmosphere of the poetry of Keats. One instinctively feels that its basic appeal is essentially poetical rather than aesthetic. That is why one can enjoy to the full fragments and morsels of Keats's poetry such as occur, like wild-flowers dropped on a foot-path, in the midst of so much that is littered and pointless and puerile.

One's culture must do what it can to get the innermost thrill out of both these things; but it would seem that while the purely aesthetic revelation manifests itself, so to speak, in isolated units, the poetical revelation has the power of spreading itself out through the enormous pell-mell of the world's life. In fact the whole turbid stream of Nature, in its wild oceanic ensemble, can be apprehended as poetry; while such vastness must remain inherently intractable and chaotic to the more mathematical aesthetic sense.

But to conclude and sum up. The profoundest gift of the spirit of poetry to a person's secret culture is the gift of peace. Poetry can reconcile a man or a woman to the simplest and barest worldly situation. As long as the forlornest patches of earth and sky are left to us to be enjoyed by the mind we can feel ourselves into the mood of Achilles crying aloud to Thetis or of Prometheus defying the wide heaven. Between the shutters of the most sordid attic the Holy Grail itself can be seen, traversing the sky, between chimney and chimney! Where a few blades of grass can grow in the wretchedest yard, there the immortal spirits of Dante's Limbo welcome their last proud initiate. Under a luminous poetic light that falls where it wills all the simple recurrent details of our days gather an amplitude and a mystic significance. Birth and death, food and fire, sleep and waking, the motions of the winds, the cycles of the stars, the budding and falling of the leaves, the ebbing and flowing of the tides—all these things have, for thousands of years, created an accumulated tradition of human feeling; and what culture appropriates from the art of poetry is the power to realize this tradition, to realize it ever more reverently and ever more obstinately!

CHAPTER IV

CULTURE AND PAINTING

If it were impossible to be a reasonably cultured human being without an intimate and technical knowledge of the difficult art of painting, few indeed would be able to claim such a title. But just as a vast number of intelligent people enrich their lives by reading books without the least notion of the technical subtleties of writing, so with this also. It must therefore be understood at the start that what the present writer is aiming at in this chapter is not any attempt to deal with the technicalities of light and shadow, planes and surfaces, perspective and pigments, but rather with certain philosophical generalizations that apply to what has been, and apparently always must be, the response of the greater number of people in the world to what this art can do by means of these technical devices in enlarging the scope and sharpening the edge of human awareness in the presence of the whole mysterious spectacle.

The difference between a cultured and an uncultured reaction to any picture remains, from this point of view, merely a matter of a greater, or less degree of sensitivity. Apart from a very small minority of professional artists and professional critics, we are all laymen in these things. The hope which those of us entertain who desire to thicken out our normal human consciousness by something that goes a little deeper, is not to become professional technicians in the problems of applying pigment to canvas, but to learn something through the medium of the artist's success in such application, of that subtler vision of his which can see in Nature and reality an inner truth peculiar to himself.

Whether this individual inner truth, or perhaps one ought rather to say this purged and exclusive truth, for its essence is more often a glow, a bloom, a dew upon the surface of things than any underlying secret, can be said to exist independently of the artist who discovers it, is a question that admits a wide solution. Probably such an *aperçu* contains both elements; namely the mind that observes and imagines, and the objective mystery that is observed and imagined.

It is just here that an answer can be found for those who are tempted to disparage the art of painting, on the ground that they "can enjoy Nature for themselves" while what poetry and music give them they could never enjoy for themselves—and the answer is this. There are countless sensations and impressions that reach us from Nature mounting up sometimes, accumulating and gathering, till they attain moments of mysterious completeness such as could never be caught or expressed by any audible sound or by any written word. And yet they are full, in their fleeting impact upon us, of a revelation that we long to arrest and eternalize in some palpable symbol. It is true that painting deals with our mere physical sensations in the presence of Nature, whereas music carries us into the fourth dimension of ideal, bodiless beauty, and words into the realm of ideas. But when one considers that the most intense and overpowering sensations we receive on earth are bodily ones, does it not seem a mad wilfulness to deny to direct sense-impressions, whether crude or subtle, that right to be gathered up into universal symbols such as is already possessed by words, as counters for thoughts, and by musical notes, as counters for disembodied mathematical beauty?

Why should there not be Platonic essences, of the rarest and loveliest kind, to be found emanating from the shapes and colours of things and the textures of things and the lights and shadows of things? If the pursuit of culture is an attempt to enlarge the boundaries of our individual perception of the universe by the visions of genius, the genius of the painter is as indispensable a revelation of new regions as that of the poet or the musician; and though it will be forever impossible to all save artists to appreciate the actual accomplishment in any particular picture from the point of view of the difficulties overcome, and the new contributions in technical and mathematical mastery of form and colour, it would be a foolish ignoring of the past experiences of the human race itself to relegate this lay appreciation of what painting reveals to us to an insignificant and negligible backwater of the subject.

Rembrandt will remain Rembrandt (as Beethoven will remain Beethoven) not because the human race will ever know by what legerdemain he overcame the difficulties of his medium (this we must leave to future Cézannes or Picassos who study his canvasses) but because of the grandeur and originality of his peculiar response to Nature and to the mathematical patterns and rhythms involved in Nature.

To cut down in contemptuous arrogance, as certain artists and art-critics do, upon every human pleasure taken in a picture that is not the pleasure of a craftsman, is to miss the one culminating sensation, for the sake of which all this subtle craftsmanship was stretched to so fine a point.

Some of the profoundest realizations that have ever come to human beings in life—with regard to the nature of things and the mystery of things—have more in common with painting than with literature because the form they are compelled to take is a series of atmosphere and images rather than of sounds or of connotations of rational thought. A water-colour sketch, for instance, of Albert Dürer, representing a road into Nüremberg in the early sixteenth century, has more power of evoking the fine edge of human consciousness at that epoch than any poem of Ronsard's, shall we say, however deftly written.

It is all very well for painters to emphasize their desire to be accepted only in the limited sphere of their purely technical achievements. The medium they use is after all no less universal than that of language, since the visual apprehension of the surfaces of things in Nature is common to all. Even when the more extreme among modern artists choose to abandon the ordinary appearances of life, as they are recognized by the normal human vision, for certain recondite aspects disentangled from the rest by a de-emotionalized curiosity, it is still our affair to follow their lead in this as far as we can and to learn from them a new response to Nature from a fresh and original slant, a slant that boldly carries our common consciousness one or two steps further, in the recognition of reality hitherto unrevealed.

When one comes to approach the very practical question as to how it is wisest, in our ordinary life, to enjoy pictures, one finds oneself confronted by the too familiar experience that this particular art has come to be associated for most of us with extreme physical exhaustion. Most of the attempts we over-burdened mortals make to deepen and intensify our stream of consciousness are liable to be attended by physical or mental weariness. But without doubt visits to picture galleries tend to be more tiring, both to mind and body, than any other cultural efforts that one could possibly make. This is because one is tempted to see far too much in a given space of time. One roomful of pictures, whether they be old or new, is about all a person of ordinary intelligence has the strength to assimilate at one time. Even the enjoyment of this one roomful should imply at least an hour's time spent in a sitting posture! It is indeed a scandalous neglect on the part of the authorities when a gallery, showing any collection of pictures, is devoid of seats. One ought to be able to take one's leisure among pictures; just as, in the presence of beautiful scenery, one leans over a gate, lies down on a bank, or sits upon a rock.

The difficulty of "too much" dealt with, there arises the annoyance of artistic guides. Such people want to make plain to any young person, who shows the least interest in the contents of a picture-gallery, all the orthodox modern doctrines about "significant form" and the unimportance of subject matter. It would seem, however, that when once this art is adjusted to one's general personal scheme of life we must be drastic in our flat refusal to suppress all human, all psychological, all poetical delight in what we see. It certainly seems to be sheer fanaticism to try to suppress our imaginative enjoyment of a picture because it contains rhythmic patterns. If we have learnt the technicalities, well and good. The pure pleasure we shall get from the thing will be an hundredfold enhanced. But even then, no knowledge of the technical difficulties, or of the art of overcoming them, ought to de-humanize us to such a tune as to make us indifferent to the other elements of beauty that the picture may suggest. Some faint touch of human imagination or feeling will, as a matter of fact, be found adhering, in spite of all they can do, to any arrangement of pure lines and colours.

One thing we may be certain of. Art is too spontaneous, too inevitable a product of the mind to be narrowed down forever to any set of drastic principles enunciated in a single decade. Poor enough would be the value of culture to us if it didn't help us, from the vantage-ground of an appreciation of values of beauty that have become demoded, to take all this modern dogmatism and derision with a Chesterfieldian pinch of snuff.

The preferences implicit here will appear in stronger relief for those who are prepared to accept the doctrine —which, of course, is a philosophical or literary doctrine rather than an artistic or scientific one—that the pictures which have the richest value for us are those which enable us to see for ourselves in Nature and to select for ourselves out of Nature the kind of chance-arranged groupings of objects which bear that imaginative light upon them which is congruous with the spontaneous craving of personal instincts. One wonders how many among the readers of this page have come to share the writer's predilection, for instance, for Hobbema and Ruysdael. Prolific of just this sort of natural selectiveness may the genius of these two painters prove to be; and moreover few galleries will be found lacking in some specimens of their work. From these "branch-charméd" avenues of monumental trees— avenues leading, surely, to Virgilian realms of Saturn—

hints and glimpses can be absorbed such as have the power
to gather into a concentrated mental perspective the vague
earth-memories of half a life-time. From the mossy purlieus of these century-old water-mills, where, in the luminous
foreground the flying spray touches some fallen trunk or
rests for a minute upon some lichen-grown rock, fragments
and morsels of forgotten impressions will coalesce, like
broken bits of a mental mirror, and all manner of side-
way thrills of ecstasy—scattered here and there throughout the years—will blend into a magical unity.

Culture is of little use to us if it does not liberate us,
in one grand stroke of what might be called positive as
distinct from negative criticism, from those aesthetic ri-
gidities which—and they are forever changing and contra-
dicting one another—would forbid us with hypnotic authority to enjoy such natural human reactions.

It is indeed the cultured person alone who has enough
scepticism and enough of the light touch to remain ironical
and slippery amid the furious dictatorships of aesthetic
fashion. Of course one knows only too well that by the
fatal tendency of the excess of the best to prove the worst,
there is a type of human mind that is a disgusting parody
of the really cultured type; and that this sham culture
and pseudo-gentility do untold harm to the Quixotic art-
fanaticism of the young. This is the worldly person's real
indifference to the whole subject; and most pitiable is it
when because of a superficial acquaintance with the verbiage
of art-chatter, such a person is clever enough to throw cold
water upon the heroic faith of youth in the importance of
the issues at stake.

The fanatical prejudices of the most violent innovator are
of course infinitely preferable to this; for in things of art,

as in things of religion, one cannot advance a step without something of the simplicity of a child.

Take, for instance, Ruskin's truth-to-Nature iconoclasm. How ill-considered was his attack upon Poussin and Claude! How irrelevant and ridiculous his quarrel with Whistler! Most cultured minds in those days, one feels sure, would have had enough ironic detachment to be sympathetic with Ruskin, while at the same time they recognized the basic limitations of this tragic man's furious error.

Claude is indeed one of the most suggestive of all painters from the point of view implied in the present writer's argument. The particular enchantment of that look of crowded mast-heads in a misty harbour; the peculiar effect of bowsprits and rigging and pennons and high-raised decks swimming in the golden haze of late summer afternoons and mingled so grandly with towering buildings and vast air-spaces—these are, in reality, what might be called eternal symbols of transitory sensations.

It is the same with Poussin. The majestic brownish-green foliage that extends above the altars of his sacred groves, tinged, as if with a rusty moss, by that particular twilight which Spengler selected as his innermost symbol of our Faustian soul, is not the pure art-quality of all this touched by something else? And is not this something else the one thing needful, both for the cultured and uncultured? These lovely pastoral men and sweet Artemis-like maidens, these goat-foot amorists and purple-stained wine-bibbers, this sun-burnt mirth, these elderberry libations, appeal to the poetry in us as well as to the craftman's eye. Why, not one of Ovid's wildest Metamorphoses but might suddenly happen in this rich moss-brown world! In the midst of the

brazen Megalopolis one catches the poignance, like delicious dew, of life's sweetness and brevity, from a mere
glance at these pictures.

But there are levels in the art of painting far higher
and deeper than any of these. A person could organize his
whole life, philosophically, morally, imaginatively, by saturating himself with the work of only half a dozen great
painters. Take Rembrandt alone. How deeply could anyone enrich his most secret reactions to life's occult panorama by brooding long and long upon the sombre reticences
of human character revealed in this great psychologue's
work! By the lights and shadows of fire-light and candlelight and by a treatment of sunshine that gives to the far
luminary of our world the concentrated earth-caught
Promethean intensity of man-made flame, Rembrandt reveals the pride and the humility of a thousand individual
souls.

But Spain is the land from which springs the art where
the absolute of beauty scattered in relative glimpses, here
and there throughout the world, comes nearest to taking
upon its inmost essence the accidents of colour and shape.
A sensitive intelligence of another race could give itself up
to at least three aspects of this divine essence by approaching the pictures of Velasquez, El Greco and Goya. The
dignity of Homo Sapiens, his natural postures, his simplest
gestures, his relaxed enjoyment of the sensual feeling of his
own personality, his sublime consciousness, be he king or
beggar, of the particular raiment, lousy rags or Golden
Fleece, by which he covers his nakedness, the way he looks
out upon the observer from the canvas—life itself grown
conscious of its incredible depths, Being itself grown con-

scious of being Being—all this and more Velasquez alone,
by a kind of sophisticated simplification of the mere ritual
of being alive, expresses with the very seal of finality.

And if the body of man, together with the symbolic ritual
of the body's raiment, finds the apogee of its expressiveness
in these haughty blacks and whites, these reserved splashes
of rose-carmine, these swart backgrounds, such as attend
like well-drilled slaves upon the fatal dreaminess of flesh
and blood, no less does the soul of man find its culminating
expression in the ecstasies of El Greco. Wildly and grandly
do they whirl up in their mounting crescendo of mystical
self-forgetfulness, these holy El Greco saints! As with the
figures of Dostoievsky there is something apocalyptic about
these luminous lacerations toppling on the verge of an unutterable threshold; but the imaginative backgrounds that
the Toledoan gives them, racks of strange vapours, icebergs
of huddled chaos, chasms of fatality, anticipate again and
again those hosts of primordial air-shapes which William
Blake saw in the fields of London's suburbs. The very madness of religion leaps up like cloven pentecostal flames from
the quivering finger-tips of these ecstatics. Long and thin
have their hands grown from the mere habit of desperate
prayer; while the contours of their God-intoxicated faces
carry the mark of such as have seen Eternity and have not
perished.

If Velasquez embodies the furthest reach that art can go
in rendering the language of flesh and blood, and if El
Greco pursues the Beatific Vision to the point where, as at
the end of the "Paradiso," it swoons into Nirvana, Goya
is the Aristophanes, the Sterne of the genius of painting.
Incredible cruelty, incredible gaiety! Yes! And something
that has as yet remained unnamed; something beyond the

magic of the earth, for it is too airy; something that resembles the dew-fresh ichor on the opening petals of young flowers, a radiant texture-bloom, only drawn out of things when the moment and the place are propitious, puts this man apart from all others, making him, medium of terror as he is sometimes, a very Diaphaneité of fleeting grace.

Considering these Spaniards, the folly of confining your pleasure in painting to anything short of a new vision of reality is made evident. And it seems as if for any picture really to sink into your imagination—so that in your secret thoughts you use the painter's very eyes and with your secret senses *his* very senses—it is necessary to carry the feeling of the picture away with you when you have left the gallery; necessary to carry it into your house, your shop, your bedroom. I will go so far as to say it is necessary to mix it with your food and with your drink; to mix it with those moments before sleeping and after waking when the mind is most virginal and receptive; to mix it with your most hurried and casual glimpses of things and with the images of your memory of things.

We all derive a mysterious satisfaction from certain predetermined formalities of design, parallel with the basic harmonies in music. Why it should be so we cannot tell, unless it is our response to something in Nature that corresponds to our own mental and physical elements. But even in the most ill-adjusted existence Nature will be found sometimes to satisfy this craving. Upon some hill-top the trees mass themselves in a certain way as we watch the scenery through a train window, or we catch a glimpse of a group of straw-stacks huddled at the corner of a field; and we respond to an organized harmony in this chance-thrown pattern of light and shade and find that it answers some secret need of our natures with startling reciprocity.

But in the greatest pictures this instinct in us which inevitably reacts to formal pattern finds its comfort in this abstract design heightened by something else. This something seems to be an irreducible, ultimate quality, evoked by the original imagination of the artist, working upon the structural mysteries of the universe. By this I mean that the absolute of beauty revealed by genius, through these mathematically organized harmonies, is free from that dark knot of human issues with which our ordinary emotions are entangled. In other words it is an unemotional, dispassionate response to beauty—beauty in its absolute being—and is thus safe from the dangers and depredations which attend those of our emotions which belong to the world of passion and desire, of joy and sorrow. But the response he induces in us to this revelation of the absolute is not merely an intellectual or abstract response; it satisfies a deep long-buried craving in us to feel a certain kind of ecstasy, like the ecstasy of the saints, which can obliterate the old shadow of distress which mingles with all earthly consciousness.

As we contemplate the delicate backgrounds of the pictures of many Italian Primitives, as we follow certain umbrageous perspectives in the landscapes of Gainsborough, a light seems to fall upon the threshold of our minds which absolves us from the turbulent dualities of existence, from good and evil, from hope and despair, from love and hate, yes! even from the last alternation of life and death. This is the miracle that those pictures work for us which come with that fresh immortal dew upon them, as of imperishably recurrent youth, such as it is not in the power of this pestilential world to fever or parch.

This is what the art of painting offers; though it may be by no means always that the miracle occurs. By no means always! For alas! As Proust so skilfully indicates in his elaborate way, the eternal being within our mortal ego must have its own peculiar food to feed upon; and this requires not only the inspired genius in the picture but some unpredictable chance of mood and hour and atmosphere working upon ourselves as we stand before it.

Painting is irrevocably intertwined with all those vague, half-sensual, half-mystical feelings that make up the accumulated burden of the interior ego, its second or spiritual body. And just because it is mingled with such ingredients it must of necessity be immeasurably varied in its appeal to differently constituted temperaments.

For that rare elusive loveliness in the world, those glimpses and touches of something that, as Pater says, "exists around us in a small measure or not at all," we must go, those of us who are secret amorists, as it were, of this strange quality, to certain delicately sensuous pictures of Giorgione, or to those long-laboured-over, equivocal revelations of Leonardo's super-human art and thaumaturgic science.

Touched by a less enigmatic inspiration and seducing us to a less ambiguous curiosity, the art of Watteau too has something of this unearthly strangeness. It is indeed a wistful nostalgia, an intimation of pleasures too rare for earth that we catch in such a picture as the "Embarkation for Cythera," a picture that might well send many a hurried visitor to the Louvre wandering slowly off along the *Rive*

Gauche in a Cimmerian mist of enchanted melancholy!

A modern artist who has the power of opening up such vistas is Marie Laurencin with her capricious wild-hare-eyed demoiselles, in their shell-pink scarves, dreaming like so many Ladies of Shalott amid their green and more than springtime leafage. And although it is a saddening commentary upon the degeneration of our milieu, from an aesthetic point of view, to descend from that winding river among the mystic rocks which was Leonardo's favourite symbol to the prairie shanties and forlorn Middle Western backyards painted by Burchfield, one feels that, even here, the power to cast over such tatterdemalion, meaningless boardings and planks, peeled and blistered by the extremities of American weather, an imaginative significance is also in its own place and time a heightening of the ordinary spectacle of things by an aesthetic inspiration. The young Swedish painter of Sante Fe, Raymond Jonson, is another modern whose work has an arresting element in it which can touch, so to speak, the nerves of the imagination with a tremor of that excitement which only genius gives.

It would seem indeed a kind of treachery to the world-spirit to allow our response to beauty to stop once for all and anchor itself by the well-worn wharves of the Old Masters.

It is not only in his Watteauesque world of magical fantasy-that the Daedalian genius of painting makes our hearts stir and move like leaves in the wind. However difficult it may be for a nature moulded upon the old-fashioned notions to respond with a really spontaneous integrity to many modern experiments, it seems that the historic sense itself should forbid our expressing our distaste with the gross facetiousness of a ponderous conservatism which can only march in the old grooves. The extreme schools of recent painting have indeed very decisively snatched a place for themselves in that wild Macedonian phalanx of modernity, whereof the glittering point of attack is the orgiastic dance; and, behind the dance, the sullen beating of tom-toms and wild brass of trombones. All these extreme modernities have a profound symbolic value. It is as stupid to disregard this value as it is silly to pretend to understand it. It is Nature. After their mad fashion these things are true. And why should not they have as much right to imitate the universe's obscene and monstrous gestures as her gentle and modest ones? No, they are not contrary to reality. With all their squares and splashes and scrawls and protrusions and dust-storms and wind-spirals, they represent a certain chaos in things which is one of Nature's own chemical secrets. The filigrees and arabesques of certain organic trails, the rhythmic patterns of earth-worms, for example, traced in wet mud, are an aspect of this, and the reckless movements of infusoria and amoeba in any drop of microscopic pond-water and the murky, entangled shadows thrown by the moon in some deep wood-side ditch. There are aspects of Nature, the formation of rock crystals, the gambols of seals and walruses, the mathematical kaleidoscopes in the contours of floating frog-spawn, the bloodied scales of a staring market-fish, the distended flanks of the acrobat hanging head downwards in the circus, which seem to have been left by destiny especially for these artists.

The art of painting has of course first and last to do with colour; and colour remains, and always will remain, the great mother's inmost expression flickering across her mysterious face. The cold and the warm, the moist and the dry, the soft and the hard, all the various aspects of her occult chemistry are palpably felt, as if they were revelations of endless psychic moods, as one stands before the best of these modern experiments.

We have to recognize the fact that although the individual painters of our day cannot be compared in sheer creative genius with the great masters of the past, there is among them a movement onwards, a movement into hitherto untried, untraversed margins of beauty, which runs parallel to the new departures, equally difficult for untrained minds to follow, in the art of music. A really cultured nature, however temperamentally old-fashioned, will not be found drawing back in sullen bigotry from these new things. It would indeed seem as if the preservation of a No Man's Land of intense and humble receptiveness is as much a part of any authentic culture as is a non-committed, ironic detachment from the vulgarities of fashion. One must be prepared to take certain aesthetic risks, and to make certain imaginative plunges into the new and the unknown, if one's taste is to expand and grow with the spontaneity of an organic nucleus of life.

The invasion of literature by the rhythmic and plastic arts is paralleled by a simultaneous invasion of Art itself by what might be called the psychic "aura" of modern machinery and inventions. Greek art found the centre of its aesthetic preoccupation in the human body, primitive Christian art in the human spirit, romantic nineteenth-century art in the magic of Nature. Modern art has discovered a completely new element for its exploitation, namely the purely mathematical and chemical structure of matter itself. Nor is it only the "logic," so to speak, of matter, in such of its movements and sequences as science can reduce to mechanical systems—or at least to mechanical hypotheses—that modern art exploits. Some of the most arresting and startling aesthetic effects which we have recently observed seem to spring from a mysterious back-wash, rather behind than within the known Cosmos, which suggests nothing less than that old ghastly "prae-life" which the human race has shrunk from so long under the name of Chaos.

It is indeed very significant that there should exist side by side in modern art both these extreme tendencies; the tendency to undeviating dynamics, as in the behaviour of magnetism and electricity, of iron and stone, of steam and steel; and the tendency to lawless almost psychic discord, such as seems to spout up with spasmodic fury from some vein of wilful arbitrariness in the nature of the universe itself.

Music and its newer instruments have, as I have already hinted, conspired with modern painting to invade those sacred groves formerly monopolized by literature. And there is yet another influence at work; for behind both music and painting one seems aware, in these days, of the occult pressure of a strange rhythmic force which is connected both with revolutionary political upheavals and subterranean class warfares, and with that revolt of youth against everything that holds it in check which takes sometimes the form of reaction and sometimes of revolution.

It is undeniable too, that the continent of Africa has begun to play an increasing cultural rôle in the heart of those blind emotional impulses that underlie our imaginative and aesthetic life.

In fine, one is conscious of a strange thudding, pulsing, rumbling movement, deep down in the nature of all modern art, which seems to resemble the distant approach, heard through the medium of the Einsteinian Space-Time, of a new cosmic religion. Spengler regards all these modern eccentricities as negligible by-products of an age of iron and steel. But is it not within the bounds of possibility that they represent, not the degeneration of a jaded and outworn civilization, but the rough, hard crude violent beginnings of a culture different from anything that the world has ever seen before?

CHAPTER V

CULTURE AND RELIGION

It is particularly difficult to analyse the relations between any intensive culture of one's ego and what is usually called religion because, under certain conditions, culture actually becomes a substitute for religion. By this I mean that any authentic culture exercises many of those mental and emotional activities usually the monopoly of religion.

Certainly it may be said that, if culture can be sometimes a substitute for religion, any beautiful and nobly rounded-off practice of religion renders culture irrelevant. Religion in its most flexible form does for us, in fact, precisely what culture does; and if we have been given a comprehensive and imaginative faith it does it far better. By this I mean that it would be absurd to besiege with the importunate propaganda of our culture-doctrines the personality of an individual whose whole being was already irradiated with the inward glow of a faith that heightened and quickened every pulse of life.

The whole purpose and end of culture is a thrilling happiness of a particular sort—of the sort, in fact, that is caused by a response to life made by a harmony of the intellect, the imagination, and the senses. If such a response is evoked by religion, where is the need of culture?

What we are here defining, therefore, as the true nature of culture is nothing less than a substitute for religion, where the absence of faith, in a modern person's being, has rendered religion unattainable.

But granting that the noblest type of religious character is already in possession of the grand clue to the situation, it is obvious that the ideally cultured man will find himself living cheek by jowl with many "varieties of religious experience" that are not by any means "ideal"! The problem therefore arises as to how such a person can most advantageously deal with religion, this exciting but very imperfect phenomenon with which he must be constantly in contact and very often in conflict.

He will find, it seems, that since religion and his own secret orientation of life run, in many places, on parallel lines, wrestling with the same difficulties, resolving the same riddles, encountering the same obstacles, there will be many moments when he can make most fruitful and suggestive use of this sister-cult. There will be many others, however, where he has to defend himself from it by every weapon at his disposal.

If, as is probable among most of the readers of this book, our culture-neophyte's abode be in an English-speaking community, he will find himself confronted by two main types of religion, the modernistic type and the orthodox type. It will be necessary for him to disentangle these two presences from each other and gather up his forces to cope with each of them upon its own separate ground.

What he can get, as grist for his particular mill, from the modernistic form of religion in these days, is, it must be confessed, very little indeed. He can, in fact, get nothing at all from it unless it happens that his culture has been of a barbarously egotistical kind so deficient in simple kindness that emotional appeals to his conscience, indicating the character of the man Jesus as an example of tenderness, shall trouble his complacency and make him more considerate.

But from orthodoxy, or, as it has come to be called in America, fundamentalism, there are many and profoundly interesting stimuli to be derived. Taking the anti-Roman kind of orthodoxy first—for I will call it "anti-Roman" rather than Protestant because I am anxious to include in what follows the Greek churches, the Church of England, and such Evangelical communities all over the world as retain their belief in the Divinity of Christ—it must be allowed, I think, that this faith in Jesus, as a Supernatural Being possessed of the supreme clue to the nature of the Absolute, contains something so startling and so beautiful in its mystical appeal that to treat it with unsympathetic distaste or with brusque, dogmatic denial, is to be traitor to that open-minded, sceptical suspension of judgment which is the fresh air of the intellect.

But granting that there is no rational standpoint from which it can be proved, as self-evident and irrefutable, that the Divinity of Christ is true, the question arises, what can our culture make of such an idea without sacrificing its integral self-respect, that is to say without giving up its suspicion that the Divinity of Christ is untrue?

What we have to eliminate just here is the popular literary notion that the dogmas of the Church are negligible but that its ritual and poetry are supremely important. If we have any psychological insight at all, we must have the wit to see that this ritual and this poetry ultimately depend upon someone somewhere having faith in the importance of the dogma. These faithful ones may be very few in number, but it is their faith in the truth of the doctrine, and

not any vague emotional feelings that we may have as to
the beauty of the doctrine, that keeps the thing alive. So
powerful indeed is such faith that it is possible for half-be-
lievers and aesthetic sympathizers to nourish their imagination in the presence of the ritual and poetry long after the
people with faith are dead. But not indefinitely. That, alas,
is certain. We cannot indefinitely exploit the faith of the
past. It is necessary, after a certain passage of years, to
know that a nucleus of believers still exists, else the sap and
pith of the whole matter will dry up.

And more than this. It is not, even for genuine sceptics—
that is to say for persons who really remain *in utrumque
paratus*, "prepared for either event"—the mere beauty and
poetry of a religious cult that fill the gap in their lives. It
is their abiding consciousness that there may be something,
some as yet unrealized and unrealizable truth, in the great
dogmas behind the ritual, which pierces to the heart of
things. It all depends upon what a person means by his response to what he calls the beauty of religion. If he means
a merely aesthetic response, such a response would apply
equally well, or nearly as well, to all the human mythologies. The imagination is stirred by ancient Greek myths,
by Celtic and Scandinavian folk-lore; but one responds to
these, unless one is a poet with the genius of John Keats,
in a manner very different from the way one responds to
the idea of the Divinity of Christ. It is doubtful whether
Keats himself ever dreamed that there was a living supernatural Being, even corresponding to Apollo or Artemis
or Hermes; but there are few Western minds—though we
are forced to admit that there are some—who do not feel
stirred in a peculiar and quite especial way by any allusion to the figure of Christ. This imaginative disturbance

does not, I think, accompany the idea of the man Jesus considered simply as an example of a beautiful, a perfect life. It is Christ, not Jesus, who excites it. And it is Christ, considered not as a supremely good man, but as a supernatural Being, a living Magician, a veritable God, who creates this vibration in our nerves. He does this for all imaginative people, whether religious or not, because He has actually become the God of the West and has come to contain, in the substance of His Figure, the passionate, and it may well be the thaumaturgic, power of centuries of desperate willing and waiting and praying.

Modernistic rhetoric, celebrating the power of love apart from the magical element in the universe which so many still feel to be incarnated in Christ, falls as ineffectively upon the ears as any other merely ethical discourse. The inner life of the ego, as it half-consciously, half-unconsciously builds up its system of culture, craves, among its other responses, some response to the miraculous and supernatural. This, of course, does not imply any unyielding assurance that these things exist. It only implies that the organic totality of our nature must always reveal, or wilfully conceal, an instinctive longing for these things.

Granting, therefore, that our culture will have something harsh, unnatural, secular, bigoted about it if it does not allow—hesitatingly and reluctantly, but still allow—at least one mental window open to the possibility of the supernatural, the question follows, what precisely will it gain from thus so obstinately keeping clear and clean this mystic aperture in its fortress-wall?

It will be a help in answering this question to enumerate some among the great men of genius who have made use of the Evangelical faith in the heart of their own inner-

most life. These men were laymen. These men were out-
siders. They were, in the common acceptance of that word,
sceptics; but the central magnetic fire of their being fed
its flame upon what it drew from the startling dogma of the
Incarnation.

It is not necessary just here to mention more than two
names. These are William Blake and Dostoievsky. Both
these great men were anti-Romanists. The Christ who inspired them was not the Christ of the Roman Apostolic
Church, but the Christ of the Evangelical heretics and schis-
matics. And in the writings of both there is much to help
us in understanding exactly what it is that the art of
culture can appropriate to itself from the Evangelical
faith.

It is in three characters among his creations that Dostoievsky embodies his strange notion of the mystical power
of Love, interpreting it from that unearthly Magian, By-
zantine slant of his, which Spengler feels to be something
altogether new in the world, something as yet not understood, and belonging, perhaps, to a fresh, psychic flower-
ing of the human spirit. This Gnostic oracle of "the proph-
etic soul of the world, dreaming on things to come," is
embodied in the girl Sonia in "Crime and Punishment,"
in the figure of Prince Myshkin in "The Idiot," and in the
personality of Alyosha in "The Brothers Karamazov." It
must be remembered that the essence of Dostoievsky's genius lies in the struggle that went on ceaselessly in his own
soul between his faith in the "God-Man" and his doubt as
to the existence of God. Dostoievsky, for all his frantic
wrestling with hideous distress, was a cultured man in the
profoundest sense of that word; was in fact a man who understood that the secret of culture is to have a knowledge

of relative values in this world. Thus these startling hints as to the nature of love which are scattered through his writings remain the passionate obeisance of a formidable, sceptical intellect before a supernatural visitant.

This, for instance, is what Alyosha felt when the premature decomposition of his Elder's body had been forgotten in the ecstasy caused by the dead man's spiritual presence:

"The white towers of the cathedral gleamed out . . . the silence of the earth seemed to melt into the silence of the heavens. . . . Alyosha stood, gazed, and suddenly threw himself down on the earth. He did not know why he embraced it. He could not have told why he longed so irresistibly to kiss it, to kiss it all. But he kissed it, weeping, sobbing, and watering it with his tears . . . he longed to forgive everyone, and for everything, and to beg forgiveness. Oh, not for himself, but for all men, for all and for everything . . . but with every instant he felt clearly, and as it were tangibly, that something firm and unshakeable as that vault of heaven had entered into his soul. . . ." 'Someone visited my soul in that hour,' he used to say afterwards."

It is in passages like this that the scepticism of the cultured encounters the movement, like the flight in the night of a dark meteorite, of something that interrupts the laws of Nature.

In the poetry of William Blake, too, one can observe the outposts of a sturdy, sceptical intellect installing themselves upon the terrain of Evangelical religion. Here is something that can be appropriated to its own purpose by any imaginative consciousness that has grown aware of the undercurrents of life:

"Jesus was sitting in Moses' chair.
They brought the trembling woman there.
Moses commands she be ston'd to death.
What was the sound of Jesus' breath?
He laid His hand on Moses' law;
The ancient Heavens, in silent awe,
Writ with curses from pole to pole,
All away began to roll."

But what culture has stolen from sceptical and secular Evangelical religion is nothing to what it has stolen from the vaguer, looser, more mystical traditions of "Natural religion." By Natural religion I mean that spiritual legacy of pantheistic feelings which runs like an underground river —every now and then spouting forth in an up-welling spring—parallel with orthodox dogma and drawing something both from Evangelistic emotion and from scholastic metaphysic.

From Plato to Virgil, from Virgil to Goethe, from Goethe to Wordsworth, from Wordsworth to Walt Whitman, there have always been great writers whose personal culture has been nourished upon this pantheistic tradition. Plato and Walt Whitman mingled it with certain polytheistic tendencies of their own. But in Emerson's essays one finds it in almost perfect purity; and Matthew Arnold's intellectual life was saturated with it.

Not less, though in a more meticulous way, did the aesthetic imagination of Walter Pater respond to its seductive liberation. This great tradition of natural religion is very old. Probably in its origin it was associated with the Orphic and Eleusinian Mysteries. But individual philosophers, from Empedocles to Croce, have been attracted by it; and for purposes of individual culture it has always had the advantage of exacting no faith in any concrete dogma.

But Evangelical religion as well as Natural religion has proved to be a veritable reservoir of living water for any spirit set upon acquiring a deep individual culture.

The Church of Rome in her proud, complicated, organic growth—like a great-rooted tree whose branches indiscriminately shelter apes, squirrels, crows, owls and doves—has offered to the wayfarer of life-awareness a no less rich, dark depository of occult experience. If one cites such figures as Dostoievsky and Blake as clairvoyant mediums through whose interpretations of Evangelistic faith we can approach life from a fresh angle, one has the right to cite the even greater name of Shakespeare as a medium for the more complicated poetic casuistry of Catholicism.

That acceptance of life in its miraculous concreteness which one gets in Shakespeare—each organic event clothed in its own circumstantial body of arbitrary mystery, and everything left unrationalized, and, as you might say, uncemented by systematized logic—is something that has a quite definite relation to the psychic atmosphere created by Catholicism. This atmosphere, so fecund of rich imaginative values, refuses to be resolved into the mere beauty of vestments and incense, of Gothic architecture, Latin liturgy and thrilling music. These have their place; but one may affirm with no tinge of scruple that, when these are referred to as the chief elements of what this type of religion has to offer, the person who is speaking has hardly begun to draw upon the historic reservoir stored up in Catholicism. What one gets from it is something far more spiritual than any aesthetic opium. A certain intellectual temper it is, or habitual artistry of the mind, an *antiquum organum,* polished smooth by long handling.

Who can deny the power of a sorcery by which those basic doubts and congenital fears so native to our perplexed mortality are relegated to a limbo at the extreme rear of the world's stage, while symbols of happier issues, set in their places by cunning "craftsmen of the spirit," are taken for granted, as if they were a part of the very foundation of life itself?

It may seem doubtful that they are such a part. But like some magic table, upon which our bread and wine is served and our candles lit, the Church bears up the weight of man's quotidian destiny; bears it, and has borne it so long that it seems a kind of violence to the good breeding of the soul to ask the uncomfortable question, how can so too-human a piece of furniture carry the burden of the Universe?

If a violent anti-Catholic were to put to a cultured person the direct enquiry "How is it that there can be anything for culture in a despotic and persecuting society?", the answer, I think, would be that, while those aspects of the Church were abhorrent to all free spirits, certain lovely qualities, both mental and emotional, could be plucked from it, just as you might pluck the most delicate mosses and ferns from an ancient place of execution.

One of the most lovely evocations of this superstition, and indeed one of the chief aspects of that sensitive temper, reverent and sweet-natured, which Catholic influence so often produces, is a felicitous blending of irresponsible humour and unashamed childish credulity. From both these things, from the relaxed humour and from the romantic consciousness of the magical side of truth, a person's individual culture can appropriate many delicate nuances.

It is certain that a cultured person will always be in danger of the blind anger of the mob, whether that mob be religious or irreligious. The pious mob will rise up against him for his atheism, while the infidel mob will stone him for his superstition.

I shall be assured by both camps, in the bitter struggle that goes on still between faith and un-faith, that a cultured person can get nothing from religion unless he wholly believes, and nothing from reason unless he wholly disbelieves. It is not true. An old religion that has gathered up into its diurnal mores so many of the hidden psychic attitudes that can undermine the malignancies of fate has the power of radiating its spiritual aura far beyond the circumference of the fold.

Here indeed, in this difficult question of the relation between religion and culture, we find ourselves compelled to face what really is the most crucial point of our present-day human situation: the problem, namely, as to how far it is possible to retain for individual lives, in the midst of the breaking up of the old traditions, those over-tones and under-tones of character which the long discipline of the centuries, under the scaffolding of a unified faith, has so laboriously nourished.

The exponents of any genuine culture in our time are forced to assume a stern and delicate responsibility: nothing less, in fact, than the building up within us of a stoic-epicurean life-system which obstinately refuses to be balked by the apparent impossibility of what it has undertaken. It has undertaken, in fact, to appropriate to itself the good of religion, while it deliberately casts away those props and crutches of infallible assurance upon which hitherto religion has depended. By "the good" of religion is not meant merely moral qualities and unselfish impulses; but, on the contrary, a residuum of something at once disturbing and illuminating, something that belongs to that element of so-called superstition which the secular dogmatists deride so fiercely.

The attitude which I am struggling to outline as the true attitude of culture to religion is not at all easy to elucidate in a few simple words. But it can be elucidated. There is nothing loose or vague or vaporous about it. It is a nice, delicate, exquisitely thin line—as thin as a fine hair—and upon this thin line, vibrant and quivering, the truly cultured mind must learn to balance itself.

Let me attempt to make the matter clearer by a definite example. Suppose that one saw written upon the notice-board of an important modern church the following inscription: "The Power of Jesus does not lie in any magical or cosmic authority, but in His natural human Love." How would a mind, cultured in the exacting and precise sense we are concerned with here, react to such an announcement?

Surely it would deny this statement! Surely it would feel that in spite of a certain sentimental and rhetorical atmosphere about these words the whole stress is wrongly laid. No one would have heard of this human love if it had not been the love of a Person regarded by the mass of men as super-human. Nor would this love—the love of Jesus—be able to exercise the spell over us that it does unless it were regarded as the love of Christ; that is to say as something different from any other man's love not only in degree but in kind; unless, to put it plainly, it were regarded as the love of a Being associated in some special and mysterious way with the dominant secret of the universe.

And if this is true with regard to the value of the love

of Christ, it is true also with regard to those ancient poetic dogmas which the world has associated so long with the idea of the Incarnation; such as, for example, the Virgin Birth. All these conceptions hang together; not so much in a theological system—that is a comparatively unimportant aspect of them—as in the psychic, emotional, and poetic body of feeling with which we react to the whole pressure of life.

It might perhaps be put in this way: Without committing himself one inch in the direction of joining any church or confessing any creed, without, in fact, abating one jot of his scepticism about the whole affair, the cultured person recognizes that it is well within the bounds of possibility that though there is no tangible human reality in the invisible world answering exactly to this Christian mythology, there may well be aspects of cosmic reality, in the mysterious system of things, corresponding to these extraordinary dogmas and represented by the vibration and perturbation —and also by the peace and calm—which these dogmas, just because they have gathered up in their long passage through history so many earth-born intimations, produce in our minds. If there should, by any chance, be aspects of cosmic reality to which these extraordinary human symbols correspond, it would seem a mistake not to leave a certain space or gap in the mind open, free from preconception, where these symbols can be allowed their scope. The great thing is to keep them in their place, in this mental gap, as one cosmic chance among many others; to treat them, in effect, with a certain lightness, so that our ambiguous interest in them should never be exploited by bigoted and fanatical persons, or by crafty and treacherous authority with the intention of imprisoning free thought.

Culture is not culture unless it induces, and sustains when induced, the one type of mind in the world which will never assist, never even indirectly assist, at any kind of mental or moral tyranny. Culture aims at producing a free spirit, in the deepest sense: free, that is to say, from the fanaticisms of religion, from the fanaticisms of science, and from the fanaticisms of the mob. If ever a cultured person were in danger of being martyred for an opinion, the only absolute opinion to which he could be forced to plead guilty would be the opinion that it is unpardonable to persecute any opinion!

It is our terrible, evil experience that the cruelty of human nature is so inexhaustible that it habitually uses—Catholics and Protestants are alike in this—these wild, strange, lovely, poetic dogmas as opportunities for a monstrous oppression. Theologically and morally, in the name of Christ they make war upon life. Life always wins in the end and always will; but in the meantime many lives are blighted and ruined.

Out of this complicated discussion, therefore, two points clearly emerge. First, that religion has kept clean and open, facing the unknown outer spaces, a postern-window in the prison of the self which common sense might only too easily have allowed to get blurred or shut; and second, that by cultivating the ecstasy of love an emotional nervous vibration has been originated on this planet which not all the brutal lusts and inert malignancies which belong to our race can ever entirely destroy.

In her obstinate insistence upon possibilities which reason is tempted to deny, religion has indeed helped to preserve alive that sacred ultimate scepticism upon which all sensitive culture is based. She has also, by her equally obstinate emphasis upon the freedom of the will, endowed the human ego with a certain pragmatic resilience, poised, taut and tense, like that of an animal crouching to spring; so that when its enemies gather fatally about it and all seems dark and deadly, it can work some interior spell that alters the whole situation.

Neither Catholicism nor Evangelicism has had the monopoly of conferring this power. There have been saints in the one cult and mystics in the other who have enabled the human consciousness to break loose from its normal moorings.

Condemn religion as you please for its abominable cruelties, it cannot be denied that it is within the circle of its consciousness that certain astonishing mental phenomena have appeared. In the sphere of what is called conversion alone, not to speak of calmer experiences, it has been amply shown, to the refutation of all cynical opinion, what the will can do, when dominated by this power, in changing the whole nervous system and transforming the unhappy into the happy.

And it seems to be only religion that can do what religion does. The cult of the senses, their awakening and refinement, can bring and can be made to bring ever-increasing opportunities of delight; but there are few epicureans among us whose presence radiates unconquerable ecstasy! The cult of philosophical endurance can bring, and can be made to bring, steady, obstinate, stubborn content; but there are few stoics among us from whose personality ecstasy flows forth like a luminous flood! But when one thinks of St. Francis's "Hymn to the Sun" or of William Blake's "Songs of Innocence" or of Alyosha Karamazov's weeping upon the earth, one is confronted by what undeniably is the greatest experience possible to sentient beings: namely, a heightening of happiness till it thrills through body and soul with a quivering absoluteness that passes understanding.

It is in the inherent scepticism of culture that the secret of our natural happiness lies; because we are then left free to be ourselves without any morbid fear. All thrilling discoveries of freedom are experiments of the will, and it is our scepticism of mechanical fate that keeps the will free.

How would the will be kept intact if we could not feel a certain philosophical doubt of every modern scientific hypothesis? Those irreversible movements of cosmogonic matter with which our grandparents terrified themselves, these newly hypothesized *quanta,* manifested in electric vortices of energy which dance their creative dance in the mathematical *continuum* of a Space-Time-Universe that coils back upon itself like the World-Snake of Norse mythology, present their bewildering physical-mental events to the sort of scepticism I am defining, and are received as a no more infallible reality than the great fantastic circles of Dante's mediaeval Paradise.

The open door into the unknown, the little crack in the starry walls of the world, which religious superstition has refused to close, remains one of the essential apertures out of the barred chambers of the human ego through which our life gets the fresh, cool, calm air which it needs to breathe. One is lucky if there are other vent-holes besides this one; but this is something, and of a value that cannot be gainsaid.

There is much more to be got for our deepest life from religion than the mere quickening of what natural and heathen goodness we may possess. Such natural goodness, with its accompanying humility, is indeed one of the greatest things in life, and no mean organ of research, as far as beauty and truth are concerned. But there is often a stratum of what Gertrude Stein calls "Stupid Being" in natural goodness from which certain wilder, stranger elements in human culture turn away, shy, baffled, frustrated, as if from a smooth rock upon which there is no ledge.

What we can derive from religion, even without wholly accepting it, is something that transcends natural goodness. Hints, rumours, glimpses, intimations touch us here, on this debatable ground, which it would seem unwise to reject—with such simple hedonists as Anatole France—when Shakespeare, Goethe, Dostoievsky give them a tremulous hearing.

It is true, we cannot deny, that to many intelligent minds religion is so involved with certain emotional and theological notions of God that it seems hopeless to attempt to get the good of it while we remain sceptical about these and even hostile to the very idea of them. But if our culture has, as in its nature it should have done, swept like an aeroplane over the centuries, and allowed the multifarious, shifting landscapes of God-worship to mingle and recede, to advance and retreat, beneath the speed of our flight, while the terrestrial recurrent nights of complete darkness blotted them all out at times, we shall have learnt the trick of separating the ecstasies produced by certain mystical feelings in the presence of the great dogmas from any formal attempt to work up what is called faith, or to proclaim what is called belief.

Although the existence of organized religion depends upon there being still left a residue of real believers, there is no need, for those whose secret culture is engaged in appropriating certain rumoured hints and hopes, to accept any pious attitude to the universe; no need to accept any formal attitude.—For as I have suggested elsewhere in this book, the nucleus of our personality, call it ego or soul, when it sinks back upon the inmost core of its awareness, is compelled—whether it desires to feel such things or not —to alternate between intense gratitude to the mystery behind life and limitless indignation. It is driven by Nature herself to feel gratitude when its being is irradiated with happiness, and by the same fatal necessity to feel defiance when the cruelty of things lacerates it or hurts what it loves. Thus all the theological conceptions of God, and all degrees of atheism and agnosticism, can be left to the surface of the mind; left to ebb and flow, to thicken and fade, as chance or occasion, as the mood or the hour, as one's malice or one's submissiveness, dominates the susceptible pseudo-logic of conscious opinion; while our real feelings, inviolably protected from the intrusion of formal belief, live and grow in their own region. And just as the real essence of what our culture gets from religion—those indescribable moments when, as Proust would say, the Eternal Being in us finds its opportunity to annihilate time— has nothing to do with our logical views, for or against the existence of God, so it has nothing to do with the question of the immortality of the soul. What this sensitized awareness of ours, which it is the purpose of our culture to integrate and refine, has really found in the wake of religion—in that long, tossing, moonlit track on the dark waters which the mystic tradition leaves behind it—has nothing necessarily to do with a life after death. It has to do with what Wordsworth describes as

"Something far more deeply interfused;
   Whose dwelling is the light of setting suns,
   And the round ocean and the living air,
   And the blue sky, and in the mind of man;"

but it is so penetrated by obstinate questionings, so saturated with doubt as to any concrete certainties, measurable by the rules of logic, that it draws back like a sensitive plant when any alien mind, working with the rational surface of the brain, calls upon it to declare itself as definitely for or definitely against the simple, popular, symbolic images of the world's hope.

The whole purpose of culture, as I have said before, is to enable us to enjoy life with a consciousness that has been winnowed, purged, directed, made airy and porous, by certain mental habits. Whatever, therefore, interferes with this free, relaxed spontaneity of mind is, according to the tone of thought adopted here, irrefutably evil.

Sometimes, undoubtedly, religion, both Catholic and Protestant, does interfere with this freedom, with this unimprisoned motion of the will which lies at the very root of our life. But before dealing with this aspect of our subject there is a certain moral question to be considered.

No man is really cultured who does not prefer culture to power, to fame, to money, to prosperous practical activity. But what about this or that noble cause?

The purpose of our argument is not to contend that culture is an aim superior to an heroic cause. It may be an inferior aim to many a self-renouncing purpose, entered upon in indignation or pity. This is a very complicated and difficult question, and one which each individual must decide for himself, knowing what he is doing and where he is going. On the face of it, it would appear most probable that the supreme wisdom consists in some kind of difficult compromise between culture and the heroic life. Every man and woman finds out sooner or later that his personal egoism clashes with his natural affections. The individual must decide. Love, as we have dared to hint—and not only the Love of the Saints, but ordinary human love—possesses, in its own right, most miraculous glimpses into the nature of both truth and beauty; and is therefore itself an invaluable organ of research, and one that culture were ill-advised to neglect. But it does remain, and it is only clouding the issue to deny it, that moments must arise in every person's life when a choice has to be made between our own culture and some laborious form of practical work by which other people are comforted and supported. If one has the conscience of an honourable man or woman, one feels instinctively that there are occasions when culture must be unhesitatingly sent to the Devil! But even in this case, though it must be whispered with some caution, it may turn out that in losing culture we gain culture! For it cannot be denied that although a concentrated awareness is what we must aim at there are many lovely and magical flashes of illumination which come sideways and indirectly. Indeed it may often happen when you are thinking of your ordinary task and are just plodding on at your monotonous human burden, that there will suddenly come over you a flood of delicious intellectual insight, bringing in its train just those very vistas and perspectives of indescribable happiness which are the final goal of the long cultural pilgrimage of the psyche!

Hitherto I have spoken in this chapter of what culture can derive of insight and refinement from its nervous contacts with religion. It now remains to speak of the inevitable hostility between the two when religion stands in the way of culture.

At this point, especially with regard to the young, it is wise to recommend a shameless Machiavellianism of the spirit! What a young mind were well-advised to do—where confronted by the opposition of stupid relatives or unenlightened public opinion—is to use the weapon of ironical submission. In other words, keep your culture to yourself, till, by practical activity, you have won your freedom; or, if you are too weak ever to win your freedom, keep it forever to yourself! This rather sinister advice does not mean that you need ever betray your interior integrity. On the contrary, you protect it by the best method with which anything great and sacred is protected—namely, by silence. Nature herself works on this plan in her vast reservoirs of mysterious life. Fight the world for others, if you will; but the moment you begin fighting the world for your own most subtle ideas your ideas will grow infected. The poison of angry self-assertive controversy will enter into them; and, even if you win, you will find your flag stained with the enemy's impure blood.

One of the most obvious marks of uncultured people is their way of blurting out what they think to be their inmost life-secrets to the first new-comer who is patient, kind, or inquisitive. It is a shrewd proof of how much more cultured, in the deepest sense of the word, illiterate country-people often are than clever city-people, that the rustic nature is cautious, crafty and slow in speaking of its interior life. Such a nature possesses an innate personal dignity and reserve in these subtle things, whereas the other gives himself away as soon as he approaches a stranger.

What does this mean, this glib chatter about the deepest secrets of life? It means the absence of that rich loam of idiosyncrasy out of which all culture springs. Aristocrats and rustics have one thing in common, and they have it in common, too, with all lovers and artists. They are unwilling to open the little postern-gate of their secret shrine for every casual traveller to stare at.

The reason why the cheap popularization of psychoanalysis runs like quicksilver through the talk-markets of the Megalopolis, is, firstly, because it disparages the power of the individual will—that *bête noir* of all mobs—and, secondly, because it brings down to a common level all the rarer values of personal dignity.

Where religion is injurious to culture is where, through the medium of stupid exponents, it offers a heavy, opaque, conventional resistance to all passionate originality. In other words where religion blocks the way is where it is false to its own Holy Ghost of original inspiration. But let youth remember—when its culture is threatened by religion—that no Inquisition can reach to the thoughts of the brain! "The mind is its own place," as says the Miltonic rebel against Omnipotence, "and in itself can make a heaven of hell, a hell of heaven."

One of the subtlest differences between culture and education, in their effect upon the mind of youth, is that the former counsels silence, where the latter is always anxious to expound, to attack, to defend. "Never argue," says the wise young John Keats. "Whisper your conclusions." What our intellectual young people should aim at, therefore, is that beautiful crystalline integrity, delicate and evasive, infinitely reserved, courteous and detached, described so eloquently by Walter Pater in his essay entitled "Diaphaneite."

Because a boy or girl is surrounded by stupid people, oppressed by a repulsive commercial tyranny, cramped by a revolting religious intolerance, there is no need for upheavals, ultimatums, overt rebellions. Sink into your own soul! Use your imagination and your senses upon the few simple elements of the Eternal that surround us all and the few undying books that you can lay your hand on, and create a new soul of awareness under the surface of your quotidian submission. There will always be earth and air and sky. Let these alone be witnesses of your silent, slow, unfevered growth.

Nor in your attitude to religious intolerance and moral tyranny, need even your outward conformity be ironical beyond a certain point. Better than irony, with its malicious after-taste, is a certain conscious transparency of natural simplicity towards life which even your cleverest enemies will find it hard to cope with. They will find it hard indeed to believe that such simplicity is not irony.

The most beautiful effect which religion has upon human character is just this very simplicity. Why should religion be allowed to retain a monopoly of it? The more sophisticated you are, the more deliberately will you aim at simplicity. You may regard it as a psychological truth of absolute certainty that the attitude of Alyosha Karamazov, or of Prince Myshkin, or of Wilhelm Meister, or of the young hero of Thomas Mann's fine novel "The Magic Mountain," is an attitude which the exponents of the moral intolerance you are dealing with find much more baffling, puzzling, and elusive, than any complicated philosophical or humorous contempt.

What intelligent youth should always aim at is a grave, detached, non-committal naiveté in its cultural explorations, a temper of spirit which keeps its sense of humour well in its place and never allows a cynical moral defeatism to poison the naturalness of its earnestness. "Earnestness alone makes life eternity," and there is no earthly reason why any intelligent youth of our day should vulgarize the freshness of his response to this mysterious world by a cheap cleverness, put on to worry and tease the simple philistine.

At the bottom of this whole relation of culture to religion there ought to lie a steady resolve, on the part of culture, to be not less serious than religion. Culture should in fact appropriate to its own imaginative life that intense dramatic consciousness of high issues at stake which is the essence of religion. Why should not culture have its own peculiar *Numen Inest,* "Deity is here," as it goes gingerly and warily through a world as full of black and white magic as ours is? The young neophyte of religion learns very soon to retain his furtive integrity under the cheap-jack fooling and brutal derision of the market-place. He soon learns to accept as inevitable the world's careless accusations of priggishness and fastidiousness. He expects to be made to look a fool and he is made to look a fool. If he has a certain psychic power of masochistic self-humiliation, so much the better. Thus it ought to be with the neophyte of culture; for if he is really sagacious, if he has the wisdom of the serpent as well as the harmlessness of the dove, he will know how to make use of all the complexes and perversities of his own nature in this ultimate quest.

He will in fact learn at last to be totally unashamed of his freedom from the warm-blooded facetious herd-instincts of his companions. He will learn at last to be as natural and simple in his intellectual aloofness as a sycamore tree among elm-trees. He will learn that the furthest reach of sophistication comes full circle; comes back to a naïveté so integral as to be totally unaffected by mockery and bullying.

Only very cultured persons possess, by a sort of grace of God, the power of being at once reserved and freely spontaneous. This is the supreme stroke of art; and it only comes to a person by a kind of heavenly luck. It means that the youth in question keeps intact the profoundest secrets of his being, while, in all the rest, he resembles clear, transparent water, free from the impurity, the meretriciousness, the dim blackguardism of any sulky superior pose.

Finally it would seem that since our pilgrim of culture, living here in Europe or America, finds himself surrounded by the psychic influences of Christianity, he would be thick-skinned and insensitive if he did not yield himself up to the profoundest of all the great Christian dogmas, that dogma which more than any other we owe directly to Christ. This is the startling doctrine of the immeasurable and equal value of every living human soul.

Certain very great men—Rembrandt, Dickens, Dostoievsky, Walt Whitman—had the genius to snatch this strange, disturbing, desperate doctrine out of the magnetic vibrations originated by Christ, and use it freely in their art. Here indeed can the lonely culture of a proud spirit bathe itself in the cleansing flood of a real, an authentic humility. The Middle Ages with their "sweet Fools in Christ" have not passed away in vain if the ecstasy of a conscious equality of all souls can still melt the barriers between man and man.

There need be no sacrifice here of that inviolable reserve

of which I have spoken, for in this ecstasy there is no question of anything but the ultimate human approach. Thou art a man and I am a man. Thou art a woman and I am a woman. Such is the magic word. The earth-bound solidarity, in misery and in happiness, of all the poor creatures of earth, that in human history has so often been outraged by monstrous arrogances and stupidities, remains the supreme religiousness of such as have come down to bed-rock.

And it is this great, poetic, natural truth to our blood, with its class-destroying, intellect-defying passion for equality, that culture must take over from religion, or prove itself not only inferior to religion but an obstacle in religion's way where religion is humanity's redemption. Not for one second does culture lose its own spirit in such moments of identity with all such as walk on two feet.

In this sweet, sad-happy drunkenness of equality it only grows clearer that to acquire culture means to acquire the art of gathering up the sensations of one's past life into a present that obliterates the first and last of all sensations—namely, that of the flowing of time! For what we recognize as the inner being of another, when this ecstasy of equality levels all barriers, is the essence of what we recognize as the inner being of ourselves, a pitifully enduring, pitifully stoical self, perpetually struggling to give the seal of the eternal and the significant to the impression-waves and thought-waves of the transitory and the meaningless!

PART II
APPLICATION OF CULTURE

CHAPTER VI

CULTURE AND HAPPINESS

One thing is certain. We cannot claim that Nature puts her seal of approval upon our culture until we can prove that it results in greater happiness for the individual who practises it. But consider our most usual unhappiness! Is it not clear that the most fretting miseries we suffer from spring from petty worries that have no connection with the larger issues of life? Here precisely is the place for an integrated and calculated art of sinking into the soul, that shall save us, not altogether or entirely—for the flesh is weak—but in a large measure, from this rankling misery and feverish restlessness.

The orientals are adepts at certain spiritual devices by which an inward calm is attainable in the midst of jolting and jarring confusion; and why should not we, who have inherited a more earthly tradition from Greece and Rome, catch the secret of some concentration of mind, more simple, sensuous, and imaginative than theirs, but not less intense?

But what will be the relation between such inward concentration and the natural happiness for which we all crave? The natural happiness? Yes! For by fair means or foul, directly or by the most circuitous routes, the fountain of happiness is what all living entities fumble and grope towards, in their troubled passage from birth to death.

And does the art of culture imply that we must retain a bold and clear awareness that we are seeking happiness, as we thus "sink into our soul," or is this a problem better left in obscurity?

Here we enter upon a region of man-traps, positively malefic with fatal miasmas and evil perils! Deep into the world-memory of our race have the dark rituals and cruel religions of former times lodged the dangerous superstition that by thinking of happiness at all we inevitably lose it. In this whole matter of our consciousness of the ecstasy of being happy and the misery of being unhappy there are occult and holy mysteries, only, it seems, to be approached without shoes! Dark and deadly has the instinct grown up within us which assures us that he "who loveth his life" shall most surely lose it. To dare to think about the question at all is like stirring up a coil of venomous cobras, as they bask, breeding, in the hot sand.

The poignant, acute difference between being happy and being unhappy is itself something that seems to make the whole subject as sensitive as a bruise upon a child's skin. But behind and beyond all this there is this dark insane sense of guilt—that it is actually impious to plot and plan for happiness.

There are probably all manner of subtle links between the erotic nerves and the most simple and delicate nuances of enjoyment which account for much of the touchiness of our feelings in this direction. Happiness, too, is such a tremulous thing; fleeting as a darting swallow, slippery as a silver-scaled fish, that one has come to dread—with a furtive shiver of suspicion—any meddling with those "arrowy odours" that seem to call it into being.

In addition to this reluctance, there is the immemorial temptation of man, the slave of casualty, to lacerate himself in order to propitiate the gods of chance! So deep has this self-laceration mania gone with us; so obsessed are we by the idea of the jealousy of the gods; that the thought of intensifying our happiness by any crafty tricks of the mind has come to seem ill-omened and a very courting of disaster.

Far more insidious than most of us realize is the great taboo about this important subject lodged in the inmost arcana of consciousness today. Modern industrial conditions, the feverish, unleisured, scrambling lives we live in the big cities, increase the power of this taboo. Pleasure begins to take the place of happiness; and thus when, at rare moments, happiness does thrill us, the feeling is so exquisite that we are tempted to regard it as a divine interposition, miraculous, unearthly, not to be sought for by human methods. Nervously we draw back from such methods; just as a devout monk, in the Middle Ages, might have to shun in haste a page of unholy magic, thrust between the innocent leaves of his breviary!

For it is as though there had been written, across the very sky of our darkness, by some terrible finger, that the thrilling ecstasy called happiness must not be spoken of above a reverential whisper.

It was the wayward opinion of Jean Jacques Rousseau, that great man whose excellent super-sensual sensationalism is so unpopular today, and whose very name is rarely mentioned without a sneer by our smart publicists, that the meaning of culture is nothing less than to restore, by means of our imaginative reason, that secret harmony with

Nature which beasts and birds and plants possess, but which our civilization has done so much to eradicate from human feeling.

As a matter of fact there are many points of striking resemblance between the undertones of Rousseau's culture and those of Goethe's. From the writings of these Nature-lovers the position could be defended that the beginning of all real self-development lies in a certain magical *rapport,* bringing indescribable happiness, between the solitary ego and "all that we behold from this green earth."

Such happiness is a totally different thing from what is called pleasure. It flows through us, stirred by mysterious memories, roused by unexpected little things, and when it comes, it comes, as Goethe himself says, "like happy children," who cry "Here we are!"

When once that sinister association between our conscious attempts to prepare the ground for such heavenly visitors and the feeling of impiety has been shaken off, all manner of mental devices—not necessarily oriental in origin—can be experimented with, by means of which one can renew the high experience.

But, before anything of this kind can even be projected, the insidious restraint of these atavistic inheritances from our old tribal prostrations before the Chthonian deities must be recognized as the evil taboo which it is.

To attain a defiant stoical calm is then the first step towards what we are seeking; for until the whole of our interior being gathers itself together, like the deep waters of a still lake, there is little hope that the magical picture of the world, purged of the horrors which we must acquire the art of forgetting, will mirror itself within us! Those ecstatic moments which we are now so impiously summoning up depend upon this "Mirror of the Psyche" being kept clear of disturbing ripples.

The mirror of our spirit thus prepared, it would seem as though the next step in our bold attempt to be "as gods discerning good and evil" were an act of sceptical detachment; detachment from that slavish submission to the chance-tossed accidents of our immediate environment, which untrained minds find so hypnotic and so deadly. By concentrating on the purer elements of this environment, upon the earth, the sky and the sun, and upon such stray presences of earth-life as fortune may have offered; by surrounding these things with the vague atmosphere of former magical sensations which they can be compelled to restore, the mind can purge itself of the troublesome pressure of litter and débris, purge itself of the worry produced by discordant happenings, purge itself of the evil taste of anxiety.

What this act of scepticism implies, with regard to the clamorous illusion of so-called reality, is the rejection of a very curious malady of the human conscience, namely the notion that one ought to accept what is offered by life, at its face-value. Not at all! It is the privilege of the solitary stoical soul to re-create such reality according to its own secret will; its privilege to make a clean sweep of what it has decided shall be irrelevant; its privilege to live surrounded by the essences of the exclusive universe of its choice. And, be it noted, this exclusive world, wherein the stoical soul obstinately wills to live, is not in any sense the mystical "over-world" of oriental philosophy. It is a world of presences which remain concrete, palpable, circumstantial, material even, although so scrupulously selected! If you call it an ideal world, it is so only in the sense in which

Greek sculpture and the Homeric poems are ideal, that is to say purged, selected, visioned in clear relief, stripped of the confusion of crass casuality.

One may admit fully and freely that for certain natures action is what brings the most subtle and tingling sense of happiness, and one may further admit that this happiness in the mid-stream of action need by no means be unconscious. One may admit too that, for yet other natures, analytical or synthetic thought, free from emotional reaction other than pure intellectual delight, is in itself happiness. But while admitting these things, it is still lawful to maintain that the most thrilling happiness possible to man proceeds from pure contemplation; and this is borne out by the fact that the highest ecstasy of contemplation, whatever its object, has a close affinity with certain great moments in love and religion, while it has none at all with either thought or action. In a certain sense the contemplation we are here concerned with is a form of action. It is also an ecstasy of thought. Its inner nature, however, remains a kind of sublimated sensuality; what, on grosser levels, is called lust, only in this case purged of the cruder elements of sex-desire and sex-possessiveness, and directed towards the great permanent poetic elements of planetary life.

The possibility of reaching a magical satisfaction of this kind by the mere process of manipulating the mind and the senses, by rejecting certain images and concentrating upon others, has been menaced in recent years by two opposite schools of thought: by the occult, which seeks to surpass altogether the ordinary phenomena of Nature; and by the mechanistic, which seeks to reduce to nothing the inner feeling of free-will. The "contemplative-poetic" method advocated here will seem to the former earthy and even materialistic; to the latter a veritable megalomania of extravagant ideal claims.

Yet it cannot historically be denied that a very definite art of happiness, at once stoical and epicurean, has been practised under innumerable names by artist, by mystic, by saint and by lover since the dawn of the earliest human culture.

Define it as you please, such resolute concentration of the spirit upon an exultation that is at once sensual and ideal offers a purpose in life which is more independent of external occurrences and conditions than any other except the religious; and for that an act of faith is required which is not given to all to make.

We must win, as Goethe says, our liberty afresh every day; and this can only be done by a very definite orientation of the will. We have, for example, to will our detachment from the hurly-burly of the world, till such an attitude grows to be a natural mental habit; till the nucleus of the psyche within us grows to be at once compact and fluid, formidably integral, and yet capable of turning into flowing vapour, so that it can glide through any thick-set hedge!

Can it be said too often that "the meaning of culture" is nothing less than the conduct of life itself, fortified, thickened, made more crafty and subtle, by contact with books and with art?

It seems to be sound psychology that what brings that swift indescribable thrill, heightening all we look upon, is a certain sudden revival of old delicious sensations, when by some unexpected touch or scent or sound these are tossed up, like deep-sea flotsam, from the recesses of the memory.

And what culture can do by its disciplined exercise of the

will is to prepare the terrain for such exultant visions. To this end one ought to be alert, even on the dullest and tamest of days, to gather grist for one's mill by assimilating these transitory essences and impressing them on the memory. Every day that we allow ourselves to take things for granted, every day that we allow some little physical infirmity or worldly worry to come between us and our obstinate, indignant, defiant exultation, we are weakening our genius for life.

It is not that we exult merely in being alive. We exult in the contemplation of that particular world of objects which we have selected from the rest, as being, for us, "the best of all possible worlds."

Memory and continuity! Into the future we are, of necessity, perpetually advancing. But the nature of this future is malleable; and if we have cultivated an intense awareness of the present and have crowded our past with delicate memories, that unknown element of chance which the unknown holds within it shall be compelled, it also, in due season, to pay tribute to the continuity of our days.

Infinite are the impressions that flood in upon us from our surroundings. Led by her dominant instinct the psyche selects from all these. In vain the trivial, the repulsive, the loathsome, besiege her and seek to hypnotize her. By long practise she has learnt the art of dealing with these things—the art of forgetting that they exist! Sprinkling them with the holy water of Lethe, that she carries under the cloak of her life-illusion, she reduces them to nothingness. They are there; but they are as though they were not there!

One of the most troublesome hindrances to this art of forgetting, which is so important a weapon of our happiness, is a very curious pathological phenomenon. We all carry about with us, but some to much more devastating results than others, an auto-sadistic Demon whose delight it is to throw foul mud at our patient aesthetic life, mocking it with perverse and monstrous profanities. This is the Demon who rejoices to hold up before our mind's eye those very things that with so drastic an effort we have flung into Lethean oblivion, hold them up and exaggerate them, till they become phobias and manias.

This is the penalty, doubtless, that any sensitized culture has to pay for its very existence; and all we can do is just to carry these demonic mud-pellets plastered upon us, as we go about our affairs; till suddenly our magic works and they have no more power over us.

It would seem, however, that sometimes a shameless vein of sheer Rabelaisian humour can be made use of, in our secret dialogues with ourselves, easing off, so to speak, the vile taste left in the mouth by the evil tricks of this auto-sadistic Demon, and swamping the devil in his own morass. We have really, in this crisis, reduced ourselves to the old dilemma of the self-persecuted ascetics of old times whose very preoccupation with their struggle to retain the Beatific Vision made them so especially accessible to the devices of the evil one. Our preoccupation is with the visible and not the invisible universe; but we too carry, as they did, our own little horned Satan about with us, whose grotesque whispers are the price we pay for our dedicated piety.

Continuity in one's interior life! That is the essence of the whole matter. Just as religious people kneel down by their bedside—and no custom could be wiser—morning and evening in the presence of their God, so we, devotees of a more secular cult, were well-advised to treat each particular day as an astonishing miracle, never to be exactly repeated, from which something unique can be added to our shrine of memories.

Without conscious continuity there can be no thrilling human happiness. That the self which awakens daily to a new plunge into the unknown should be surrounded by a magic circle of memories all orientated towards the same ecstatic sense of life, this alone is real self-culture.

It is not that we need ask of these never-recurring days any startling or exciting occurrences. That cry is the tragic cry of youth's eternal restlessness. The more culture a person has managed to attain, the more independent he is of outward circumstance. A man or a woman can be confined to one remote village-street; they can be bed-ridden at one village-window; it will still remain that a passing cloud, a glow of sunlight, a few blown leaves, a little leaf-mould in a flower-pot, will be enough; as long as the mind that contemplates these things has been gathering for years with intense awareness the hoarded treasures of its memory.

And now let us turn to a difficult and complicated aspect of personal happiness where culture can really be of immeasurable service. I refer to the part played in our life by what is called pride. Let me hasten at the start to define this pride as an integral feeling of self-respect associated with what we may call a person's life-illusion. One's life-illusion is that view of one's self, taken by one's self, which includes both one's rôle in the world, as it applies to others, and the part played by one's self, in secret solitude, in regard to the universe.

Now it is quite clear that nothing militates more murderously against one's self-respect than that helpless defeated sense that one is, as the saying goes, a failure. This feeling of being a failure implies that in the depths of our being we have accepted some objective, if not some worldly, standard of efficiency in life. If however our culture were sceptical and sagacious enough, and individualistic enough—as it ought to be and can be!—to hold in deep contempt all the opinions of the crowd and all objective and worldly standards, this ultimate pride of personality within us, this self-respect by means of which we lie back upon an unassailable life-illusion, could be perfectly content with itself apart altogether from external success, or fame, or prestige, or any reputation in the eyes of others.

We should, in Mr. Wilson's fine words, be too proud to fight. We should in fact be proud of our personality for no other reason than that it is what it is and that there is no other exactly like it. We should fall back upon that noble and primordial life-pride which animals, birds, fishes, and possibly even trees and plants, experience. We should stretch our limbs with pride and open our eyes with pride. We should be proud to be bipeds, endowed with the power of eating and drinking, of uttering human speech, and of walking to and fro across the earth!

It is precisely here that a real sceptical culture, by inspiring us with a philosophical contempt for all human grandeur and all human praise, may throw us back upon a deep, noble, simple, childish life-illusion according to which what we are exultantly and inviolably proud of is simply the fact of being alive, of being able to go walking about, touching things with our hands, blinking into the sun, feeling the wind on our face, the ground under our feet! The sort of pride a really subtle and poetical culture will supply us with is the same sort of pride an ichthyosaurus would feel as it wallowed in the mud; the same sort of pride that a horse or cow or a fir-tree may be supposed to enjoy.

This is as a matter of fact the great Homeric secret of happiness—the happiness of having for your life-illusion something that is inalienable from your basic bodily personality.

When the god Ares for example—that arch-swaggerer and villainous roisterer—had been so well lambasted by the heroic Diomed that he fled howling to Olympus, no sooner had the heavenly unguents eased him of his distress, than (so we read) he sat down by his divine sire "rejoicing in his lustihead." As a matter of fact this blustering bully-boy of a god-of-war had so wise a life-illusion that his pride was completely satisfied by the mere feeling of well-being. How proud he was to be able to strut about, to drink nectar, and finally to sit down glorying in his strength by the elbow of the All-Father!

What wholesome natural wisdom in this sly god's childish power of forgetting Diomed and his sharp spear! More than half the misery in the world springs from stupidly placed values. It is not a moral question—we have seen what a childish rogue Ares was! It is a matter of simple animal cunning. Quite apart from idealism, quite apart from virtue, it is the merest life-wisdom, drawn from the ancient earth, to place one's pride, one's self-valuing, one's life-illusion, where it cannot be knocked over—in other words, sturdily, simply, childishly, on the ground!

Here lies the whole secret of being happy. Ambition is the grand enemy of all peace. "By that sin fell the angels!" There are certain cool springs of happiness barred to all but the humble. But one need not practise humility. I do not

refer to these now. But the great art of life consists in placing one's secret personal pride where it is inviolable; where
it is unassailable.

This procedure may not be easy. But if we value happiness this is what we must do. There is no other way. Nor
does it in the least mean that one need de-humanize one's
self or deny one's self any natural response to such personal
triumphs (of the ambitious sort) as chance throws in one's
way!

This is no admonition to sanctity or heroic asceticism.
But one's deepest pride has to be given over, committed,
absorbed, grown "native and endued," to an absolutely different level of experience from the level of worldly rivalry.
What the ambitious man regards as thoroughly foolish and
is prepared to denounce as self-indulgent, dreamy, absent-
minded, a confession of personal failure, to a really cultured man, to an authentic stoic or epicurean (for these
opposites amount to one and the same thing when they are
contrasted with the values of the world) is the true purpose
of life and an eternal fountain of abysmal pride.

The whole difference between an educated man and a
cultured man is to be detected here. An educated man con-
fines his mental and aesthetic life to periodic visits to galleries, theatres, museums, libraries, lectures. When he goes
for a day's pleasuring into the country it is as a sportsman,
a golfer, a motorist. He is then taking his holiday; taking
it from education quite as much as from business, but not
by any means escaping from energetic action.

But in a cultured person's life holidays, like the lady's
love in Wilhelm Meister, are a case of "never or always."
Every day is a holiday! Every day has its own particular
margin of lovely relaxed sensations, upon the deep quietude

of which no practical, no educational disturbances are allowed to impinge. To the cultured person, that day is utterly wasted where one has been cheated of all time to one's self.

To an educated man's mind the pictures of Constable or Corot, of Hobbema or Ruysdael are all in the Museum; Homer's "Odyssey," Wordsworth's "Prelude," T. S. Eliot's "Waste Land" are all in the shelves. But the man or woman who is using literature and art as a means of enhancing certain thrilling sensations to be got out of life has (consciously or unconsciously) assimilated a feeling for that morning freshness, dewy and diaphanous as liquid mist, through which the legended figures of Corot move with such wistful grace.

This birch-coppice by the banks of an American creek whose heavy July-greenery invades the old dark woodwork of a water-mill, finds an added response in a cultured person's imagination, not only because of something Ruysdael-like, or Hobbema-like, about the way a thousand little objects are grouped there, but because of something in those rounded moss-grown branches, of something in that floating greenery, which suggests the kind of poetic romance that we associate with the Odyssey.

It is above all the sign of a cultured man to be enough of a connoisseur in the art of past generations not to be fooled into fantastic dogmatism by the art-theories of his own age. Although a violent and fanatical championship of modern art has a lively value in stirring things up and making conversation illuminating, as far as happiness is concerned, the more sceptical, easy, uncommitted enjoyment of every particular epoch we chance to encounter, for some special grace in it, seems the maturer method.

How many lovely and never-returning vignettes of Nature one might have missed altogether, if, moving through the world with a steel armour of modern-art arrogance about one, one had hardened one's heart to certain quaint old-fashioned inartistic methods, which nevertheless have, on occasions now totally forgotten, entered into the imagination and profoundly moulded it.

It is in fact a grand imaginative power, this liberation from restraint of the right of being thrilled by endless enchanting things, in both art and Nature, that break all the aesthetic rules! And it needs a most holy ignorance or a most sophisticated wit to reach this consummation! What real culture, in fact, can do for personal happiness is to simplify existence down to bed-rock, to heighten in fact those great permanent sensations which belong, as Wordsworth puts it, to "the pleasure which there is in life itself."

This achievement is of course a matter of habit. But it is a habit well within the scope of every son or daughter of Adam. To attain it one must be at once stoical and epicurean; stoical in one's power of hardening one's sensibility to "the ills that flesh is heir to," and epicurean in one's power of lively response to the simplest recurrent sensation.

The coolness of sheets, the warmth of blankets, the look of the little blue flames dancing on the top of a fire of hard coal, the taste of bread, of milk, of honey, of wine or of oil, of well-baked potatoes, of earth-tasting turnips!—the taste of the airs, dry or moist, that blow in through our opened window, the look of the night-sky, the sounds of twilight or of dawn, the hoarse monotone of a distant pine-wood or of pebble-fretted waves—all these things as one feels them, in the mortal pride of being able to feel them at all, are the materials, eternal and yet fleeting, of the art of being a man alive upon the earth.

Assume that one lives in a great city. Is there a particular street near us where the morning sun turns the pavements into aqueous gold? Is there a particular street near us where the sinking sun gives to every figure that moves out of that glowing furnace the opaque blackness of a goblin of the abyss?

Never, even amid the most obtrusive and tyrannous masonry, do the fluctuating lights and shadows of one day exactly reproduce those of another! The cultured man is the man whose interior consciousness is forever obstinately writing down, in the immaterial diary of his psyche's sense of life, every chance-aspect of every new day that he is lucky enough to live to behold!

CHAPTER VII

OBSTACLES TO CULTURE

The life of culture is really a pilgrimage; and, like Bunyan's Pilgrimage, a person can make his start upon this long journey at any moment in his life or from any conceivable situation. One's actual years make little difference. Whenever the start is once made our cultural wayfarer is bound to encounter dragons and giants, Sloughs of Despond and Dungeons of Despair.

Let us consider some of these perils. The melancholy thing is that the worst of them seem implicit in the process of culture itself. Take the mental condition known as "defeatism" for example. Here is a case of an important aspect of culture, its sophistication and its intellectual scepticism, turning round with an adder's bite upon the very roots of one's being. This weary, disillusioned note of futility in our life may take many different forms. One among these is aesthetic and besets us when the art-for-art's-sake view of what is most precious in works of genius dominates the field of our response and casts a blighting suspicion on every other kind of appreciation.

Writers like Huysmans, Maurice Barrès, the De Goncourts, Baudelaire, D'Annunzio, Oscar Wilde, and the particular kind of half-brutal, half-barren sophistication, represented by the garish over-crowded stage of Huneker's exotic "little flowers," tend to throw a rank withering death-odour over the natural up-shooting, the fresh green growths, of a sensitive mind's development. The cure for this spiritual wilting is not to rush into the arms of Robert Browning, or even into those of Walt Whitman; for nature can scarcely be expected to endure such violent oppositions, but rather to turn to Pater or Proust, or to Matthew Arnold or Landor, writers who are epicurean enough in all conscience, and heathen enough, but of a different emotional timbre.

At the very opposite pole from the tendency just alluded to is a much more widely extended peril, a terrible trap indeed for the poor pilgrim of culture. I refer to the mechanistic, anti-religious, "de-bunking" tone of mind! If the arrogant snobbishness of the art-for-art's-sake code poisons and blights, the elephantine philistinism of this "de-bunking" temper stamps with its clod-hopping heel upon a thousand delicate wood-mosses and meadow-weeds. In place of a patient ironic indulgence in the presence of human aberration this school of "treat 'em rough" puts it into our heads to go rampaging around the world like so many irascible policemen, rapping with our bludgeons all the nervous human craniums who see and feel what we cannot see or feel!

The great mistake these people make with their rough, blunt "honest, honest Iago" accent, is the mistake of assuming that not to be interested in religion, or not to be shocked by sex-lapses, or not to be averse to drink, are in themselves hall-marks of an eminent intellect. Unfortunately the road to wisdom is not so easy. But meanwhile this pathetic desire to be wholly and gloriously "de-bunked" often does the human mind much absurd harm. In fact one might easily uphold the position that a new and important stage has been reached in one's culture when one wakes up on some relaxed morning when the wind is in the right quarter to the illuminating idea that the great thing is to be "de-bunked" ourselves once and for all of this ill-bred pose of "de-bunking."

But alas! Such obstacles as these—obstacles laboriously placed by culture herself in her own path—are not to be compared in their power to do evil with the vapid and silly chatter of ordinary sociability among men and women. Dull conversation, stupid conversation, the conversation of those innumerable occasions when neighbours' hearts appear to melt towards those present while they chuckle over the delinquencies of those absent, the conversations of relatives who are not in the remotest degree interested in each other's minds, the society-talk of social climbers—it is this that can leave a person's whole interior being completely untuned, debauched, ruffled, outraged, with an acrid taste of dead-sea ashes in the mouth!

What happens under these conditions is that the mind gradually becomes hypnotized by one of those curious mental atmospheres that acquire a sort of horrible truth as they seep into us; the truth in this case being a certain level of the grosser human-animal consciousness, a level which we all share but out of which it is the rôle of culture to lift us! As Gertrude Stein explains, everyone has in him a certain amount of what might be called "stupid being"; but with the especially luckless persons this "stupid being" is the main thing! Well! Could we not assume that in most gatherings of people, however genial and warm-blooded such encounters are, the "aura" projected is simply that of "stupid being"? And may it not be the presence of this very "aura" that drives so many young people into black moods of reckless reaction; moods that are so disturbed and so embittered that the calm voices of the gods themselves take on a strident harshness when they are heard through such sick reeds?

A much more insidious obstacle to culture than this, however, is an over-respect for a certain smart, clever, cynical common sense when applied to matters of literary taste. A situation arises here that might well be named "Worldly Humour as the skeleton at the feast." Pitiful is it to see so many really sensitive youthful minds prejudiced against some of the finest and rarest of modern intellects by this "manly" jeering. Young natures are very like boys at school in these things; and when a rough-and-ready contempt is expressed for certain proud, elaborate, difficult fastidious artists—like Pater or Proust or James—such little black sheep have a cowardly tendency to crowd behind the bully who is making such a fuss and applaud his silly jibes to the echo. It is just here that a commonplace sense of the comic can betray a naive intelligence into the delusion that what is rare and delicate is unnatural and affected. The real affectation may often, we submit, be entirely on the other side; for the most annoying sort of schoolboy-wag loves to put on that airy tone of superior facetiousness with which "men of the world" are wont to carry off their own obtuse ignorance. Writers like Proust and Henry James and Dorothy Richardson are far too occupied with their own curious visions of life to find time for any genial propitiation of the average man's facetious camaraderie; and the result of this is that all these great originals can be made easy fun of for having "so little sense of humour."

Certainly when one contemplates the general condition of mental life in a large city, it seems as though it needed an inhuman obstinacy to avoid being sucked down by the vortex of vulgar sensationalism that seethes around us at every moment. When one considers the psychological fact that written and repeated brutalities hit the mind more deeply and vulgarize the spirit more grossly than those that we see in real life, and when one contemplates the unbelievable crowds of people that every day are saturating themselves with the illustrated tabloid sheets and thirstily imbibing the raucous comedy, the hoarse publicity, the incredible sentimentalism of their "Radio Selections"; when one finally considers the mere invention of such monstrosities as the ordinary "close-ups" in the movies; the wonder grows that any human beings are left in these places whose debauched wits retain the least resemblance to old-fashioned human minds.

Nothing but an extreme and an almost misanthropic individualism can save us from the ubiquitous atmosphere of all this psychic vulgarity. We must accept the situation. We must harden our hearts against social-mindedness. We must welcome proudly all accusations of priggishness and pedantry. The worst prig in the world is a less despicable animal than these besotted slaves of a "sense of humour," these flunkeyish lick-spittles of folk-foolery, these gesticulating Robots. Commercialized opinion, naturally enough, has turned against the teaching of Greek and Latin, those useless, anti-social subjects, in the schools. And what is the result? A facetious popularization of the old mythologies has become a modern craze; and while the real poetry connected with Helen of Troy is a forbidden affectation, the story of the woman herself lends itself most horribly well to a comic Freudianism!

The point to get lodged in the mind of any youthful

person, whose fatality has begun to urge him to take life seriously where his neighbors take it flippantly, and to take it ironically where his neighbours take it seriously, is that ignorance may be a most blessed advantage in the pilgrimage of culture. Merely to have reached the point of not being ashamed of ignorance, especially in current topics and the latest shibboleths of aesthetics, is a great mastery. Consider, for example, the difference between some eccentric bachelor who has discovered the very arcana of his most secret taste, of his quintessential soul, in some form of curious erudition, some mania for a particular art-epoch or thought-epoch of the past; compare, I say, such an one as this, whose leisured interludes are full of a mellow, a spontaneous, a whimsical fantasy, with the kind of shallow, encyclopaedic mind one meets on social occasions, whose lively chatter about a thousand clever nothings is more boring than the ramblings of doting senility.

How true it is that the greatest of all obstacles to any deep, banked-up, sensitive culture is the inability to obtain leisure, the inability to be alone. This is where any impecunious, over-worked person has every reason for becoming a ferocious Jacobin, a savage revolutionary. Of all practical problems connected with the pilgrimage of culture, this is the most difficult. You may, however, be perfectly certain that you are on the right track when your craving for solitude becomes a kind of desperation; a thirst that at all costs, and on every day of the week, must somehow be satisfied!

It is again no easy matter to deal with that gross indolent inertia, which every human being is subject to, even in his heavenliest solitude, and the causes of which are bodily rather than psychic. This is when the imaginative will, to which allusion has already been made, must play its part. Up from the innermost recesses of our being this imaginative will must be summoned; and it must be summoned until it obeys the call. What, when it appears, it deliberately concentrates itself upon is the idea of the cold, black, overwhelming darkness of death; the death namely of this body which is now proving so recalcitrant! Nothing restores that lost glamour, that blurred fine edge, to the spectacle of life, more than a sharp awareness of the exceeding great chance that tomorrow—or the day after tomorrow—we shall be struck down and all will be over. You may long for such a consummation as devoutly as you please. The certainty of its arrival quickens the body's pulse as nothing else can do. When, however, the body's inertia, that "dull whoreson lethargy," which proves so stubborn an obstacle to our intellectual pilgrimage, has been lifted a little by concentration of our consciousness upon the certainty of death, the will were well advised to focus its forced awareness upon what might be called the ego's embrace of its universe. Life can be forced into intensity only when the whole of our nature is strung up to wrestle with life and embrace it. The body falls into its place then, whatever its infirmities may be, and becomes a yielding, tremulous medium for that ultimate act of contemplation which resembles so closely an erotic ecstasy.

Thus it may happen that the very fact of our having to make a special interior effort to overcome our physical inertia results in a fuller flood of the magic of life than we should have known had the apathetic hour never pressed down upon us. It is in fact a sagacious trick of the mind never to allow any weary, insipid, lethargic unit of time really to pass away, without having clutched it before it vanished and sucked from its grey Cimmerian apples some particular juice, different from all other juices!

The expression "imaginative will" is intended to outline that integrated gathering together of the self within the self that would seem to correspond with what Cardinal Newman meant by the singular phrase "illative sense." What this "imaginative will" really does is to take the kingdom of heaven by storm; in other words, to fling wide open the closed casements of the ego to the inrushing airs of life. The strain, the tension, the interior effort is confined to this opening of the shutters. Once flung back, the effort, for the time, is over; and what follows is just an enchanted passivity, a relaxed and abandoned drifting upon a flowing sea!

The instinctive refusal of the interior ego to submit to the lethargic heaviness of these weary, apathetic moods, its revolt, in fact, against the gravitational pull of matter, becomes, at last, by frequent repetition, an inevitable automatic habit. So naturally, as the individual grows more cultured, does the inner ego respond to the challenge that the situation eventualizes at length in this, that the mere fact of any time-unit becoming inert and dull automatically releases—unless we fool away such a chance by yielding to the weight of "stupid being" in us—the very forces destined to rescue us.

One of the most prevalent obstacles to a growing self-development in sensitive personalities is the difficulty of striking a balance between the process of banking up our own peculiar taste and the process of extending that taste in new directions. In the one case our psyche has to harden itself into an inviolable core of resistance to innovation. In the other case it has to dissolve into a floating vapour of curious exploration. Until we have acquired this magician's trick with our inmost identity, our culture will lack its dynamic secret of growth. It is at this point that a good deal of harm has been done to the instinctive rubric of self-development by those favourite modern catch-words "rhythmic life" and "creative life." The exponents of this "rhythmic" method are very dangerous guides. Their advocacy of an unceasing *rapport*, always consciously maintained, between soul and body, is a grievous error. Such a *rapport* is invaluable only as long as we are banking up our identity against invasion; but when it becomes a matter of extending the circumference of our universe a completely opposite method is required. Then, as I have hinted, it is necessary to turn our inmost ego into a cloud, a mist, a vapour, a nothingness, a pure receptivity. At such moments, during such de-personalized ecstasies of exploration, it is only a tiresome drag on the event to cling to any conscious "rhythm" of soul-and-body. Then again, with that pompous phrase "the creative life," we can only too easily betray our real culture. There must, in fact, be always a systole and diastole in these mental movements. The fidgety "creativeness" of certain young artists is more than anything else an obstacle to their growth. At a time when the youthful Keats was passionately studying and even imitating Spenser, Milton, Shakespeare, these "creative" ones are playing at being "Dadaists," "Sur-realists," "Instrumentalists" and what not. The only way to overcome this obstacle is to cultivate the art of becoming nothing. Here, at last, we approach the secret of a certain passionate humility in the life of the intellect, a virtue which can be carried to the extreme limit without the least danger, since the great centripetal-centrifugal law of one's spiritual pulse-beat makes it inevitable that every rapture of humility shall be followed by a corresponding rapture of self-assertion.

We live in an age of cultural chaos; with the result that there never have been so many dogmatic guides. Not one of these guides but has some private angle of vision that may serve one's turn. The reader however will certainly have misunderstood the whole tenor of this book if he thinks that to become a disciple of Keyserling or Valéry or Unamuno or Santayana or Tagore or Claude Bragdon will relieve him of the necessity of cutting his own coat to suit his own cloth!

A devilish hindrance to any real culture is the snobbishness of preferring culture to personality. The least possible amount of culture, when what it does is to set free and round off the natural movements of the individual psyche, is better than the greatest possible amount of it when it hangs heavy and stiff upon the outside of one's skin.

Finally, there must be noted that fatal tendency, to which so many of the most charming Americans succumb, of sacrificing their culture to their native goodness of heart. One almost hesitates to refer to this, because there is something about natural goodness so much more attractive than anything except the finest and mellowest phases of the cultural life. It does remain however one of the saddest of human spectacles when natures, obviously predestined to a delicate and exquisite appreciation of the imaginative life, are betrayed, year after year, by their unselfish warmth of heart, into frittering away the unreturning hours listening to the egoistic confessions of others, in giving to others their nervous sympathy, their emotional energy, their very life-force. Why! The holy saints themselves always insisted upon having some moments of their own in which to "enjoy God," independently of their acts of social kindness. But our poor modern victims of "service" seem to be permitted no respite. From person to person, from group to group they move, letting their spiritual life-blood flow away in streams. And the tragedy of the whole situation lies in this, that, as the kindliness of these victims increases and the pleasurable glow of their too-human intercourse deepens and spreads, something precious, original, unique in the depths of their being gradually fades away. A meagre, impoverished, frustrated, diluted expression looks out from their "serviceable" eyes. This look is accompanied, and in a measure redeemed, by that glowing "brotherhood warmth" in the presence of which all human distinctions melt into something spacious and equal; but even this is in danger of becoming a kind of over-sweet drug; a drug which at all times must be supplied by fresh human contacts; and deprived of which, in any enforced or unprepared-for loneliness, these people are left empty and desolate.

But active goodness is not the only danger to the integrity of one's being. There is such a thing as a desperate pursuit of "Truth"; a pursuit fierce, relentless, absorbing, which is even more destructive than warm sociability to any peaceful self-realization. Certain physicists, certain metaphysical logicians follow the vortices and spirals of Nature's serpentine coils with a ferocious intensity that leaves all personal human life a thing of shreds and patches.

The obstacles to culture are often as insuperable as they are numberless. Our long pilgrimage is perhaps more like a voyage than like a journey. Below and around the harsh jagged reefs of practical necessity flows the full-brimmed ocean of life. On its surface drift and sway the nameless horrors—cruelty, monstrosity, distorted shapes of decomposition, lurid phosphorescence, fins of sharks, spawn of cuttle-fish—and the mind can torture itself to madness with these things if it will; and only by good luck or by great effort can it forget them. And yet it remains that if once one acquires the trick of taking all the material necessities and all the practical necessities with a certain lightness and a certain detachment, the habit of enjoying the sensation of life itself will gradually absorb one's consciousness and make an unassailable ship's keel if only one holds fast to the rudder, from the deck of which the eternal elements can be watched and wondered at as the vessel steers by its pole-star.

CHAPTER VIII

CULTURE AND LOVE

Since the art of self-culture is concerned with precisely the same stream of intimate impressions as that which is disturbed or quieted, quickened or retarded by every emotional shock, it will be found to be especially affected by the most formidable of all such shocks—namely the experience of love.

Let us approach this complicated problem, then—of the effect of love upon culture—by considering the normal case of the opposite sexes' attraction for each other.

The unfathomable abysses into which it is necessary to plunge our plummet before we can bring up enough salt sea-tangle for our analytical purpose is proof in itself of the deep intermingling of the culture-urge with the sex-urge.

The oldest among songs are the love-song and the war-song, among dances the love-dance and the war-dance; and when two well-chosen lovers or mates exchange opinions upon life, the heightened dialogue that ensues between them partakes of the emotional vibration of both these. Two minds, in a most literal sense, are better than one; and it is the very hall-mark of a certain thick-skinned type of conceited male or ironical female to throw away, out of lack of emotional humility, the richest chances of mental enlargement.

The primal origin of the liberating effect of sex-excitement upon our intellectual being sinks down into those obscure regions of animal-life and plant-life that lie at the background of all human consciousness. The intuitive instincts of the female, clair-audient to the furtive oracles of Nature, gets into touch with a thousand occult rhythms in the system of things that masculine logic misses. But how dumb, how inarticulate these flashes of wisdom remain, if not given shape and form by the synthesizing tradition of masculine reason. That devastating irony which is every woman's first instinctive retort to the pedantic patterns of man's sapless logic-forms, how richly it can be precipitated into a precious body of the most illuminating intimations as soon as there emerges the phenomenon of *sex-love* to orientate the two parallel methods of approach!

It must be remembered that the problem confronting us here is not the purely scientific one of the worth of any particular pragmatic hypothesis, but the subtler human one of personal growth in general planetary wisdom. A richly cultured mind, like that of Goethe, can fall into many specific errors, just because of its refusal to harden itself against a certain feminism in its own being (such as eternally rebels against the dry assumption that the mathematical laws of cause and effect can deal adequately with the mystery of life) and yet, in spite of such specific errors, can steadily grow more formidable in massive adjustment to the pulse-beat of the universe.

And what Goethe could do, with his more highly charged intellectual equipment, any pair of ordinary lovers can do, in their own measure and in their own place.

The potentialities of sex-love as a stimulus to culture can hardly be exaggerated when one recalls the profoundly magnetic unction with which two naturally predetermined mates are wont to heighten the syllable "we" in relation to their mutually built-up and banked-up system of inclusions and exclusions. The essence of a vitally growing culture lies in the accumulative force of its instinctive "yes" and "no," as various new claims are made upon its attention. A clever person loves to parade his topical and current knowledge upon this and that; whereas in the inarticulate depths of a cultured taste there are original elements that reduce the mere pretension of knowing the appropriate catchword to a negligible banality. It is the very fact that any well-assorted couple must needs spend so much time in thinking aloud which gives to their reaction on any definite aesthetic point an orientated bias that carries more weight than the wayward judgment of a solitary intelligence.

But it is in the actual psychic play of Eros-heightened self-assertion, when each of the two lovers is instinctively evoking an original vision of things for the sex-interest of the other one, that their combined culture unfolds like an organic growth. And such culture, a matter at once of vision and taste, will of necessity take to itself a mellower and riper quality than the purely masculine or purely feminine body of feeling such as they would be imprisoned by if they lived in isolation. For instead of any toning down of the two extremes of their separate perceptions, of the feminine intuition, for example, against the masculine logical formula, the mere fact that they are in love will intensify these differences to the limit; and the combined vision will not resemble an insipid compromise between exciting opposites or a vapid neutrality between living intensities, but a point of view that is as much alive as a child would be alive. Such a fusion of the imaginative perception of two people does in fact give birth to something that is completely new in the world; to something that would never have existed if they had never met; to something that may altogether perish with their perishing.

The recognition of this mysterious something need not imply that you must encounter the two together. Wherever either of them is, there this united vision of theirs functions. For just as any man or any woman carries, when in love, an illuminated aura to which complete strangers are attracted, so this Eros-heightened vision, this psychic offspring of their love, flings forth such an arresting gleam upon every kind of subject, that the dullest conversation is quickened by it and the most tedious platitudes transformed by its fairy light.

Since the true meaning of culture is a quickening and vivifying of a person's deepest and most secret happiness; in other words the attainment of as thrilling a response to the magic of life as that person's temperament allows; it is obvious that sex-love, an urge so perilous and potent among the obscure roots of our being, should affect it from centre to circumference.

Among the exactions that come between a person and any deep adjustment of one's personality to the magic of the universe, none is more evilly draining than a sex-partner whose basic life-illusion is contradictory to one's own. Different it may easily be; and the most delicate harmony be the result. But there are aspects of contradiction that seethe and ferment with a deadly fume; so that by their action the very roots of both identities are poisoned and all spontaneous cultural life menaced by a kind of psychic cancer.

Perhaps the profoundest liberation achieved by a happy

and lasting love-affair is the liberation from wandering lust, than which few distractions are more obsessing and none, except the swamping of a girl's personality by the subtle influence of her parents' home, more murderous to culture. The obsession of de-personalized lust has, it might seem, very much the same effect upon the culture of a man as parental vampirizing has upon the culture of a woman. In both cases what the condition of being in love restores is a lively awareness of the mystery of the *inexhaustible margin* . . . by which I mean the flowing stream of those simple not-to-be possessed elemental things that make up the background of all human life. It is the turbid fogs that sweep over our imaginative landscape, when possessive desire drives us, which obliterate these things and render them negligible. Lust-tantalized, lust-obsessed senses turn upon the earth and the trees, upon the sun and the moon as they overhang the streets, upon candlelight and firelight as they transform the walls of rooms, the same lacklustre eye that an ambitious man of affairs or a pleasure-engrossed woman turns upon them. It is sex-love alone, when it has absorbed into its being the restless hunt for sex-sensation, that restores to these elemental presences of the background of our days, their poetry and their mystery.

And the same thing applies to the deeper sorts of books and the more formidable works of art. It is the lover rather than the pleasure-seeker whose culture is roused to make the inevitable effort to overcome that natural human indolence which prefers the sensational to the beautiful.

Love, being the most magnetic of all things, is of all things the most effective in absorbing the pressure of the commonplace. The art of culture cannot find a more potent sorcery wherewith to evoke those illuminated groupings of people and of objects from which everything mediocre and meaningless has been purged away. Life and Nature are forever tossing forth significant and symbolic situations, full of tragedy, full of delicate humour. These situations contain platonic essences capable of nourishing our deepest memory; and it is only the disorganized litter of the day's crass casuality which snatches them from us and drowns them in oblivion.

The state of being in love—and even, in certain fortunate cases, the more permanent state of loving—rouses and stirs up that secret nucleus of our personality which it was once the custom to call "the soul." It compels this ultimate "I am I" to gather its forces together and to exercise, over the pell-mell of life's disorganized and casual happenings, its own creative will. Without love the mind's awareness of what is happening to it is continually being drugged. Lust, ambition, work, pleasure—all of these drug, drain and absorb it. Liberated by love, at one grand stroke, from these superficialities, the mind experiences an incredible relaxation. This relaxation very soon lends itself to a vibrant sensitivity in which impressions are received and values noted of a kind that are fresh, thrilling, original. What love can achieve for a person's life-culture is on a par with the miracle that a heavy dew can work upon a thirsty garden. The juices and the saps of a million frustrated growths bestir themselves within their parched stalks. Dumb, silent shudderings of vegetative awareness dream upward towards the drooping petals and downward towards the dark unconscious roots.

Thus it is that when one ponders upon the effect of love upon the furtive culture-habits of any man or any woman, one comes to throw aside the withering moralistic assumption that without offspring, or care for offspring, love must necessarily be sterile. It is, in fact, just at those moments when our deepest culture is illuminated by love that we are startled by a very singular intimation—the intimation, hinted at in certain mystical writers, that some momentous transaction is at such times actually reaching its consummation; reaching it on a level of experience stretching out far beyond ordinary human consciousness. Whether it be that when we are in love the masculine and the feminine vision fuse themselves in a clairvoyant synthesis, or that each of these distinct visions is heightened separately to the limit of its own orientation, there can be no doubt that, in the presence of some delicate landscape-nuance or of some rare aesthetic appeal, the imaginative lover has a subtle advantage over both the ascetic mind and the vicious mind. The complicated ataraxia of some balanced moment in a perfect dance, the mysteriousness of one of those lingering prose-periods that carry a perfume in their reluctant modulation, the fatal mathematical finality with which some musical phrase rounds itself off—these things yield up an essence to a consciousness quickened and sensitized by love—even by hopeless love—which is far richer, in its dim, green, springtime than anything experienced as a purely aesthetic recognition.

It is the fact that when in love we are confronted by the mystery of the whole macrocosm, confined and incarnated in a living microcosm, that quickens and ripens our development. The whole essence of personal culture lies in an intensification of the cosmic-sense. This cosmic-sense need not imply the predominance of any vague, loose mystical planetary emotions. It may concentrate itself upon a most

concrete, particularized, earthy series of small diurnal rec-
ognitions—upon the little things, in fact, of our normal
human life, grasped in their symbolic significance. But
whether planetary or particular, what it does imply is the
sense of awe, astonishment, wonder, amazement, ecstasy.
No lover can pass by unmarked such things as that Byzan-
tine spaciousness of faint watery gold evoked by certain
twilights, or that dusky blueness, rich as the coif of the
Mother of God, in which certain spring evenings end. The
lover takes nothing for granted in Nature because he takes
nothing for granted in the one he loves, who is for him
Nature's epitome. Awareness, awareness! That is the
essence of a cultured life, just as it is of the essence of a
lover's life. Uncultured people live in the world without
being conscious that to be alive at all is the one grand mystery. Driven by necessity, as we all are; driven by hunger, by
desire, by economic anxiety, as we all are; the cultured
human being never lets a day end without sifting and win-
nowing his store of accumulated cosmic-sensations. Miserable he may have been; uncomfortable he may have been—
but he has not been unhappy. He has said to the universe
—"Whatever you inflict upon me, I can still enjoy your
mad beauty! Even while you are making my life miserable
I can still enjoy this or that . . . and again, *that* and *this*!"

The cultured consciousness uses the Universe precisely
as an intelligent lover uses his dear companion. He secretly
enjoys its miraculous beauty, even while he suffers from its
unpredictable waywardness.

Fully must it be admitted that the tragic shocks of jealousy and pitiable decline of love are charged with cataclysmic threats to our deepest life-illusion; whereof what we
name culture is only the conscious development. The heart,

as one knows too well, can be taken, by the loss of love, out of Nature, out of Literature, out of everything except Music, which, in its strange absoluteness, lifts even desolation itself into the realm of the ecstatically accepted. It is therefore as crucial for culture as it is for happiness to work the magic that will prevent this loss. Some measure therefore of the art of love becomes an essential part of the art of culture if we are to retain what we have won. It is indeed just here that the deep saying of William Blake, "I forgive you; you forgive me; as our dear Redeemer said —'this is the wine; this is the bread'," becomes so profoundly applicable. For the only solution to that bitter knot of contrariety that tightens in such a deadly serpent-coil round the tree of life, when two egoisms clash, lies in this irrational plunge into illogical forgiveness. And such a plunge, although the water be ice-cold at first, proves quickly enough its own incredible reward. Each of the two egoisms feels the magical solution at the moment either of them makes the initial plunge. Between two natures, the weaker may prove the stronger in this daring venture; and the strange thing is that it is not only one of them, but both of them, that are liberated by it from that quicksand of mental possessiveness, where sex-hate is almost as active as sex-love. Strange too, in these perilous regions, is the fact that the secret inviolability and basic integrity of each separate psyche is preserved to an incredible freedom by this act of interior abandonment. Victims of one another the two seem destined to remain—until one or other of them has the wit to make this plunge; and, beyond all reason, to accept and forgive. But when once one of them has made it the profoundest interior self-possession is restored to both of them, and the buried body of Eros rises living out of the grave. It is then that once again, only now with a yet more unearthly lustre, the strange light of *sub specie aeternitatis* descends on the familiar landscape. On the great passages in poetry it descends, on the mysterious lines and colours of the rare works of art that the two have discovered together, on those invisible patterns of rhythmic mathematic whereby the art of music lifts the very pity of their misunderstanding into an ampler ether, and on their double vision of the world.

What is so withering to people's life-illusion and to their secret culture is not the obsession of love. It is the possessiveness of love. This possessiveness is something quite different from sex-attraction. It is a projection of that maternal or paternal cannibalism which desires to hug what belongs to it, even unto death. Who does not know the subtle way in which parents "set down the pegs," as Iago would call it, of the proud self-assertion of their offspring? To this gloating, levelling, cannibalistic "love" the victim's faults and weaknesses—yes! its worst vices—are equally accepted as "dear" and "darling" with its most desperate idealisms. Who has not watched a mother stroke her child's cheek or kiss her child *in a certain way,* and felt a nervous shudder at the possessive outrage done to a free solitary human soul?

When the real original culture of a boy or a girl first becomes consciously important; when, thrilled by vague delicious dreams, dreams of a reality of magical essences, hidden behind the cruder reality of his home, he takes to his parents a scrawl, a jingle, a toy-erection, a painted bird or flower or ship—let the parent note well that the significance of this does not lie in the "cuteness" or pathos of the thing itself, but in the dream-attitude towards reality, the dream-ecstasy of finding a different reality, of the child's thoughts as he was making it.

The number of unknown original geniuses who have been destroyed and brought to nothing by this levelling possessiveness would be staggering if the truth were known. It is this vicious "love," more than any other force, that blights, poisons, devours. It feeds, like a deadly caterpillar, upon the green sap-filled leaves of youthful culture, attacking them when they are tenderest, most sensitive, most helpless. Massive, slow-moving, super-masculine writers are the ones to escape this curse. Like wily badgers they shuffle backwards into their holes and there lie *perdu*. But where they gain in independence they lose in critical help; for in fleeing from the female harpies they sacrifice that mysterious cosmic-feminine influence of which Goethe makes mention at the end of Faust.

But sex-love is not the only kind of love; though undoubtedly, that element enters into many more human relationships than we guess. It certainly blends most bafflingly with almost all forms of passionate friendship.

Where passionate friendship is concerned all that I have just been saying with regard to love holds true. It is, however, a very different thing when we come to consider ordinary friendship. Friendship undoubtedly has a perilous and double-edged influence upon one's culture. And although nothing, no influence, no environment, no mockery or derision, can divert from the path the person who is born to tread the path, yet there is a certain margin of sensitivity where our culture can be helped and hindered to a startling degree by the personal friends that chance has selected for us.

The influence of friendship upon culture differs from that

of love, in that it assumes the basic idiosyncrasies of personal taste to be unalterable. Love, in spite of all rational knowledge to the contrary, is always in the mood of believing in miracles. By believing in miracles love works miracles; and in this matter of a person's deepest cultural tendencies it is astonishing what changes, for good or for evil, love can effect.

But friendship takes these fundamental personal characteristics for granted. It rejoices in them or it condones them. It has no desire to change them. Thus the effect of friendship upon culture is something concerned with such influences as can be brought to bear upon the outstanding temperamental traits; not to change them; only to exploit them, enjoy them, share them, contradict them; dispute, criticize, analyse and steer them!

It gives us an interesting hint as to how absolutely different are the various arts in their emotional effect upon us, when one comes to recognize that one gets so much less from one's friend in the arts of literature and music than in the plastic arts. From repeated arguments with a friend about some modern sculptor or painter—Brancusi, let us say, or Picasso, or Matisse—one's whole attitude to such an artist might gradually be changed. One might return again and again to the gallery, ponder on the works in question and quite likely come eventually to the conclusion that there was far more in the clue he had suggested than one had dreamed of.

But in literature and music it seems to be a totally different case. These things sink into one's being through some sixth sense not used in the plastic arts. One's whole nature must be saturated with these in a manner far more absorbed and abandoned than with those. No arguments with a friend, however often repeated, would seduce us from our allegiance to Proust, say, or to Stravinsky. This is because literature and music gather up into themselves a thousand floating impressions quite independent of the eye, morsels of mysterious feeling, drawn some of them from our unconscious atavistic life and some of them from those blind obscure motions of the blood that seem to belong to darkness rather than to light, to time, shall we say, rather than to space.

The influence of a friend upon one's deeper culture seems, too, to find its natural boundary when it touches our ingrained attraction to certain particular periods in the past. It is just here, where love would be peculiarly clairvoyant, even wickedly and destructively clairvoyant, that friendship is often brusque, hasty, impatient, apathetic. Our mania for a particular *genre* in art, let us suppose, for a special school of early Italian pictures, may easily have become an habitual *aperçu*, by which we have learnt to feel ourselves into some particular aspect of Nature—the peculiar effect, say, of sharply-cut silver-blue leaves against an ethereal horizon or of violet hills against blue space—but this aspect of Nature may be the very one against which our friend has long been, so to speak, defending himself, in his predilection for the wild-tossed, greenish-brown branches of later, romantic landscapes, heavily charged with the impending expectancy of mythological events. A lover, under such circumstances, would instinctively dream of some miraculous metempsychosis, by means of which either your secret-illusion would be transformed, or his (or hers) would be transformed. A profound uneasiness would trouble both your impassioned minds until, in the hidden depths of your opposed instincts, some mysterious psychic change *did* occur.

Finally, to sum up all this, it would seem as if the ideal situation for a cultured man or woman is to have a lover of the opposite sex with whom "deep might call unto deep" in regard to the basic mysteries of beauty, while at the same time he had one or two intimate friends whose explorations into completely new fields of aesthetics would constantly enlarge his discernment and supply other *points d'appui* from which he could carry his guarded, exclusive, and banked-up preferences into "fresh woods and pastures new."

CHAPTER IX

CULTURE AND NATURE

The most important aspect of all culture is the gathering together of the integral self into some habitual way of response to Nature, that shall become ultimately automatic by means of fuller and fuller awareness. What, as we have seen, should be the background of all one's days and of all one's experience, is a certain habitual philosophy of life, resolving itself into a confronting of the "not-self" by a consciously integrated self. This habit of feeling, this attitude of the self towards the not-self, would remain the same, even if our scepticism of objective reality were carried into an extreme solipsism; in other words, into regarding all the impressions that come to us as merely the dreams, *in vacuo,* of our own solitary ego.

Of these conscious gatherings together of the scattered sensibilities of the ego, in face of the "not-ego," the most important, then, is our response to Nature and to whatever it may be that lies behind Nature. Few, among even the most unfortunate of us, whether in slums or hospitals or asylums or prisons, are bereft of all glimpses of Nature. Something at least of what "prisoners call the sky," during some moments of the day, must be revealed even to the most unlucky; and if not even that, there will always remain memories of what we have already felt.

The great test of culture, even for those who have the

use of all their powers and are free to go forth as they please, is always the conscious way in which they make use of memory. Memory remains forever the mother of all the Muses; and in our response to Nature it is the accumulated memory of all past responses that gives weight and poignancy to what we feel at the moment. Comparison enters so much. This particular grouping of things, this especial perspective, this patch of sky with floating clouds, this fragment of a hill-side, or a cliff, or a road, or a field, is added with so much more definiteness to our store-house of prevailing impressions because of vague or vivid memories of similar visions in the past.

No refining of one's taste in matters of art or literature, no sharpening of one's powers of insight in matters of science or psychology, can ever take the place of one's sensitiveness to the life of the earth. This is the beginning and the end of a person's true education. Art and literature have been shamefully abused, have been perverted from their true purpose, if they do not conduce to it. The cultivation in one's inmost being of a thrilling sensitiveness to Nature is a slow and very gradual process. The first conscious beginnings of it in early childhood are precious beyond words as the origin of dominant memories; but the more deliberately we discipline our sensitive grasp of these things, the deeper our pleasure in them grows.

The first conscious aim which it would be wise to concentrate upon is the difficult art of simplification. The difference between cultured people and uncultured people, in regard to their response to Nature, is that the former make a lot of a little, whereas the latter make little of a lot. By this I mean that the less cultured you are the more you require from Nature before you can be roused to reciprocity. Uncultured people require blazing sunsets, awe-inspiring mountains, astonishing water-falls, masses of gorgeous flowers, portentous signs in the heavens, exceptional weather on earth, before their sensibility is stirred to a response. Cultured people are thrilled through and through by the shadow of a few waving grass-blades upon a little flat stone, or by a single dock-leaf growing under the railings of some city-square. It is an affectation to boast, as certain moralists do, that a city-dweller can get the same thrill from dingy sparrows and dusty foliage as from a rain-wet meadow full of buttercups. Better were it, than any such pretension, simply to recognize that in the deepest levels of culture city-dwellers are at a disadvantage compared with country-dwellers. Better were it, if it is your ill-luck to live in a city, to hasten into the country, at least once a week, and spend all your dreams during the other days in remembering that happy seventh-day excursion.

But granting that, by hook or by crook, we can obtain some daily or weekly glimpse of Nature free from masonry and pavements, it seems that the best way of deriving lasting enjoyment from such glimpses is to simplify one's pleasure to the extremest limit possible. By this I mean that it is always wise to avoid show-places and choose for your excursions into the country the simplest and most natural scenery you can find. To a cultured mind no scenery is ordinary, and such a mind will always prefer solitude in an unassuming landscape to crowds of people at some famous "inspirational" resort.

Fate itself usually decides what kind of scenery it is that we are able to reach without hardship; but, if the element of choice does enter, it would seem to enter as determining the sort of landscape which is most profoundly congruous with our temperament. There is undoubtedly a deep affinity, probably both psychic and chemical, between every individual human being and some particular type of landscape. It is well to find out as soon as possible what kind this is; and then to get as much of it as you can. There must be many hill-lovers and many sea-lovers who suffer constantly from a vague discomfort and suppressed nostalgia, although such feelings may be completely unconscious, as year by year they are condemned to spend their lives in some pastoral or arable plain. On the other hand there must be plenty of people, born for placid undulating luxuriant country and yet doomed to live in some austere, rocky region where all the contours are harsh and forbidding.

There can be no doubt that the primary satisfaction in regard to Nature is sensual. People ought to cultivate sensuality where scenery is concerned. One ought to touch it, to taste it, to embrace it, to eat it, to drink it, to make love to it. Many people when they spend a never-to-be-given-back day in the country lose all the imaginative good of their experience by talking and fooling. It is almost impossible to get any really deep impressions—whether sensual or mystical—from such an excursion unless you go alone or with one other person—a blood-relation or with some one you are in love with.

It is strange how few people make more than a casual cult of enjoying Nature. And yet the earth is actually and literally the mother of us all. One needs no strange spiritual faith to worship the earth.

Religious people—and quite properly—go to their Mass fasting. Delicate and rare are the mystic feelings they have; but not less exquisite are the sensations of those who walk

in the pastures of the Great Mother. She too, as well as
the Mother of Christ, deserves the worship of an empty
belly. The real initiates of this cult will never sit down to
breakfast without having walked at least a few steps in the
open air. After a night's sleep the senses are virginal. Objects and sounds and fragrances ravish them then, as they
cannot do at a later hour. Between the life of the earth,
freshened by her bath or sleep, and the life of any of her
offspring, there is a mysterious reciprocity at such a time.
A grass-blade is more than a grass-blade in the early morning; the notes of a bird more than a song; the scent of a
flower more than a sweet fragrance.

Each of the other hours has its own secret too. How
porous and insubstantial are the moments just before and
just after sunset. Who does not know, even among city-
dwellers, that peculiar wash of dark blue air which seems
to flow in over the whole earth and become a new firma-
ment between earth and heaven until the first stars appear
and the night falls? What an unique delight there is too
in giving reckless scope to the delicious feeling of drowsiness that will overtake you sometimes on a warm thyme-
strewn bank or by the edge of a hot corn-field! This noon-
drowsiness, this magic noon-sleep, is an experience by itself.
It is heavy with the rank saps and the gross juices of the
Goat-foot's engendering. It has certain primeval relaxings
and releasings. Heady, tonic revelations it has too, hardly
to be revealed to the profane.

But it is rather in the twilight than in the heat of the
day, or perhaps just before the twilight, when the sun
falls horizontally across the earth, that the deepest buried
springs of memory within us are stirred. What is there
about those lengthening shadows when they fall across

lawns or meadows from motionless tree-branches that stirs the mind and makes a person feel strangely kind to his worst-hated enemy? What is there about a long white road, disappearing in the twilight over a ridge of hills to some remote, unseen destination that touches the imagination in a way so hard to put into words?

There is no necessity to answer such questions; but there is a deep necessity for waiting long and long for the experiences which are so inexplicable. He would be an arrogant fool who dared to call himself a cultured man without ever having made an intense and special cult of enjoying these rare moments. It will, I believe, be often noticed that when a person wants to *appear* cultured what he does is to profess aesthetic or artistic admiration for certain arrangements of form and colour in Nature. Nothing is more annoying, more teasing than this. It seems so irrelevant to drag in these pseudo-art-motifs when the life of Nature is so satisfying in itself. What the real Nature-lover does is to lose himself and all his most passionate art-theories in an indescribable blending of his being with the plough-land or meadow-land over which he walks.

Some essential portion of his identity, some psychic projection of his ego, rushes forth to embrace this patch of earth-mould, this tuft of moss, this fern-grown rock. He does not really think about what the poets would call its beauty. In fact, whenever you hear anyone begin to murmur about "the beauties of Nature" you are justified in doubting whether that one is possessed of the real clue to them. Such people are summer-lovers and holiday-lovers. A few October rains, a few November storms, and off they go, fleeing in discomfort to their cozy pavements and reassuring fire-escapes.

No, the real Nature-lover does not think primarily about the beauty of Nature; he thinks about her life. Beauty of course he does find in her, and a thousand suggestions for art too; but what attracts him, what he worships, is herself, her peculiar identity. Whether at the particular moment she is looking lovely or sinister, cheerful or sorrowful, peaceful or tragic, he loves her for herself. Her winds may be bitter, her rains cold, her frosts keen, her skies lowering, her streams swollen, her roads rough, her mud deep, her swamps miasmic, her uplands barren; to her constant lover it is enough that she is what she is.

And her lover ever desires to have her to himself. The real initiate of Nature will naturally avoid the main highways and prefer to travel on foot. Not that he will be the type of person who has a mania for showing to the world how far he can walk. Such an individual is a freak-athlete, not a lover of the earth. The physical exhaustion of such exploits and the tenseness of so much strain dull the finer edges of one's receptivity and turn a natural happiness, full of delicate, lightly caught sensations, into a stark preoccupied endurance.

The whole essence of this great Nature-cult is to store up and lay by thousands and thousands of impressions. The memory can hold much more than most people give it credit for; and the quickened awareness of our days depends upon our memory. The feelings that can be roused in us by innumerable little physical impressions, coming and going upon the wind, lost in the air, are feelings that bind our years together in a deep secretive piety. Nor need we ever be ashamed of such a secret life, hidden from the uproar and clamour of the world, nor be bullied into regarding it as selfish. Who knows? Who can tell? It may well be that Nature herself—or at least our own planetary Earth —depends upon such subtle ecstasies in her offspring for her own indescribable self-realization. The feelings that move us at many moments when we are alone with Nature, "with thoughts that do often lie too deep for tears," seem to bring their own justification. They associate themselves inevitably with generous human emotions, with indulgence towards all creatures, with pity for all creatures. And although not consciously directed towards any form of definite action, they give to all our actions a large, transparent background such as provides an inward escape.

A life deliberately given up, in the secret levels of its being, to such a cult as this is not a wasted life; it is a triumphant life. It fulfils some absolute purpose in things that are outside and beyond the troubled fevers of the world.

Let us suppose for a moment that the reader of this book lives in some easterly quarter of the United States. It seems to me of the greatest importance to make exactly clear what from our present point of view a person's mind really gets from its contemplation of Nature in such a place. Let my reader permit me, therefore, a palpable example of what I am trying to hint at. One leaves the streets of a town or city, let us say, and after a few sub-urban avenues one reaches the outskirts of the adjoining country. Here there may still be a few houses, even those absurdly freakish ones, in the erection of which the un-civilized rich and their aggressive "realtors" combine to make modern architecture so barbarous a monstrosity; but between these houses the open fields begin to appear and one catches scattered glimpses of arable horizons or wooded hills. There is grass, too, now by the side of the road; and even if the road itself is cemented for motor-traffic there is mud, wet or dry, in the ditch and possibly a dirt-path, foot-trodden and hoof-marked, running beside it. Here precisely is a situation wherein one may mentally test oneself as to the presence or absence in one's inmost personality of the sort of culture defined in this book.

If you are totally alien to such a cult it will be only by some unlucky accident that you find yourself on foot at all just here. According to your habits you would be rushing past this wayside plane-tree, this wooden bridge, this dilapidated cattle-shed, this patch of swamp-marsh, this group of wind-bent pines, insensibly gripping the wheel of your car and thinking of nothing but your affairs. That you are on foot at all in such a spot, if not due to pure accident, witnesses adherence to the cult of Nature. And then how instinctively you will find yourself debouching from that hard, concrete roadway and hastening to feel under your boot-soles the yieldingness of the flesh of the earth! Your whole nature will soon be absorbed in watching that rack of clouds in the northern horizon, that undulating pasture where a few black-and-white cattle are grazing, that vast corn-field, now interspersed with melancholy, piled-up corn-stalks, forlorn amid the close-cropt stubble.

Let us assume the month to be November, so often sad. Turning your back to the traffic in the highway and standing for a moment at the road's edge you may chance to see a thistle growing there or a solitary dock-leaf or a faded, flowerless sprig of iron-weed or milk-weed. This abject and forlorn plant, let us imagine, is growing on the crest of a sandy bank wherein at a glance you can see embedded certain common fossil-shells—ammonites perhaps—and beneath the stalk of the plant and a little above those stone fos-

sils you can catch a glimpse of the trailing roots of a neigh-
bouring elder-bush whose tarnished leaves and dried-up
seed-husks outline themselves, like the head of that thistle
or the leaf of that dock, against the grey horizon. As you
gaze at these things, innumerable memories, drawn from a
thousand impressions of childhood, flow into your mind.
The blurred edge of that sandy bank, here a grass-blade,
there an empty snail-shell, the grey spikes of that thistle,
the texture of that dock-leaf, gather to themselves a symbolic value as you stare at them. They become represen-
tative of the whole mysterious face of the earth, held up in
that November greyness, haggard and tragic, to that curved
dome of grey vapour which is all you can see of the over-
arching sky. And as you continue to look at all this, concentrating your whole nature upon it, and forgetting all
else, it gradually comes over you, that between your secret
identity,—part physical, part psychic—and the secret identity, physical and psychic also, of these stalks and leaves,
of these sand-grains and stone-fossils, there is a reciprocity
beyond all rational understanding. It may easily be that
the feelings you have at the sight of these things do not
amount to anything in the least resembling an ecstasy of
happiness; do not amount to anything in the least resembling a mystical emotion. That does not matter. What
matters is that in the calmest and most earth-bound manner
you should concentrate your thoughts upon the whole ron-
dure of the turning globe as it transports all its living burden through measureless space-time, of which burden, just
now, this thistle-head, these ash-roots, this tarnished dock-
leaf, together with your own flesh-covered human skeleton,
are transitory fragments.

It is thus not merely the beauty of these little objects—

though there may be beauty enough in the silveriness of the thistle, in the metallic lustre of the leaf, and in the yellowness of the sand—which will arrest your thoughts. You are more than an aesthetic or artistic admirer; you are a lover! What you will come to feel is a singular identity between your own inner being and the inner being of these things. Nor is this sense of identity, thus arrived at by a process of quiet, steady concentration, any fantastic, mythical, or even mystical experience. It is the calm recognition of an absolute fact. Intuition and reason are at one in regard to it. Your whole nature, in its physical and psychical totality, responds to these other forms of mind-matter thus presented to you, so vividly outlined, against this grey November sky.

There is indeed a strange and profound satisfaction in feeling this consciousness of identity between your own transitory life and the transitory life of other earth-products, whether organic or inorganic. Concentrating upon such identity, there may even sometimes steal over the mind a "sense of something far more deeply interfused," the idea of a lastingness in fact of some essence in them and in yourself, independent of the annihilation to which all alike are moving.

It is true that nothing mitigates one's fear of death more profoundly than to be saturated with the processes of the seasons and the chemistry of earth-life. If they knew that they were destined to die in the open air it would be an incredible relief to a great many people. It is because the difference between the condition of life and the condition of death is so slight in the world of vegetation that any contact with all these roots and stalks and leaves and seeds and flowers fortifies one against the fear of death. The contemplation of the heavenly bodies themselves, of the sun, the moon, the planets and the stars is not so protective against the fear of death as is the contemplation of the smallest patch of green moss growing on an old stone wall. This is because there is more direct affinity between any green-growing thing, full of sap and sweet and bitter juices, and ourselves, than between us and those remote, scoriac, chemical luminaries. The expanse of the starlit sky can be regarded as a poetic experience or as a scientific phenomenon. In the one case it is stimulating, in the other it is ghastly.

When one looks at a herd of cattle feeding in a green pasture, under massive and aged trees, one experiences an inflowing rush of *confidence* in regard to the basic friendliness of the system of things, just as the sight of a butcher's shop produces dismay and distrust. One is well advised to remain very sceptical about the philosophic value of such feelings. But the feelings are there, and they have their place among the many contrary impressions that life brings. Because of a certain mellowness in the hour and the occasion, sights of this kind almost cajole us into a homely trust in Nature for which there is little practical justification and no rational support.

But what makes the thought of death a matter of easier contemplation when we have saturated ourselves with earth-odours and have drunk up the sounds and sights of the country till they have sunk into our very bones, is a certain dreamy affiliation with the sub-human longevity of rocks and stones and trees. When you are drowsy with the hot noon-sunshine or soaked through and through with driving autumn rains; when you have felt the dead leaves blown against your face, or have stumbled long in the darkness among fallen trees, or plodded stubbornly for hours through sand or mud, a curious lethargy, sweet and wholesome as the weariness of animals, patient and acquiescent as the enduringness of tree-trunks, takes possession of your consciousness, lulling it gently into a passive *amor fati* or love of fate, which seems to accept death and the idea of death with a singular equanimity.

It is just here that an adequate culture will make use of whatever snatches and fragments of classical literature may have come its way. For no writers express this sunburnt, wind-bent, sea-hardened acceptance of our common mortality with more majestic dignity than do the old writers of Greece and Rome. A very limited knowledge of Homer and Virgil will be enough to prove how this kind of fate-loving resignation, saturated with the sounds and sights of Nature, can give a person a certain magnanimity in the presence of death.

It seems somewhat of a disgrace to our race that we so often need the prick of some kind of sporting instinct to drive us to spend long continuous hours in the country. It is, of course, true enough that many people, led on by a passion for sport, imbibe indirectly and as it were sideways, a more insatiable craving for Nature, than many more harmless men and women ever possess. But how unnecessary it does seem, from a philosophical and humane point of view, to blend our happiest moments with the sufferings of such vibrant fellow-sensibilities and kindred nerves!

There is some excuse if you want to eat what you kill; but in the case of catching fish there is really something that one feels to be repulsive about using worms or any other live bait; and most fish can be caught without recourse to such devices.

There is no necessity to make a pedantic cult of the sturdy self-conscious epicurism of prolonged walking-tours. There is however a certain type of bachelor or spinster who enjoys these solitary excursions with a delicious gusto; and it is certainly true that there is nothing that makes a deeper dent upon the mind, or comes back upon the memory with a more magical thrill, than the sensation of entering some unknown town or village in the falling twilight, when the lamps are just being lit and one can see the roofs and the chimneys against the evening sky—especially if one enters such a town over an old river-bridge!

The particular type of egoistic, solitary wayfarer, to whom I allude, may indeed be a very learned man or woman. One must insist however that such an adept in lonely walking-tours has no cause to assume any superior airs over the less adventurous individual whose walks are confined, like those of the poet Cowper, to the banks of his own stream or the purlieu of his own village. In fact, when this subtle Nature-cult, wherewith this chapter is concerned, is made a secret source of pride in the depths of a person's life-illusion, such pride should take but one form alone. It should take the form of being able to derive thrilling ecstasy from the most common, ordinary, and familiar natural objects; objects that it is not necessary even to leave one's doorstep to encounter; objects like earth-mould, tree-tops, grass-blades, flower-pots, privet-hedges, walls and chimneys against the sky, and always the sun and the moon and the heavenly bodies, in their irreversible order!

The lover of walking-tours, of dreamy sojourns in propitious wayside inns, of meditations in old graveyards and historic places, of bivouacs among precipitous ascents and lonely summits, of long wayfarings by the sea's edge, will often be found to be a great reader of books. He will even, like the present Pope, Pius XI, be sometimes an extremely erudite philosopher.

But perhaps what lends itself best of all to such an inveterate epicurean cult is some leisurely old discursive book, such as a volume of Montaigne's "Essays," or Sterne's "Tristram Shandy," or Rousseau's "Confessions," or the "Essays of Elia," or even perhaps the "Essays" of William Hazlitt, which one can pick up and lay down at any moment.

One might suppose that one or other of the tragic plays of Shakespeare, or one or other of the longer novels of Dostoievsky, would serve the turn of these solitary wayfarers; but as a rule, I fancy, their particular psychology is, like that of George Borrow, optimistic rather than pessimistic. They are no "Melancholy Jacques," these people. They will be found selecting Rabelais rather than Swift to prop against their beer-mug at the "Valiant-Sailor."

One cannot help reverting to these pleasant, selfish rogues, these pilgrims of "the Ideal Road," with a certain tenderness. But they are congenital eccentrics. They are indeed, just as Borrow was, often very conceited eccentrics. They are devoid of the ultimate, authentic *seriousness* as far as the human spirit is concerned. Thoreau was not a little tarred with their brush. There is a tincture of priggishness in it. They have their own originality, these wilful tollpike fellows; but where real liberal culture is concerned, they lack a certain universal humility and natural humanity, which make Homer and Shakespeare, and even Sir Walter Scott, better teachers of wisdom than Robert Louis Stevenson.

In fact all sorts of very interesting psychological nuances

deserve to be analysed here, and the longer one considers this problem of self-culture in relation to Nature, the further one comes to recognizing the importance of a Quakerish quietism in these delicate matters. What I mean is, one suffers so often from a sort of fussy, chatty, bustling, over-genial *camaraderie* in regard to this open-air cult; an attitude which considers itself akin to that of Walt Whitman, but has really not the remotest connection with Walt Whitman's formidable planetary acceptance of vast streams of cosmic life.

The real Nature-worship is very different from these priggish affectations; and is so important to the person who practises it that he is prepared to sacrifice many precious feelings for the sake of the sensations he loves. There are passages in Wordsworth, for instance, that seem to lead up to an almost inhuman stoicism, and indeed, here and there, to an inhuman subsuming of all natural personal affections in a certain feeling for the mysterious Earth-Spirit.

Such a pantheistic experience is a frequent and very natural accompaniment to lonely walks in the country, and is certainly something that ought to be enjoyed to the extreme limit, irrespective of any logical restraint.

But on the other hand we need not feel we are lacking in any grand secret of culture if a certain scepticism in our inmost being refuses to allow us this mystical abandonment. What has been called cosmic emotion is not the only way of embracing Nature; nor is the pantheistic ecstasy the only ecstasy allowed to lovers of the earth.

To minds devoid altogether of that philosophical background which is the beginning of wisdom, it may appear absurd that we should be driven to find names for the different types of feeling to which we give way. But those who know anything of human nature know that it is by means of the condensation of mental images around some particular pivotal point that new life is given to things. Such a pivotal point is a name. A bird, a flower, a star, while it is un-named, is for the human mind endowed with only half of its possible reality.

Let us, for instance, take the case of that peculiar approach to Nature that might be called polytheistic. As soon as a person begins to recognize that the feeling he has for a certain field, or mountain, or valley, or stream, or even for a certain tree or plant, carries with it nothing of that sense of a great Universal Spirit at which Emerson and Wordsworth are always hinting, and yet has something in it beyond mere material pleasure, it will give to that person's emotion an added intensity when he realizes that what he feels has had for thousands of years its own name and is in reality identical with that old animistic inkling of superstitious suspicion, that the world we gaze at is, so to say, full of gods.

It is in the poetry of Keats, beyond all others, that this mythological way of apprehending Nature finds its consummation. Matthew Arnold uses the expression "natural magic" to describe it. What it really implies seems to be that hidden in the separate identities of Nature, in each tree, each plant, each rock, each stone, each tuft of moss or lichen, there dwells some sort of particular Genius, the soul, as it were, of that individual thing, born with it expressing its living essence and destined to perish with it.

I have already referred to the importance of names even in the matter of philosophical conceptions. How much more are they important in the matter of plants, birds, trees, animals, fishes, butterflies, and the constellations of the stars at night! Here indeed is one of those instances where culture absolutely depends on knowledge. Without knowing the names of these things—at least their ordinary, popular, English, or local names—how is it possible to enjoy Nature to the full? If it is not a silly affectation when people declare they enjoy these things more freely without knowing their names, it is certainly an ignorant and foolish boast. Each planet, each plant, each butterfly, each moth, each beetle, becomes doubly real to you when you know its name. Lucky indeed are those who from their earliest childhood have heard all these things named. This is no superficial pedantry. Deep in the oldest traditions of the human race dwells the secret of the magical power of names. Only by knowing the names of demons were such beings controlled; and the legends which indicate the mystery and secrecy which hung about the names of certain of the gods bear witness to the same strange potency. If one named a supernatural personage by his true name one did not conjure or invoke him in vain.

Let it be understood that it is by no means necessary for the purposes of an imaginative life to possess any elaborate knowledge of what are called the scientific laws of natural history. Technical botany, for instance, is of no importance to real culture compared with field botany. The purpose of culture is to enhance and intensify one's vision of that synthesis of truth and beauty which is the highest and deepest reality.

A cultured person, therefore, regards Nature with what might be called a Goethean, rather than a Newtonian, eye. He trains himself to see and to feel, rather than to analyse or to explain. His attitude to Nature is indeed what Milton said all poetry should be, "simple, sensuous, and passionate." The ecstasy he derives from Nature will vary, of course, with each individual temperament; but it will have this in common, that it draws its life *from life,* rather than from the dissection of the cadaver of life.

Two men, let us say, are standing together upon a high promontory overlooking the sea. The one is preoccupied with a scientific analysis of the organic chemistry of the verdure on the edge of the precipice. The other grows from moment to moment more aware of the ultimate mystery of land and water, and of the planetary roll of the whole terrestrial orb, as in its motion it follows the solar path through space. Must it not be allowed that it is this latter, rather than the former, who has the richer and deeper culture? To take nothing in Nature for granted—that is the root of the matter. To awake in the morning to each new day as if one were only just born—born afresh with a mature intelligence, and as if the earth and the sea and the air and the sun were miraculous new experiences, realized for the first time at their face value—such seems to be the method of true wisdom. Many scientific specialists, full of intense curiosity in their laboratories, fall into the most philistine dullness of perception the moment they pass into the normal experiences of life. What culture ought to do for us is to sweep away that crust of quotidian familiarity which blinds us to the thrilling magic of life, and bathes us afresh in the luminous pools of being.

There is not the remotest reason why we should not treat Nature sentimentally or even idealize her extravagantly. It does indeed appear from the very latest discoveries of science that not one particle of so-called material energy exists in the world without some concomitant psychic attribute, commensurate with what we call semi-conscious or "vital" energy. Just as today philosophers speak of "space-time" instead of time *and* space, so physicists appear compelled to speak, not of "force" or of "atoms," but of "mind-matter," as the residual stuff of reality. What, therefore, used to be derided fifty years ago as the pathetic fallacy, namely that Nature feels, in some intimate way, even as we ourselves feel, must now be regarded as something approximately true. Fast and faster every year is the purely mechanistic conception of life receding and being discarded; and thus the instinctive old-world response to Nature, as something living, in the same sense as we ourselves are living, that poetic response which correlates the ideas of Homer with those of Goethe, and the ideas of Leonardo with those of Einstein and Eddington; that response which is made, not by reason alone or by imagination alone, but by what Matthew Arnold so admirably called the "imaginative reason," returns upon us today as the most comprehensive as well as the most simple reaction which our mind, under its present mortal limitations, is able to experience. It is indeed only when we are, for a little while, quite alone with Nature, that our basic philosophy falls into focus and we are able to see things in a true perspective.

Let any reader of this volume gather together the forces of his inmost being as he stands under any sort of tree upon any patch of bare earth or uncut grass, and let him feel himself as a human animal, unique among his fellows in his own peculiar personal sensations, carried through Space-Time on the surface of this terrestrial orb! Let him obliterate from his mind all the tiresome preoccupations of his job, of his money-difficulties, of his worldly, professional, or domestic cares. Let him visualize his life from its conscious beginning to this actual moment in its general outlines, with its miseries and its compensations glimpsed spaciously, felt largely, as from an airy height. Let him recognize the essential residue of what real love he has for what real living or dead companions. Let him face the reality of death, as he has never perhaps faced it, in all its ghastly finality. Let him at that moment practise the art of forgetting to its extreme point; so that whatever the particular horrors in life are, the ones that have worried him the most are calmly set aside upon his mind's rubbish-heap or flung into his mind's oblivious Limbo.

Then let him give himself up to the warmth of the sun as it falls upon that tree-trunk and that patch of earth, or to the greyness of the clouds and the chill of the wind as these things press upon him and make desolate this place of his retreat. From both the generative warmth and the sorrowful wind a strange happiness will reach him if he retains his concentrated receptivity of mind; for the deep fountains of his memory will be stirred simply and solely by that passive attitude of his which has obliterated worry and care. Then will all manner of old obscure feelings, evoked by both sun and wind, warmth and cold, earth and grass, air and rain, rise up in his mind. And he will remember certain street-corners where the evening light has fallen in particular ways. He will remember certain bridges where the rain-wet stones or the mosses have taken on a certain delicate sadness, or have pierced his heart "with thoughts beyond the reaches of his soul." He will remember the tarry smells and the salty breaths of this or that harbour-mouth, passed carelessly enough at the time, but returning upon him now as of the very essence of his life. He will remember how he once came up the slope of a far-off hill, following some half-forgotten road; and there will come upon him vague memories of remote gates overgrown with elder-bushes and with tall nettles; memories of bare beech-trunks, God knows on what far uplands, of stranded barges in stagnant back waters, of green seaweed on lonely pier-posts, of glittering sun-paths, or moon-paths, on sea-waters and river-waters, of graveyards where the mounds of the dead were as drowsy under the long years as if the passing of time had been the passing of interminable flocks of sheep. Thus will he tell like beads the memories of his days and their long burden; while the unspeakable poetry of life will flood his being with a strange happiness.

If he waits long enough, thus standing alone, thus staring at earth and sky, there will even, perhaps, come over him that immemorial sensation, known to saints and mystics from the beginning of time, wherein the feeling of all outward things is lost in a singular ecstasy. If he is a lover, or has a friend he loves beyond all, the identity of this friend or of this love will be with him in this ecstasy. It will be as if he carried this friend, lodged in the *cor cordium* of his own being, so that it is with a double nature that he embraces the secret of the universe, freed from all care!

Some peculiarly constituted persons, as was the case with the mediaeval ascetics, feel that they cannot attain such ecstasy in the presence of Nature without some degree of fasting and prayer. No rationalist, no free-thinker, has a right to quarrel with this austerity unless it seriously injures the health of those who practise it. A limited degree of asceticism is a natural concomitant of such sweet practises. But if a person's physical disposition is congenitally so well-balanced as to make it an easy and unforced habit with him to forget completely the chemistry of his body when he is very happy, what is the use of fasting?

And if a person's culture has long given him the habit of sinking back upon the depths of his being and upon the ultimate mystery of self and not-self, so that it has become a custom with him to hold a secret dialogue with the hypothetical first cause, it is with him, already, as though to breathe were to pray. It matters little under what mental image or conception he has come, by reason of his original temperamental bias, to visualize this first cause of all life. As has been already suggested, his attitude towards it will partake of a double gesture—a gesture of boundless gratitude and of stoical defiance. This, if he be honest with himself, will surely be inevitable; for must not such an hypothetical first cause be at once the fountain of all good and of all evil?

The probability is that at these moments of ecstatic fusion with Nature nothing but the former of these two gestures will prevail. The defiant gesture will remain temporally in abeyance, only to return when the ecstasy is over.

If it is a sure sign of an uncultured mind to allow one's own casual chattering to interfere with one's enjoyment of Nature, it is a still surer sign of this lack of control to permit one's thoughts to dwell on worrying topics in place of compelling oneself to look at every detail, to smell and listen and to touch everything; keeping all one's senses alert for changes of wind and weather and for the most vague and flickering influences of place and atmosphere.

Nothing is more important than to acquire some habitual way of regarding Nature, some way of gathering together all one's consciousness and sensibility, so as to react to Nature in the exact manner, that over a long period of time we have learnt to be the most satisfying. This attitude of ours ought to become at last more than a deliberate thing. It ought to pass from a conscious habit into an automatic, instinctive gesture, such as the totality of our being inevitably makes the moment we are alone with Nature. Nothing is harder than to feel alone with Nature when really we are with our companions; but this art also we must gradually acquire.

Now what is the best habitual way of reacting to Nature? What does this gathering together of one's sensibility in her presence really amount to? In the first place, it seems to me, it must imply that basic gesture of our solitary ego towards the hypothetical first cause; that dual gesture of unbounded gratitude to life and unbounded defiance of life. This first attitude deals with whatever we can imagine to our limited mind as existing behind Nature and being the cause of Nature. In the second place it must imply, so it seems to me, an intense and growing awareness of the surface of Nature. We touch here upon a very crucial and important point. It must be admitted that to many human minds there is a peculiar satisfaction in feeling as if all the outward things, such as earth and water and sky, were penetrated by some inner spirit or force, which, as Wordsworth says, "rolls through all things." If this way of feeling is natural to you—and indeed there must be admitted to be a thrilling pleasure in it—there is no earthly reason why it should not be indulged to the extreme limit. Since it is so deeply involved with the psychic processes of so many minds, and since it belongs to an immemorial human tradition, it would seem probable enough that like the kindred idea of the existence of God it represents some truth in the system of things that refuses to lend itself to the exact requirements of logic and the precise exigencies of reason.

But while this spiritual view of Nature, or this irrational feeling that there is a spirit in Nature, has a powerful influence over such personalities as are fated to feel its sorcery, there is no reason why such as do not feel anything of this kind should be ashamed of their limitation. It remains quite possible, on the contrary, that such people are right; and that the whole notion of a Spirit interfused through Nature is an illusion. In either case it would seem the part of a wise man to concentrate the chief powers he may have upon those things in life which are objective and tangible and sure—though in reality they too may easily be of the stuff of dreams. To be of the stuff of dreams is perhaps a much more solid degree of reality than to belong to a vast all-penetrating spiritual force which must forever remain uncommitted to any palpable shape or form.

On the surface of Nature's forms and shapes there are a thousand undulating emanations, flowing here, floating there, dependent upon the innumerable caprices of chance and occasion. These emanations, wherein the shadows of clouds, the flickering of broken lights, the motions of winds, the winged atmospheres that come and go around us, blend with something that emerges from each separate individual living thing, and make up together that mysterious essence, that some have called the magic, of the universe. This magic seems to rise up from the appearances of Nature and to sink amid the appearances of Nature. It is indeed the flickering and the flowing of a presence that is at once psychic and material; and though non-human in its essence is so deeply associated with our nervous life

that it over-brims in every direction our conscious awareness and excites magnetic vibrations which touch our sub-
conscious memory and rouse up strange responses in the
imagination.

It will be noted that this magic of the Universe always
emanates from the surface and always returns to the surface. It is the breath, the bloom, the fragrance, the flickering expression upon the surface of life itself, and always
seems more authentically the secret of Nature than any
hypothetical spirit to be sought for below life. We thus
arrive at the conclusion that what might metaphorically
be called the soul of Nature dwells upon the surface and
not beneath; and is associated with the lights and shadows
that flicker across the surface rather than with any subterranean energy seething below. And not only do we reach
the conclusion that the soul of Nature dwells upon her material surface rather than in any "spiritual" depths, but
that it dwells on this surface rather than in any structural
anatomy of things or any inorganic chemistry of things.
In other words it is in the breath and bloom of the ani-
mate and in the lights and shadows, the tones and tints of
the inanimate, rather than in any electric or chemic forces
underlying these, that the poignant reality of Nature lives
and moves. It therefore presents itself as irrefutably true
that the real lover of Nature is of necessity preoccupied
with the appearances of things as they attain their symbolic
significance. The superficial is thus the real essence. Nor is
this a wanton paradox.

The superficial aspects of Nature are the entelechy of
Nature; and those who give themselves up to them most
completely are those who have been initiated most deeply
in Nature's creative ways. The character of things and

their true symbolic value is not to be found in the manner in which things originate, but in their issue and consummation.

One of the deepest secrets connected with any habitual awareness of Nature is her gradual influence upon the resistant and stoical elements of our being. This particular influence works best when the kind of landscape around us has certain qualities of austerity. Walking along lonely roads, walking across bare prairies or barren uplands, walking along solitary sea-banks or desolate sands, there is a grim feeling of communion with the primeval elements such as one misses altogether in luxuriant or picturesque scenes. Something stark and steadying comes to us out of the driving rain, out of the burning sun, out of the tossing wind, in such lonely walks; something that seems to force us to resemble the character of wind-beaten tree-trunks or of weather-stained rocks, something that by slow degrees conveys to us a strange power of deriving happiness from the mere process of resistance. It is indeed nothing less than resistance that becomes then the ultimate secret of life. And well it may. For when anyone regards life philosophically and from the deepest stratum of his being, resistance comes very soon to sum up the ultimate situation of all human entities. There is the self and there is the not-self; and these two confront one another at such times free from every mediator.

At such times too, the force of the wind, the wet of the rain, the hot fury of the sun, the touch of the earth, sand, grass or rock simplifies one's human personal history.

The other people in one's life grow then more emphatic. They are more intensely thought of, realized, considered, placed. The one person, if there happens to be one, who is dearest of all, is at such times carried on the shoulders of our consciousness, very much as the celestial Babe was carried on the shoulders of St. Christopher. Those affairs, relations, matters in our life which call for certain restrictions and restraints in us, perhaps even sometimes for a vein of renunciation, are accepted at such times, under the influence of these stark elementary powers, with an easier mind. These great simple powers as they work upon us— this wind, this earth, this sea, this forest—come to enable us in a curiously stoical manner to accept our fate.

And not only to accept it. If we have reached the point of deriving a certain stubborn happiness from the mere process of resistance we actually come, not only to accept our fate, but in a strange way to love our fate. It is perhaps only by long subjection to the elements, by putting up with rains and winds and frost and sun for a long while, that we come to share the stoicism of trees and animals. Nothing goes deeper into the heart of things than the stoicism of a wind-bent tree or of an old horse. It is this that explains the expression one often sees upon the faces of very old people in country places. It is an expression of nothing less than a sort of non-human love of fate. Country people have many mean and vicious characteristics from which town people are free. Continual contact with Nature evokes evil qualities as well as good qualities. But there gradually comes into existence with country people, as the result of intimate association with the changes of the year, with the morning and the evening and the night felt to be living presences, and with rains and dews and burning noons, a certain obstinate patient passivity, a certain lying back upon life, which is a great mastery.

There is yet another thing that our intellectual culture can get from living closely with Nature, or even—if our fate has lodged us in a town—from spending one day a week in close contact with her; and that is a sense of imaginative proportion. By imaginative proportion I mean a vivid realization of the tragic disasters that happen to all living things and a recognition of the extraordinary value of mere normal well-being. In a town the ambulances so quickly dispose of hurt men and women; and now that machines have taken the place of horses the tokens of accident are more quickly obliterated. But in the country, faced by the realities of Nature, you are surrounded constantly by shocking evidences of disease and death. Dead rabbits, dead sheep, dead crows, dead snakes, dead trees waylay your steps; and the consciousness of the terribleness of what may at any second happen to yourself tends to throw the issues and the dilemmas of life into a certain drastic perspective. All these grim sights of tragic birth and tragic death, and the deep solitary endurances among the beasts of the field and the birds of the air, make a person regard certain human contacts with a stark, hard eye; while at the same time one's feeling for one's parents, or offspring, or mate, grow more rooted as the years go on. What any close contact with Nature really does for a person's culture is to get culture itself into focus; so that no tricky affectations or morbid self-consciousnesses, no melodramatics with regard to art or with regard to one's own originality, spoil one's stark, simple, natural, proud-humble contentment at being exactly what Nature has made one to be. Beside a sick sheep—with the look one knows too well in its eyes—beside a dead rabbit or a hawk-killed bunting

or an old labourer with his legs pitilessly curved by in-
durated rheumatics into two spindly ox-horns, one loses
the finickiness of much fussy self-assertion.

Contact with Nature has, in fact, a profound effect upon
that portion of our character which has to be drawn upon
when we decide on any drastic integrated resolution. There
is a certain fidgety preoccupation with other people's feelings which disappears in the presence of the indomitable
loneliness of so many living things. One cares less and less
what other people think of one. It is this that gives to many
old carters and shepherds such a strangely isolated air,
as if they possessed some secret *rapport* with levels of existence where human conventions count for much less than
they do among the rest of us.

There is also another very important effect upon one's
culture that such closeness to Nature gives; and that is to
make one realize the value of a certain fundamental power
possessed by the will. This power of the will is limited in
its control over outward events; but it is almost unlimited
in its control over the motions of one's own mind. The
more often one uses it in this direction the more formidable does its strength become. It would seem that the grand
master-effort of the will should be directed—such, at least,
appears to be the tendency one gathers from animals and
birds and plants—towards keeping clearly before one's consciousness the idea of a certain thrilling calm of mind. This
is the consciousness that a state of ecstatic peace is the
deepest secret of the universe at which we can arrive. If
the will is stubbornly orientated towards such ecstasy, one's
inner self does actually begin to grow happier and happier.
This or that thrilling moment will, of course, come and
go as it always has done; but the stiffening of the will into

a certain pattern of obstinate quiescence carries us a long way towards this calm energy of peace.

The endurances of animals and birds and plants, each in its lonely isolation, brings one finally to a stark conclusion —the conclusion, namely, that the will has an almost unbounded power over one's own secret and private reactions to life. Any long practise of these primordial wrestlings produces the feeling in us that the whole stringency of the cosmic situation is an affair of the solitary individual's consciousness. Whether one is happy or unhappy comes more and more to be the one single issue over which one has a nearly complete control; and it becomes too, more and more emphatically, the only sure and certain help one can offer—except the magical power of love—to "the stream of tendency that makes for righteousness." All outward actions, every overt thing we do, every splash we make in the great tide, has a fatal tendency to produce as much harm as good. We observe this daily and nightly if we live close to the earth. The only two things that we finally come to distinguish from the rest as invariably resulting in good rather than evil are our own deep individual calm, obstinately preserved in spite of all blows of fate, and the sort of love for other individuals which is compatible with our leaving them alone. The love that interferes and knows not how to leave alone is a love alien to Nature's ways; and, as everyone knows who has looked into the eyes of snakes, birds, toads, geese, and sea-gulls, there is an upwelling from the heart of Nature of a resolute will to be happy in spite of all, which is stronger than any creed, deeper than any philosophy, and more potent than any renunciation.

Finally, in a philosophical sense one can derive for one's

culture untold benefit by living close to Nature. The philosophy which serves one's turn best is, as has been already hinted, a philosophy that sweeps away every mediation that comes between the individual ego and the unknown First Cause. Unknown, unknowable, this non-human, good-evil power evades all definitions. It is so strong and yet so weak; so kind and yet so cruel; so comforting and yet so ghastly; that one can only think of it in opposites and approach it in images. But when one walks, for a long while, alone over grass or sand, over rocks or forest-floor, one seems to become aware that every individual growth, every living leaf and stalk and tendril and grass-blade is enduring and waiting in mute expectancy; bearing its peculiar mystic burden at the great cross-roads of our finite Space-Time; while all the time it is secretly drawing a strange, magnetic, unspeakable contentment from some level of existence altogether beyond those boundaries. For this happiness it returns thanks to that first cause; in its long endurance it defies that first cause.

The singular thing about the influence of Nature is that it enhances the intensity of this dualism between gratitude and defiance by giving one the feeling that all around in every direction living sentiencies are experiencing the same double emotion. Mysterious gratitude—mysterious defiance —such seems to be the attitude of Nature herself to the unknown Power that begat her; and this attitude, we, her innumerable offspring, share with our great unscrupulous Mother. But although the ultimate gift of Nature to our culture is this double-edged response, it remains true that what one naturally feels in any kind of reaction to simple scenery is an obscure impression—not of any First Cause at all—but of a floating, airy company of invisible presences, the Genii and tutelary Spirits, as it were, of the streams and rocks and plants and trees among which we move and pass.

It is so important that the impressions of Nature, such as I am attempting to analyse, should be felt in a clear and unambiguous way that, if my reader will permit me, I will recapitulate and sum up again the whole situation as I see it. I will set him in some open-air spot as vividly imagined at this moment as the fancy of author and reader, exerting themselves together, can manage to conjure up. It shall be, if you please, in the presence of some fence, or wall, or hedge, at the edge of a field, over-grown with a variety of tall, straggling weeds. Let us suppose that the day is windless and that all these entangled growths are motionless in the undisturbed air. In dead silence one stares at this inaudibly-breathing vegetation; and, as one stares, the impression gradually emphasizes itself that the dominant feeling of all these growths is a mute expectancy. Expectancy of what? Ah! that none can tell! But something in one's own heart and one's own psychic mood answers in intimate correspondence to this curious waiting, this waiting with indrawn breath. And as we stand there, allowing our identity to sink back upon the final mystery of life, it seems as though, in a wordless dialogue with the eternal, we at the same time accuse that unknown of the sufferings of all sentiency and offer thanks to it for the happiness of all sentiency.

But this is only the underlying pulse-throb of what we feel. Along with this there spreads about us, upon that hushed air, a vivid awareness of the magical effluences proceeding from those leaves and stalks. Vibrations and quiverings, half-material, half-psychic, flow through them and through us, and an innate reciprocity—to use a phrase of Hardy's—establishes itself between us in that small cubic dimension of matter and ether.

Nor is this the end of it. Following upon all this, any man or any woman, thus worshipping the whole of Nature in a patch of entangled weeds, begins to grow vividly conscious that Nature is much more than a dimly-realized Whole. Nature in fact begins to present herself as a vast congeries of separate living entities, some visible, some invisible, but all possessed of mind-stuff, all possessed of matter-stuff, and all blending mind and matter together in the basic mystery of being. It is, in fact, just here, as we continue to stare at these entangled earth-growths, that there is borne in upon us the boundless polytheism of the universe. The world is full of gods! From every plant and from every stone there emanates a presence that disturbs us with a sense of the multitudinousness of god-like powers, strong and feeble, great and little, moving between heaven and earth upon their secret purposes.

Liberating however my already exhausted reader from the tension of awareness to which I have subjected him, does it not appear, granting to the full the immense divergency between different temperaments, that what any intense preoccupation with Nature can do for our human culture is to enlarge its capacity for mystic-sensual enjoyment? The basic purpose of this book is simply to hint at ways and methods by which the subtle antennae or sensitized feelers of personality can exploit our common experiences.

When one notes the extraordinary manner in which life is mingled with disease and with death in Nature, almost all living things bearing about with them the burden of something that is fatally diseased or that is already dead,

one is encouraged to use one's will more resolutely in abating no jot of hope. Nature and the much-enduring creatures of the Earth can convert us by degrees from every morbidity, from every one of those subjective madnesses from which we all suffer, each after his own fashion. If withered weeds, if lightning-struck trees, if wounded animals and hurt insects, if mangy dogs, rats with three legs, moths with lost wings, fish with bleeding gills, beetles attacked by parasites, thorn-bushes bent double by relentless winds, rocks cracked by volcanic convulsions, blinded hawks, caged birds, snared rabbits, cattle destined for slaughter, can all manage somehow, in their enduring stoicism, to draw some obstinate and stubborn satisfaction from the mere fact of being still alive; and if, as one has an inkling is the case, such lives can tap at moments strange thrills of happiness from one knows not what levels of existence altogether below the reach of their distress, how much more can we, with our more cultivated powers of will and our subtler mental devices, work the same indomitable sorcery.

It is most evilly true that pain is deep. Physical pain, mental pain; deep is this accursed conspiracy encompassing all life. But from Nature we get eternal whispers that happiness is deeper than pain. Yes—what we call culture is in reality only an elaborate, intellectual cunning, directed towards the snatching of happiness under the very jowl of the dragon. If there is any device, any crafty trick, any residual wisdom to be gathered from Nature it is surely the art of forgetting. No natural entity one ever encounters but has acquired, by a laborious process of experience, some measure of this sly art. To be able to forget, to start fresh, to renew our days with a profound *vita nuova,* such is Nature's hint,—forever repeated in a thousand-different tones.

The sun scorches up the past, the rain washes out the past; the wind blows it away, the earth swallows it up. My brother, Llewelyn Powys, feels that there is in life a perpetual sinking down and sinking back, an everlasting landslide, of all sublunary things; a slide of the reasonable into the unreasonable, of the formed into the unformed, of the distinct into the indistinct, of what has come out of the shapeless, back again into the shapeless!

But while we make use of Nature in these various ways to enlarge and to steady our philosophy, it must be remembered that Nature can be an enemy to culture as well as a friend. This dangerous and evil influence of Nature is something that is as insidious as the seeds of hen-bane and as fatal as the juices of night-shade. No one who knows anything of existence in the country is ignorant of certain malign and ill-starred powers at work there, powers as hostile to any harmonious human life as the worst criminals and the worst smart people of the metropolis! How often does habitual work on the land turn to flint or stone the inherited sensibility of a farmer, of a peasant proprietor! How often does the breeding of beasts for the market brutalize a man's mind and dull the sensitiveness of his imagination till he resembles a clod of dung! What callous, vulgar wretches so many among our colonial settlers are, full of such ferocious preoccupation with their exports and their cargoes that their hearts have grown harder than fossilized sea-urchins! One has not had much experience of life if one still cherishes the illusion that when a man's body has been long subjected to the influence of the elements, his heart and his intellect must necessarily have grown subtle and sensitized. It requires a shock too miraculous to be quite natural to convert the tough ruffianism of the Peter Bells of this world. The real Peter Bells usually perish as they have lived, impenitent, insensitive, sly as foxes, greedy as hogs, vindictive as rogue-elephants, blood-thirsty as weasels. Nor does great creative Nature pause for one minute to discourage such scoundrels in their villainous malpractises. Rather, if anything, does she encourage them.

We must therefore make a mental note of the significant fact that while it is from Nature that certain large, lovely, luminous visions of life rise up before us, it is also from Nature that hard hearts learn to be harder; ferocious vices find hideous justification; loathsome insanity is pushed on to nourish itself on kindred madness; while inert, hopeless despair is led to drain the last dregs of its destiny.

Yes; the mind that seeks to gain control over its fate upon earth will do well to beware of Nature. Like all the greater gods, Nature has to be dealt with in a certain very crafty way, the full secret of which is revealed to few. Nature, as Leonardo declared, may be the mistress of the higher intelligences; but if the higher intelligences do not draw upon a certain magnetic force that seems to dwell beyond Nature, the great feline Mother will soon corrupt them with her own sub-human treacheries! Upon Nature and through Nature, each undivided mind must work out its fate; but our culture has been a too compact and too tightly contracted thing if it has not come to feel that there is always a certain portion of its being that can detach itself from Nature.

A true culture will never be entirely committed to any particular religion or any particular mystical theory; but on the other hand it will never cease to make use of the long struggle of the human spirit to lift itself above the ferocious life-and-death contest of Nature's savage arena. It will never lose touch with the cumulative tradition of pity and tenderness which is our final human protest; a protest which draws its force from some far-off Unknown, and is lifted up against both the inert malice of matter and the deep unscrupulousness of the great mother of life and death.

CHAPTER X

CULTURE AND THE ART OF READING

At the bottom of all culture lies some fundamental attitude, half-conscious, half-unconscious, to the hypothetical first cause of all life. One is forced to use the modifying word "hypothetical" because the very concept of cause itself may well, as Hume hints, be an illusion; but since the only causative energy we are aware of, so to say from the inside, is the causative energy of our own interior being, it seems as if any drastic introspection is bound to land us in some sort of ultimate dualism, wherein what we feel to be ourselves confronts what we feel to be an all-inclusive not-self. And it is to this ultimate not-self that our basic soliloquy with life is directed, sometimes, as has been already indicated, in ecstatic gratitude, sometimes in calm, stoical, implacable defiance.

Gathering up our forces to cope with the shifting stream of impressions that flow in forever upon our waking hours, we come by degrees to realize that our ultimate virtue lies in forcing ourselves to feel and to be what is called happy; and to be this in spite of all obstacles and accidents and miseries. There have been great metaphysical and religious systems teaching that a certain calm indifference, a certain imperturbableness, what the Greeks called *ataraxia*, is the true end—to be unmoved, in fact, by both misery and pleasure. This resigned indifference does not seem to the present writer to satisfy the natural demands of living, sentient beings as fully or as freely as the old simple Homeric zest for life.

There is a profound defeatism and a deep, suicidal nihilism about this calm resignation, this *ataraxia,* which does not seem at all to correspond with what we observe and note in the ways of animals, birds, fishes, reptiles, insects or plants. To these other children of the earth as well as to us there is an irreducible vein of tragedy twisted in and running through the bitter-sweet body of life. Hunger and thirst, cold and heat, suffering in the flesh, suffering in the mind and nerves, horrible drudgery and horrible persecution, few of us but have at least tasted these evils. Some, for no fault of their own and for no reason at all except the wantonness of pure chance, have been driven to drink them to the very dregs—fate, chance, providence, society —all these things seem to combine in certain cases to crush people to the ground. There is nothing more expressive of a barbarous and stupid lack of culture than the half-unconscious attitude so many of us slip into, of taking for granted, when we see weak, neurotic, helpless, drifting, unhappy people, that it is by reason of some special merit in us or by reason of some especial favour towards us that the gods have given us an advantage over such persons. The more deeply sophisticated our culture is the more fully are we aware that these lamentable differences in good and bad fortune spring entirely from luck.

It is luck: luck in our heredity, luck in our environment, luck above all in our individual temperament, that makes the difference; and moreover at any moment fortune's erratic wheel may turn completely round and we ourselves may be hit by some totally unforeseen catastrophe. It is luck too, springing from some fortunate encounter, some incredible love-affair, some fragment of oracular wisdom in word or writing that has come our way, that launched us on the secret road of stoical-epicureanism, on the stubborn resolution to be happy under all upshots and issues, which has been so vast a resource to us in fortifying our embattled spirit. At any moment we are liable, the toughest and strongest among us, to be sent howling to a suicidal collapse. It is all a matter of luck; and the more culture we have the more deeply do we resolve that in our relations with all the human failures and abjects and ne'er-do-wells of our world we shall feel nothing but plain, simple, humble reverence before the mystery of misfortune. The nobler and the more imaginative our culture is, the less do we pride or plume ourselves over these social and temperamental differences. Least of all do we allow ourselves any arrogant pose of intellectual and aesthetic superiority. The only superiority worth anything is the superiority of being happier; and it may often happen that a fish, a cow, a king, a cat, a glow-worm, a communist, a sparrow, a pig, a millionaire, might be happier than we are. It is only at the very beginning of culture, in its rudimentary A.B.C. stage, that groups of people allow themselves to feel intellectually and aesthetically superior; and in the presence of the abysmal irony of what the Chinese call a really "superior man" such arrogance grows aware of a startled, uneasy suspicion of its stupid limitations!

But of all the activities culture pursues, in its effort to deepen our awareness of the multifarious magic of life, the one which ought most profoundly to influence us in the direction of humility is the reading of books. When one thinks what one owes to books, when one discovers again and again the extraordinary illuminations that have come to us from reading books, one's pride in one's own originality finds itself forced back to the honest, primordial ground where it has alone a right to expand and expatiate, the ground, namely, that we are what we are, different, peculiar, unique, but not superior to anyone.

Happiness, which is the sole end and purpose of culture, is liable to be menaced more crushingly by blows to our inmost self-respect than by anything else in the world except physical suffering and the fear of physical suffering; and the only way by which these blows to our self-respect can be avoided is to sink down upon a basis for our personal self-esteem so deep, simple, and primitive that it cannot be outraged by any psychological shock. Such a basis is the perfectly legitimate pride we have a right to take in just being what we are! Our body is different from every other living body in the world. Our mind, our feelings, our nerves, our secret reactions to life, all are different from those of any other animal, or any fish, or reptile, or insect. Here we sit, or lie, or stand, or walk, looking out upon the mystery of the world; and we have a perfect right to be thrilled with unspeakable pride that we can see and smell and touch and taste and hear in a manner completely different—and who can refute such a contention?—from every other living thing.

Bring down your pride, O man of aesthetic superiority; bring down your pride, O woman of intellectual superiority; till it stands firm and sure on the unassailable ground of eating and drinking and stretching your limbs, and walking to and fro upon the earth! None of the children of the earth enjoy these primitive enjoyments exactly as you do. When you walk along a pavement or down a lane you have a perfect right to stride and strut and sway and bend with a delicious exuberance of pride. It is true you are a miracle, a wonder, a mystery, the paragon of animals, one single unique and inimitable living thing. It is a great achievement to be able to walk about and enjoy yourself in the sweet air! It is a still greater achievement to enjoy yourself over some hideous, monotonous task in an office, or a shop, or a factory, where you cannot walk about and where the air is anything but sweet.

One thing certainly everyone has a right to be proud of; namely, the power of continuing to be happy under blow after blow of malignant fate, under insult after insult of brutal people.

But this deep simple pride, pride which is so rich an element in the art of happiness, need not stop at the natural material things I have named. It can extend to the supernatural. There is no man or woman in the world who does not experience vague feelings of mystical power, of cosmic power, bringing him a strange sense of belonging, even in his most miserable objective weakness, to the company of the immortal gods. He does belong to them; he is of that company. Not the wretchedest man or woman but has a deep secretive mythology with which to wrestle with the material world and to overcome it and pass beyond it. Not the wretchedest human being but has his share in the creative energy that builds the world. We are all creators. We all create a mythological world of our own out of certain shapeless materials. What we really mean when we speak of the universe is not something static; it is simply a congeries of these personally created worlds wherein animals and birds and fish and plants and insects all contribute a fresh, vital element of change, as they carry the whole teeming caravanserai forward, into an indetermined, unpredictable, and perhaps not even irreversible future.

Not one of our fellow-creators in this vast congeries of personal lives that we call Nature is devoid of some sort of instinct, corresponding to the accumulated weight of habitual consciousness which it is the purpose of our culture to supply with selected memories out of the past of our own existence and the existence of our race. Animals and even birds and fish have a continuity of accumulated habits which answers to the sort of culture I am trying to define in this book.

For those among us who are lucky enough to have been born and bred in the country, there ought to be scant need for those savage premeditated shocks to the megalopolitan herd-conventions which writers like D. H. Lawrence and Robinson Jeffers find such a zest in giving. That whole school of what might be called the cave-man cult—and such a great book as Whitman's "Leaves of Grass" belongs to the same general category—comes with an exultant feeling of release to anyone who has been "cabined, cribbed, confined" in some narrow human bondage. But to anyone who from childhood has cast a not-unseeing eye upon the ways of pikes and weasels and magpies and foxes and sparrowhawks and sheep and cattle and horses and upon the tilling of the fields, there will be found something over-strained, over-violent, megalomaniacal about these heaving gestures. Nor will the call to prefer Nature to humanity disturb very much the type of rusticated pastoral mind that has never separated, in its most casual thought, humanity from Nature.

What, it seems to me, an ordinary person of average intelligence can gain from this super-vital cult, with its straining after bodily violence, is a simple and frank enjoyment of the physical sensations of his own body. These sensations need not be so extreme, either in the direction of lust or in the direction of mysticism, as the impulses described by some of these writers; but it is an enormous gain to our culture when we allow ourselves time to enjoy with a certain indolent and dreamy passivity the mere animal sensation of being alive. Very soon after these primordial sensations in which we revert, through long atavistic stages, to the feelings of the ichthyosaurus and the diplodocus, we shall come, if we read Wordsworth, to make much of many more gentle and less primeval feelings. Here, too, the rocks and stones and trees will draw us back and down, to the beginnings of things, to the dark, old secrets of flood and fell; but these primal presences will now be associated with the frailer lives of flowers and mosses and grass, and with the movements of cattle and birds.

Flickering shadows upon white stones by the wayside, gusts of wind over the bending corn, winding lanes leading across hilltops into unknown landscapes, yellow stone-crop and harts'-tongue ferns upon old ruined sheep folds, great dreamy bumble-bees murmuring through long hot noons in the heart of foxglove-bells, the metallic coolness of glittering celandines in a mud-dark ditch, the dew-fresh pallor of cuckoo-flowers in long, lush hay-grass, the roll of great thunder-claps in high mountain gorges; all these, as we ponder upon Wordsworth's poetry, become more and more an intimate part of our life.

Wordsworth, more than anyone, if we acquire the trick of putting completely aside his pieties and his moralizings, has the power of initiating us into those aspects of Nature that are not what we call beautiful at all; but are nevertheless full of the breathing life of the earth; the life of grass-roots and moss-spores, of lichen-scales and puff-ball dust, of frost-marks and the creaking and groaning of withered thorn-trees as the wailing wind sweeps over the uplands.

The best way to make the reading of books really valuable is to use them as I am now suggesting Wordsworth should be used. Discount shamelessly and unblushingly a writer's ethical propaganda and concentrate your attention upon what he reveals to you of the life-motions of the earth. Even in the margin, so to speak, of his propaganda, you can often find the most delicate revelations of this sort—in poems for instance, like "Michael" and "Ruth" and the "Leech-gatherer," there is a stoical acceptance of destiny, mingled with a resolution to enjoy certain simple physical pleasures in spite of destiny, from which a most valuable wisdom can be gathered.

Refining, so to speak, in more and more subtle reactions, the primordial ground-swell of purely bodily sensations, it is in the poetry of Keats and in the prose of Charles Lamb that those rich imaginative regions can be traversed, so tremuluously suspended between earth and sky, wherein a thousand magical trophies of recondite art are mingled with the very life-sweats of Nature, with the stickiness and clamminess of honey and mushrooms, and the rank pungencies of mud-grown hog-weed.

Such are the regions where tender, pastoral, Virgilian deities, full of a certain dreamy autumnal wistfulness, mingle without incongruity with the tavern-smells of Eastcheap. Here the quaint ways of old ledger-dusty London clerks are brought into contact with high poetic images from Milton; while "child-angels," free from all blame, take their places beside fallen Titans and trees "branch-charméd by the earnest stars."

It is interesting to note as a psychological commentary upon the unhumorous, noisy, hollow gaiety of our time that the word "solemn" has become a word of reproach. One ought to be solemn sometimes. If we read any great, powerful, modern book, such as that most suggestive and monumental work, Spengler's "Decline of the West," in a mood of grave receptivity, a mood full of memories of the older solemn books of our own race, books like those of Sir Thomas Browne and John Donne and Jeremy Taylor, we shall be much more ready to refrain from clever catch-penny critical objections, much more ready to give ourselves up imaginatively, freely, to a few world-shaking speculations, in which we can listen to the heavy, rumbling undertones of the brooding fates.

It will not matter to us so much, then, in what particulars this great book is perverse. Culture is always ready to take very lightly those fantastic faults of mystical exaggeration of which expert pedantry makes so much. And this is the case because what culture is concerned with is a certain stimulation of one's imaginative reaction to life. Any writer, however wild, grotesque, or heavy-handed, who makes our daily sunset more of a surprise to us and our lunar crescent more of a miracle, any writer who rouses our sense of the vast tragedy of the generations, any writer who makes us feel the earth to be a divine presence and the night to be a palpable god, wins our whole-hearted respect.

The gathering together of minute facts of knowledge, verified and checked and re-checked by expert instruments, has no doubt an incalculable practical value; but in the reading of books and in our choice of books what culture demands are large, bold, startling generalizations, or startling refutations of older generalizations, such as quicken our sense of life.

Any writer who takes such ultimate things as the problem of space and time, or the Einstein doctrine of relativity, and renders them vivid, portentous, consoling, or appalling, is doing for us what it was the rôle of the old prophets and poets to do. That is why in making any selection among pseudo-philosophic modern books such an one as Wyndham Lewis' "Time and Western Man" has an important place. Not because we need go one single step in agreement with his conclusions; but because our whole intellectual arena is illuminated by a fierce, lively, agreeable search-light, as we read such a wayward book.

In other words what culture demands of us in our reading is simply a heightened sense of the grandeur of the epic of human life upon earth. The more the obliquities and perversities of human destiny are held up to ribald scorn, the more stubbornly our imagination reverts to those majestic simplicities that no scorn can touch. It does not matter to real culture whether a book be lucid as transparent air, or sullenly obscure as pitch-black midnight. If it stirs us up to feel the throb of the great life-engines, down there in one abyss, it has completed its task.

Thus the maddest obscurities of Joyce's latest work, just because there is something in the surge and sweep of that wild philological dithyramb which releases the cosmic dance of our blood, have a certain value for us, even though we understand this cosmopolitan "Olla Podrida" of erudition and obscene slang no better than if it were the gibberish of madmen. What one is wise to do with books is to saturate oneself with their imaginative atmospheres. Thus after re-reading the four great novels of Dostoievsky one is obsessed by the feeling of the presence of strange and passionate characters, each man, each woman a wandering dark star of convoluted mystery, moving along roads in the outskirts of towns in rain-swept woody plains or between tall houses in sombre northern cities.

To all this one must add what one gets from the heroic Greek tragedies, a sense of super-human men and women on lonely olive-covered heights and high, bare sea-promontories, wrestling calmly, stubbornly, austerely with the dark powers of the nether-world, and visited at moments by pure immortal incarnations of the sun, the moon, the sea, the rivers and the earth. All these impressions derived from reading are of little value unless we can mingle and fuse them with the actual feelings we have as we walk about, or look up for a moment from our work at desk or counter or factory-machine.

What culture can do is to liberate us from the pressure of that odious, false reality which is the poisoner of and the assassin of all thrilling and exciting thoughts. It is a good thing to read books which create an atmosphere wholly and entirely different from the one in which we are doomed by a maladjusted society to labour. Thus it is well worth the tedium of his long-windedness to linger slowly over the rambling romances of Sir Walter Scott. Dull though much of it may seem, stilted though much of it is, there is a massive genius in this solid Antiquary of Folklore, for the creation of quaint, homely, whimsical, idiosyncratic personages, such as do really resemble in an astonishing verisimilitude many persons that one may encounter today if one looks out for them.

It is not because of any silly "high-brow" priggishness that a cultured person avoids like the plague the countless clever, witty, lively, lurid, fantastical stories that flood our bookshops and our popular magazines. It is because the human mind is fatally sensitized to such influences; especially if the subject of them possesses that topical and immediate appeal which crime-stories and adventure-stories in the daily newspaper possess. It is not from pride but from humility that any nature, anxious to nourish itself upon food which the long experience of the generations has proved to be most stimulating, gives all these insidious temptations to the Devil. There are no doubt original and fastidious geniuses who instinctively loathe these mean and meretricious viands; but average sensitive people are wise to steer clear of them even if they feel attracted. Life is short and the number of books is appalling. It is a kind of insanity to satiate oneself with short sensation-tales and detective-tales and leave untouched the great, slow, deep-breathed classics.

The whole point of the difference lies here. These flashy, clever, lively modern books distract one's attention not so much from the vulgar, false reality of the superficial show of things, for this, as a rule, they delight to emphasize, and indeed rejoice to reproduce with photographic minuteness; but from that deeper, lasting reality which might be called the Platonic essence of our long human experience. This they neglect, this they avoid, this they expurgate, lest their work be rendered dull and tedious to the eye that loves best the fever-mists at the edge of the bottomless pond.

Culture would not be culture if it were not an acquired taste. A new sort of barbarian has been evoked by our megalopolitan civilization; the barbarian of tasteless taste. In the old days all books, even what are called broad-sides and chap-books, had a solid value. In their most Rabelaisian grossness there was a certain tang, and a certain smack of the restorative earth. They had the value of good dung-heaps. But with the inrush of modern cheap printing, combined with the standardization of vulgar city-psychology, what we are confronted with today is a magnetic emanation, passing like radio-waves from mind to mind, of the crudest superficiality; an emanation given off, like a miasmic effluvium, from the surface-scum of the agglomerated mob-mentality. In old days the lewd under-side of things was represented in blasphemous pamphlets, Gothic gargoyles, and the quips of dissolute pedants, rustic idiots, lascivious scholars. Today this inherent and indestructible satyrishness of the human race is presented with the hard, brutal, malapert facetiousness of uncultured city-scoffers.

The choice of the books one reads is indeed one of the few important gestures one is permitted nowadays to make, in the great war that is always going on between the children of light and the children of perdition. To make people feel deeply by legislation is impossible; to try to reduce them to wisdom by savage satire is usually but beating the wind and digging trenches in the sand. But if one is driven by ungovernable distaste to make some sort of protest, what one really can do is to eschew with stubborn austerity all this raw, steaming product, insidious as carrion to emperor-moths, of the ovens that bake our corruption.

The secret benefit that both men and women can derive from confining their reading to the deep, imaginative books is a richer, subtler knowledge of each other. However fiercely feministic a woman's philosophy may be, she will find her insight into the restricted group of men she knows enlarged beyond expectation by the psychological clairvoyance of the great writers. What cannot a woman get by saturating herself with the work of Proust, for example? She may well have been completely puzzled by a Monsieur Swann or a Baron de Charlus, however shrewdly her natural instinct may have pierced to the marrow the Madame de Verdurins of her circle. And, for a man, what enlargement of his insight into the feminine nature will have been evoked by the figures of Aglaia Epanchin, Nastasia Philippovna, Grushenka, Sonia, Darya and Lise, from the great novels of Dostoievsky? Once a man has grasped to its tragic extreme that "terrible passivity" that finds examples all the way down the ages, from the Homeric Helen to Hardy's Tess, is it possible that some kind of added considerateness, some kind of added tenderness, will not accompany his wayfarings among women? It is not only that men and women learn more of each other's secrets from the great writers, they learn to respect each other better, and to feel more reverence for the primordial comic-tragedy of the difference between them.

One can easily grant that a crafty, suspicious man and a shrewd, dissimulating girl can learn more of each other's tricks and subterfuges from close contact and near observation than from all the books ever written; but what they cannot learn is that these tricks and devices, these vanities and touchinesses, are as old as the world. What they cannot learn—unless they are born original thinkers of rare quality—is a certain tender and poetic reverence for all these naively revealed everlasting characteristics. The abysmal vanity and incurable pompousness of men, for example,—would not a bookish woman learn something about that, and about how to be tender to it, from long leisurely hours spent listening to the crazy theories of "my father" in "Tristram Shandy"? Would she not inwardly digest too a certain childish guilelessness in her man, all the more pleasantly from following the innocent protests of "my Uncle Toby"?

And would not a man, who heretofore in his experience of women had encountered none that were not either of the maternal or of the courtezan type, be driven to a new and quite unexpected recognition, when in reading Conrad he came across that "wounded elf" variety of girlhood, so beautifully revealed in Flora de Barral in "Chance" and in Lena in "Victory"?

The reading of books worthy of the name, if both are passionately addicted to it and have somewhat the same predilections in the matter, may quite conceivably, over and over again, save many a ménage from disaster. No lover of good books—in other words no cultured person—can feel continuous hostility to another reader of the same sort. The mere sight of that engrossed look, that absorbed and rapt delight, would, one may well suppose, disarm the most vindictive hate.

It is deplorable the amount of stupid, unenlightened taking-for-granted that goes on between people, especially between a man and a woman who have lived side by side for many years. This is a sort of pulling wool over the eyes of the Sphinx, covering the candles of the altar with a wet blanket, scratching the figures of an almanack upon the canvas of the Virgin of the Rocks, and using the three fates for a milestone!

Human beings have only a limited amount of vital energy, of that resilient cosmic magnetism *"qui fait le monde à* *la ronde*"*; and the mere repetition of the same routine, unless one is a genius of the hearth or very much in love, has a tendency to cover up with a thick layer of cement the delicate foliations and deeply cut hieroglyphs of another spirit. But if both man and woman, both parent and child, are readers of the old, great books, the faintly-caught music of the spheres steals nearer; and under the spell of the muffled march of the generations the blurred outlines of those familiar physiognomies begin to emerge in full relief and life grows rich and thick once more.

The more Greek and Latin books people read, either in the original or in translations, the more cultured they can become; that is if their natures are destined for such nourishment. And this happens because the ripe and mellow heathenism of these works, their poetical earthiness, their calm acceptance of life and death, thrusts a critical wedge of profound detachment between our minds and every mystical or moral cult that seeks to convert us or corrupt us. And the mystical element which the classic writings supply in place of such modern fantasias is their living mythology.

Since the whole purpose of culture is to enable us to live out our days in a perpetual under-tide of ecstasy, it is clear that culture has entirely failed if it has not helped us to see men and women walking to and fro over the earth in the likeness of gods, if it has not helped us to feel that the sun and the moon (whatever the last scientific theory about them may be) are mysterious personal powers to whom it would seem natural to pray. Greater than any printed book is the vaulted scroll of the constellations; and from whence is this cosmic folio drawn, where it is not Chaldean or Arabian, if not from classical mythology?

People who do not read books, or who read only the

fashionable books of the hour, are driven to depend for their mental activity upon what passes for conversation. Almost all modern conversation, when not between lovers or book-lovers, is a silly interruption of the secret ecstasy of life. That is where certain wise sensation-lovers, like Wordsworth and Miss Dorothy Richardson, can be of such value to our culture. They make us realize the ghastly waste of time that we indulge in when we give ourselves up to frivolous badinage.

Who does not recognize the shock and clash of a wicked outrage when one watches a young unspoilt mind emerging from the pages of its book and the delicious dreams that its book has called forth, and being compelled to encounter the noisy chatter of a great roomful of lively roisterers, where gramophones and radios and feet and tongues all are rending and tearing those gossamer threads, those filmy mists, those delicate fibres, those green tendrils, that have the very dew of creation upon them?

Let us have done with this vociferous, hypocritical humbug about real life being so much more important than books! The noisy persons who use these bracing expressions will never know, with all their bluster,—never in twenty years!—such quivering ecstatic raptures as one silent boy or one reserved girl draws in an afternoon from the pages, or from between the pages, of Rousseau's "Confessions," or Proust's "Le Temps Retrouvé," or Thomas Mann's "Magic Mountain," or Spengler's "Decline of the West." It is not the outward variety or the material bustle and clatter of experience that count—it is the subtlety and the intensity. Culture in fact can do what nothing else but love and religion can do. It can take the quiet, gentle, attenuated impressions of life, impressions thrust back, as it were, one remove from the first raw impact, and make them into far better planetary symbols of the great secret life-forces than all the dance-halls and night-clubs and baseball-matches and horse-races in the world are able to provide!

Lovers of books will be found to be of almost infinite variety. In their methods of reading, in the slowness or the speed with which they read, in the nature of the books they re-read again and again, in the type of books they never return to, they differ from one another in almost every point. One might imagine for instance four brothers, all great readers;—and one might be found reading Montaigne's "Essays" again and again, another Goethe's "Conversations with Eckermann," another the poetry of John Donne, another the novels of Hardy. And just as there are these irreversible differences in taste between book-lovers, so the revelations about life which various people derive from reading lie as far apart as the poles.

But all have their living value. All are true in their hour and place—a voracious reader of Balzac's impassioned Vulcanian quarrying will have received one startling revelation at any rate upon which to muse. He will have learnt that a man who gives himself up to the love of a woman or girl must be prepared to yield willingly, nay! voluptuously, to an abysmal possessiveness the like of which can only be equalled by the maternal instinct. He will learn that if he abandons himself body and soul, in full unreserving trust, to this instinct of hers all will be well. He must let her sew for him, cook for him, create the atmosphere of his ménage for him, manage his money, sift and select his friends, share his ideas, his ambitions, his philosophy, his religion, his very memories—and then all will be well. An indescribable background of psychic satisfaction will rock him then to rest like the waves of a great, smooth flood. He will be happy and she will be happy. Out of two beings one being will have been made. And yet in the midst of this incomprehensible unity there will still exist, separate and distinct, down to the very nadir of the universe, that unbridgeable difference between them which is the *fons et origo* of all!

Such a devoted reader of Balzac and of several other great novelists—for it is in this art that psychology utters its most penetrating if not its most massive oracles—will discover too that much of the savage insistence which we find in such writers as D. H. Lawrence, as to the sublime, irreconcilable war between men and women, springs from the fact that the predestined mate is so hard to discover. There is indeed only one test—so we gather between the lines as we read—of this perfect mate; namely that without a jot of suspicion or misgiving a person can fling himself absolutely, for good and for ill, upon her mercy. In full premeditation must we say for ill as well as for good; for until a man puts his conscience, as his final and ultimate offering, at the feet of his love, in her heart she knows that the consummation has not yet been reached. Towards this absolute issue, like a winding river heading for the salt sea, she directs their affection. As long as he holds back, in the depths of his being, one single uncommitted water-drop of his enamoured will, the flood of that river will be delayed, stirred up and darkened with silt and mud, in its deepest bed.

The mind of a book-lover, meditating long and long upon such things, as he contemplates the Platonic essence of life in these formidable writers, will soon learn to read the great book of Nature for himself. He may, for instance, in this business of mating have found his experience of women reduced to the narrowest limitations.

It matters nothing. The writings of Balzac, Henry James, Turgeniev, Dostoievsky, Emily Brontë, Proust, Stendhal, will have supplied him with the experience he requires. Taking a hint from one and a hint from another he will soon find himself reading the secrets of creative Nature without further assistance. It is then he will discover—to carry our primitive example a step further—that having made the one grand interior motion of submission to his mate, she will be pliable and easy in every detail. As soon as she feels he has held nothing back—not even his very soul; as soon as she feels that she herself has lodgment within the circumference of his very soul, she will yield to him in detail without scruple or hesitation. Pliable, docile, flexible, will she be. His philosophy will be her philosophy, his friends her friends, his ambitions her ambitions, his peculiarities her peculiarities. There is no doubt that in all those famous examples of docility in woman of which the history of great inspired artists is full, such docility, for instance, as was displayed by Catherine Blake to William Blake, the secret below the secret of their relations was that the man, prophet, artist, saint, lover, held nothing back, either mental, spiritual, or material, in the depths of the association.

Here and nowhere else is to be found the explanation of those curious cases where a devoted wife or mistress allows her mate full liberty in the matter of alien sex-pleasure. It will usually be found that in these cases the faithful-unfaithful man tells his woman. People therefore who do not wish their light-o'-loves to be known to any but the sharer of them were wise to steer clear of men and women who have found their life-companion! Women are not nearly as jealous as men with regard to wandering amorous caresses, or even with regard to the final act of love. What hits them to the heart is for other women to know; because this knowledge by others is a token that they are still outside the inner circumference of their love's consciousness.

What renders the anger of women so terrible is that with all the irrationality of its immediate occasion it manages to get behind it the whole flood of some primordial force in Nature; and it succeeds in doing this because what a woman unconsciously feels to be the justification of her raging fury is the fact that somewhere in the depths of his being her man has escaped from her or is in the process of escaping from her. The true ultimate anger of frustrated possession is fortunately rare. No reader of Russian books, however, wherein, as in Dostoievsky for instance, the anger of women is so beautifully and formidably exposed, will be without some sort of clue as to the difference between this ultimate possessive anger and its comparatively harmless substitutes.

In that great scene in "The Idiot" where Aglaia Epanchin and Nastasia Philippovna face each other at white heat in the presence of the Prince, the anger of both is entirely this ultimate possessive wrath. And well indeed might they both feel it, for the luckless Myshkin was assuredly holding something back in both cases. He loved Aglaia with his natural instinct. He loved Nastasia with his strange "Fifth Gospel" pity. It may thus have been quite true, as his friend Yevgeny so sternly said to him, that in the depths of his being he loved neither of them.

Another thing one may soon learn, if one reads Nature for oneself under the inspiration of these immortal writers, and that is that every man overrates the moral importance of every woman's anger. Out of the womb of the Great Mother herself, of Gaia-Demeter, the mistress of life and death, there springs forth a certain natural, elemental irritation, the organic ferment in the reservoirs of the universe, which is an inevitable accompaniment of cosmic gestation. Such irritation, such irrational outbursts of startling anger over unbelievable trifles, need not be taken as ponderously and gravely as most men are tempted to take it, answering it with solemn arguments and pedantic appeals to reason and justice.

Nothing infuriates a woman more, or in her malicious fury, delights her more, than these portentous and only too logical reasonings. It is almost as bad when the good man assumes an air of outraged, martyrized virtue. What a man should call up at such moments—and if he is a cultured man, and has pondered long upon the classics, this is what he *will* summon up to his aid—is the primordial opposite to this Gaia-ferment, namely the stolid, massive, whimsical, detached humour of the Hephaestus-craftsman at his anvil.

But a really cultured man, who has been led, not only by the classics but by the sly, fantastic humourists of the north to consider Nature's tricks with some acuteness, will instinctively practise a certain retort to this seething ferment of the Great Mother's irritation which has an even better effect than the stolid, humorous patience referred to above. I am alluding now to an assumed, pretended, but very stern masculine anger, which, like the rattling of the terrible quiver of the son of Latona, can quell the tumult even of Chthonian Deities!

It is interesting to try to analyse why it is that we all naturally find it so much easier to read a modern novel of the second or third class of quality than to read any classical work. It is not at all that the former is simple and the latter obscure. Very often, if our translation is good, the latter is by far the less obscure. Is it not primarily because the play of character and circumstance, all the little details, all the topical questions, all the scenes described, belong to our own time? This contemporaneousness of detail relieves us of all imaginative effort. Everything is done for us. The writer is thinking, describing, jesting, whimpering, holding his breath, in a medium so familiar to us that the mind has to make no effort to get the undersense of what is happening. Take for instance a book like "The Bridge of San Luis Rey" and compare it—only, of course, in this particular connection,—with a book like "Middlemarch"; and will it not be clear that, for those among us who enjoy average fiction, this masterpiece of George Eliot's is a work less easy to read than the clever modern work?

Raise the standard on both sides of the shield higher! Compare Homer's account of the duel between Paris and Menelaus and of Helen's looking down from the walls of Troy with Thomas Hardy's "Jude the Obscure." Who among us who retained his honesty in these matters would not confess to find "Jude the Obscure" far more exciting, absorbing, and easy to read than those great Homeric scenes, even in the simplest of translations?

Does it not almost seem as if a certain effort of the imagination were required when one is reading a classical book, whereas when one is reading an exciting modern book no effort of the imagination is needed? One now begins to realize what, in this affair of book-reading, culture really means! Culture means the power of making just that very effort of the imagination which is required in order that we should get as much satisfaction out of those passages in Homer as out of "Jude the Obscure."

Now this effort of the imagination is not acquired all in a moment. It is a matter of practise and training. The more often you taste the Pierian Spring the more deeply will an insatiable craving for its waters follow you about. You will find yourself, when on a journey, seized with a mania for Homer's poetry that *must* be satisfied, even if it means hunting through all the local bookshops for some miserable school-edition. And with what delight you will open the thin volume when you've got it in your hands! How, if you are in a strange place, you will lay it by the side of your plate in some unknown tavern; how you will mingle its reverberating ocean-mutter with the twittering of sparrows in some small-town square or with a budding lilac-bush at the edge of some city-garden!

And how will your imagination go to work in this magical trick of making what seems so dull to the uncultured mind grow to be thrilling and exciting? In the first place you must realize that this Homeric writing is dealing with life and death on the very simplest terms. When that lamentable little step-son of theirs killed the other children and himself it was a blow of a malignant, perverse, and an almost mystical cruelty to the luckless hearts of Jude and Sue; but when Hector says farewell to Andromache for the last time the situation represents the most natural, ordinary, primitive state of things that could be imagined.

If we desire to reach the cultured attitude to books and reading, we must grow conscious of this same natural, ordinary primitive state of things as something that surrounds us at every moment, as something that is, in fact, the Platonic essence of reality. And this remains true even though some vividly described character in a powerful modern book may be far more alluring to our intellectual curiosity than Hector or Andromache, than Achilles or Odysseus. The "Ulysses" of James Joyce, for example, that much-enduring Leopold Bloom, might easily arrest the attention of anyone's analytical contemplation far more than his great prototype!

But what these modern books cannot do is to satisfy a certain acquired taste which culture has given us; a taste for contemplating life and death in their most natural and normal simplicity and associating them with beauty, love, jealousy, wrath, and allowing them to take their place, grandly and monumentally, free from all moral *arrières pensées,* against a background of earth, air, and sea; of sun and moon, and the day and the night.

One could almost repeat, word by word, the sort of spontaneous creed which a very bookish person might be driven to confess. It would probably be a different creed altogether from that of a bishop or a soldier or a statesman or a judge. One can indeed easily conceive it running as follows—"I believe in many gods. I believe that there may be immortality. I believe that virtue is charity—I believe that the secret of life is happiness." But the grand device of a lover of books, whatever his creed, is to mingle his pleasure in reading with the other pleasures of his life. Deep and subtle are the various sensations that come to us in this way. Perhaps the most wonderful of all thoughts, except those of love under certain very especial circumstances, are the thoughts that come to us when we have been reading some particularly thrilling book and then stop for a second to observe the shadows on the hills, or to look out upon the lights of the streets, or to gaze down at the sea. For some reason or other the effect of long absorption in reading—and let parents and authorities of all kinds note this well—is to purge the mind of annoying and teasing thoughts and to leave us amiable, genial, benevolent. It is a wicked thing that so few of the proletariat have leisure to read for as long as they want. Not to have time to read is such a miserable deprivation that one can well understand the revolutionary mood of those who have suffered it.

When a rich person declares he "has no time to read," it is as if he said "I have no time to eat," or "I have no time to wash," or "I have no time to say my prayers." All we children of men, to the most abject and exploited drudge among us, find time for some sort of love-making—however remote and attenuated it may be—and for a person with the least rudiments of those slowly acquired habits which we call culture the necessity of reading resembles the necessity of love.

What one is apt to forget is the curious loneliness of so many people. How many a girl finds herself as isolated among her brothers and sisters and in the presence of her parents as if she were marooned on a desert island. How many a young man awakens one morning after the first glow of his married life has waned to realize clearly and decisively that between himself and the woman he is now linked with there is no real mental understanding. Nor need we take these exceptional and tragic instances. Under the most genial circumstances it is not easy for any man or woman, for any boy or girl, to find a perfect mental companionship. One's relatives are affectionate, one's acquaintances are good-natured, one has one's measure of pleasant, amorous delight. But something is missing; and this something is unfortunately the one thing, most necessary—someone with whom to exchange ideas!

It is just here that books, and books alone, enter and save us. All intimate and intense reading is a kind of secret dialogue between the writer and one's own soul. After a long, furtive, impassioned, Platonic love-affair with Goethe, or Walt Whitman, or Keats, or Lamb, or even the translunar Emerson, what a contrast it is when we fall back upon ordinary casual fooling with our less exciting friends!

Think how narrow, in reality, is every mortal person's circle of human acquaintanceship. And we all are possessed, even the least intelligent among us, of peculiar mental twists and quirks, of peculiar imaginative reactions, which could easily go down to the grave with us, unsatisfied, unrecognized, unappreciated. Entering the world of books, in place of a restricted circle of a dozen intimates, we find offered to our fellowship a vast and spacious Limbo, crowded with the undying dead. It will go hard if among these we do not find a few, at least one or two, adapted to our fastidious requirements in a way impossible with any living friend—unless chance has been good to us far beyond the luck of most. If only these divine immortals could speak to us in the flesh; could answer certain sharp, bitter, tragic-comic questions, touching the poignance of our actual experience!

In the matter of books, as in the matter of religion, there is no palpable voice from beyond the banked-up walls save what a miraculous faith can bring; and for how few is this miracle worked. For a few it does sometimes almost seem as if some strange, occult exchange of mental vibration went on between the remote idol and the living idolater; but for most of us, as in the case of our communion with the ultimate first cause, our dialogue with the dead remains lamentably one-sided.

In the actual process of reading books how can any guide give rules or directions? Some natures are on the alert for one kind of nourishment, others for others. To some the style—that rich palimpsest of mysteries, that white magic—is everything. To others the style is nothing, compared with certain definite opinions, characters, ideas, philosophies, moralities that our favourite books contain. Some abominate preciosity; others love it best of all. Some adore a plain, direct, sledge-hammer method of going to work. Others find such a thing tedious, didactic, lacking in grace and charm. Some lap up with wicked voluptuous relish the satiric vein whenever it appears. Others loathe it and hurry on to something more positive, more illuminating, more inspiring. Some hover above a book, like a kestrel-hawk out of the sky, and pounce swiftly on just what they want, leaving the rest like so much dead carrion. Others find it advisable to read very slowly, following carefully every single page, saturating themselves with a book's very atmosphere till it becomes a portion of their inmost being. Some natures find an immense enlargement of their personalities by reading much in a foreign tongue. Something French in their spirit corresponds to the French language; something German in their imagination to the German language. A person may have felt an exile in a strange country until he had the felicity to begin a study of Latin or of Greek. Then, like a little postern door opening upon an unguessed-at earthly paradise, he uses this old tongue to pass free and content among characters, ideas, conceptions, images, even a very air and landscape, exactly adapted to his exiled, maladjusted and persecuted nature. It is a great mistake to assume that one person is necessarily more cultured than another because he is a good linguist. It might easily happen that by feeling and thinking with a certain versatile volubility in many languages one gradually lost the power of identifying one's whole being with any. To be a superficial adept in many tongues is to be a living master of none. But it does certainly remain true that there are many most sensitive personalities of pure Nordic blood who with a desperate spiritual yearning pine for aspects of culture entirely denied them in their Nordic surrounding. Many lonely natures, if only they had the wit to realize it, are, by a kind of atavistic adoption, children of some long-past epoch of the human pilgrimage. They may live in some little wayside town in Iowa or Colorado, while in all their most integral instincts they belong to Periclean Athens, Imperial Rome, the Florence of the Medici, the London of Ben Jonson, the aristocratic salons of the eighteenth century, the revolutionary Europe of Heine, of Byron and Shelley! There must be little local Carnegie Libraries all over the United States full of bad mixers, odd fish, misfits, queer ones of every wounded sort of wing, who are taking refuge there in regions totally unknown to their neighbours, wonderful Elysian Fields of escape, into which no exacting employer, no debased public opinion can ever pursue them.

The world of books is, in fact, the Grand Alsatia, to which all the hunted ones of the herded tribes of men can flee away and be at rest. The mere presence of real culture in certain communities is a stone of stumbling and a rock of offence. A cultured person is a person doomed by nature to a considerable degree of social ostracism in our modern world. This is due to the fact that culture itself, even in its simplest, earliest stages tends to adopt a certain detached bird's-eye view of human life and its bitter controversies, an attitude of contemplative, critical discrimination, which is more than anything else hateful to all partisans. Not to take sides—not to see the devil in one camp and God Himself in the other—what could be more suspicious?

After the great poets and novelists—after Homer, Shakespeare, Dostoievsky, Proust, Henry James—it would almost seem as though works of history—memoirs, chronicles, biographies, legends, folk-lore, studies in the growth of religions and religious heresies—were the most fecund in the sort of imaginative interest which brings the best grist to culture's mill. And the way to read these books is to resign all attempts at reaching any objective impartial judgments. The thing to do is to give yourself up wholly and totally to the most violent prejudices of the author until by degrees the particular emotional *aperçu* which has stirred him and obsessed him reveals to you that unique, unrelated expression of the Protean face of truth which has been all the while his secret inspiration. Quite the opposite expression of the same Protean countenance will be caught when you proceed to give yourself up with equal sympathy to the argument of his antagonist. But if there be such a thing in this world as an approximation to absolute truth in human affairs, it will be found in the act of placing side by side the two most extreme points of view that can be discovered. Everything in life is dualistic and the truth of human history is no exception. Between one taboo and another swings the great pendulum of the psychic contraries of history. Truth lies, if anywhere, in the bringing close together, in full illuminating contrast, of the most opposite interpretations; and in allowing them to remain uncoördinated, unreconciled, unrelated, save as we are forced to imagine that they are two sides of the same shield; but a shield the nature of which, apart from their propinquity, it is forbidden to us to discover.

The desire to reconcile, to synthesize; the desire to interpret the magical divergencies of things and the issues of things—which are their entelechies and their essences—in terms of vague, colourless, hypothecated neutralities, such as no man has ever seen or will ever see; is a desire against which true culture must always be contending. The petals of life's mysterious flower must always carry upon them the bloom of inexplicable paradox. Their scent, their colour, their very shape, seem always to differ from moment to moment according to a darkness which is so much a thing by itself, and a light which is so much a thing by itself, that we can never behold the substance that changes with their alternation. Culture must do with its books of history as it does with the opinions it encounters on the lips of living men; it must accept them on their own terms. The views of every man and every woman are different; different with that divergency of innate psychology which separates all lives from one another by such impassable gulfs.

The universe is not static; it is a congeries of growing organisms, each one of which is an absolute creator. There are indeed as many universes—that is to say fluctuating temporary adjustments of "selves" and "not-selves"—as there are living organisms; and it comes more and more to be evident that there are no *lacunae* of chemical or magnetic energy—no blind oases of matter—that are not portions of the mysterious organisms of living things.

If that primal father of energy we call the Sun could inscribe in eternal hieroglyphs upon some cosmogonic Rosetta Stone the history of its long journeying, such a book would be no more a piece of absolute truth than a similar scroll inscribed by the Moon or by Saturn or by Aldeboran. It would be the Sun's rendering of his burning reaction to the "not-sun"; it would be the diary of his half-successful, half-frustrated struggle to create his own world, and of a thousand cosmic impingings, some warded off, some yielded to, upon his huge, dreaming life-illusion.

Just as to be cultured among men means to have a sense of the mystery of life more vivid and intense than that of others, so also does it mean the possession of a deeper scepticism than that of others. In a person's choice of books this becomes very quickly evident. Uncultured people read only the religious books, the moral books, the philosophical books, that reflect their own ideas. The rampant secularist, the crusading mechanistic iconoclast, shows himself to be just as uninterested in the theories of his opponents as the most rigid fundamentalist. How refreshing, how thrilling a moment it is in one's intellectual life when one realizes the equality of all truths!

A world "fixed up," once and for all, on religious or theosophical or metaphysical lines is a world lacking in certain tragic but strangely beautiful possibilities. A world "fixed up," checked and counter-checked by tangible sensuous evidence, is a world with all its artesian wells, and all its volcanic chasms, and all its black holes in space, and all its psychic dimensions, cemented over and smoothed down with an adamantine layer of concrete.

How absurd it is to have such a dogmatically uncultured mind that one misses the reality-value in the half-truths of mythology, folk-lore, ghost-stories, religious superstitions, and moral taboos! Those pages of Lemprière's "Classical Dictionary" entitled "Mythology" are quite as "true," when taken literally as explanations of this peculiar world, as are the latest theories in dynamics and physics.

There are certain cynical, frivolous, unpoetical, modern writers who compose, in a demi-semi-facetious manner, silly books upon Black Magic and the like; airing their sadistic fancies and venting their cheap wit on old tribal legends of which neither the truth nor the beauty touches deeply their jaded, life-weary, languid nerves. Such superficial exploiters of old earth-legends and old poetic myths are in their hearts not sceptics at all; for they have not the least real belief in the possibility of these things. They are in truth dogmatic unbelievers who, out of a kind of fanciful roguery and a faint aesthetic titillation, play with the poetry of life. They do exactly as the *nouveaux riches* do, who fill their vulgar reception-rooms with bric-à-brac stolen from the shrines of dead gods. In the matter of the choice of books a youthful mind that desires to be really cultured will of all things shun and avoid a certain frivolous humour that is in fact anything but humorous. It is the wan, bleak, hollow gibing of a corpse-nature that can only give back a thin leprous suppuration as the winds of morning and evening shake its gibbet-tree! Real humour is like that of Rabelais and Sterne and Cervantes and Shakespeare—something that has the pith and sap of a vital life-ecstasy in it. The reading of books can be indeed a veritable path to perdition if its trend is towards an inherent frivolity. The most savage and blasphemous, even the most furiously obscene writing takes its place along with the greatest, if its sardonic wrath and cataclysmic imagination springs from the stirred depths of the writer's soul.

Passages from Jonathan Swift and from James Joyce hold such a place, because such noble, devilish fooling springs out of the lacerated abysses of the human heart. Where the youthful mind, let loose in any great library, is apt to go astray, is where it falls under the catchpenny spell of the kind of mind that is cynical rather than sceptical, frivolous rather than blasphemous, and corrupt and defeatist all along the line.

A big library contains many queer books. It is the greatest mistake in the world to assume that all the evocations of genius provide good nourishment. Many provide the most delicate poisons. Some resemble the plant called hen-bane; others the plant called wolf's-bane. The assumption that the human mind is enriched by all the virtuosity it imbibes is as stupid as to put Pantagruel or Candide upon the forbidden shelves. There are frivolous, cynical, hollow-hearted books, written by clever modern aesthetes— we are not of course referring to Oscar Wilde or to James Branch Cabell—that fall into line only too well with the silly pseudo-sophisticated patter of the most unpleasant smart people.

Just as the worst thing that could be done to a youthful mind is to give it the impression that the old, great, simple books are declassed, passé, dated, out-moded, done-for, and that the revelations of the *Zeitgeist* are to be found in the frothy nothings of the hour, so the best thing that could be done to a youthful mind is to get lodged in it forever the assumption that every great classical work is inexhaustible and that there are still endless aspects of it, deep and subtle, left for the latest reader to discover. For a youth just beginning to find out a whole new world of ideas and sensations the writings of Walter Pater, especially in that noble Macmillan edition, are in a sense more precious and more important than is any particular poem or play or history in the Greek or in any other language. No young "intellectual" were wise to disregard Pater; for his critical method—whatever our modern literary guides may say—has one incalculable value: it associates mental ideas with sensuous impressions. Pater does this whether he is referring to the relation between ideas and images in the artist's own mind or to the relation between his written word and our own sensuous sensations as we appreciate it and appropriate it. In the matter of collecting books—I mean *owning* them and having them on one's own shelf in one's own room—I would put Pater's works in the very forefront of those a person were wise to buy.

Pater's philosophy of critical appreciation will never be outmoded for a mind sensitive to rare and gentle things. As a philosophy of life it will hold good when hundreds of cleverer, more scientific, more startling systems have vanished like bubbles. It is much more original than those who disparage it, and it contains a much more complete way of life. In one thing it is extraordinarily original; and for this, more than for any other reason, I would rejoice to see a boy or girl saving money to purchase these spacious and stately volumes. It is original, I mean, in the reiterated emphasis it lays, implicitly between the lines as well as explicitly in every line, upon the primary importance of selection in the intellectual life. It avails little for Pater's disparagers to upbraid him for this selectiveness as if it were a species of finicky affectation. Certain self-conscious preciosities in his premeditated style—they are all intimately characteristic and many of them are charming—do not affect this main tendency. The point really at issue is this— can you build up any intellectual life at all, can you nourish it, feed it, make constant and deliberate efforts to keep it alive, without selectiveness, without being—and why should we be afraid of the word? —fastidious? The intellectual life is not at first as natural as breathing.

Afterwards, when it is a second habit, it does become so. But not at first,—not for a long time. There are certain quite definite efforts that have to be made; efforts as unpleasant as the effort of waking yourself up and getting out of bed. Take the case of selecting books for a journey. How much easier is it to choose the last novel by Willa Cather, or Sheila Kaye-Smith, or Martha Ostenso, than to carry off in your pocket the "Loeb Classics" edition of Homer or of Virgil! And yet when once you have made that effort and have opened the "Odyssey," let us say, at that scene in the house of Alcinous where Nausicaa waits for Odysseus half-hidden by the side of a smoky pillar, to waylay him returning from the bath to a crowded hall-fire to boast of his deeds among these mackerel-catchers and apple-growers, and the girl challenges him as to what his feelings for her are who has just now saved his life, how the old, invincible, salt air of that great poetry blows round you again, with all its high, penetrating exultation, transforming this raw, cluttered, noisy world and remoulding it nearer to the dreams of all noble spirits.

And then at some later moment of your excursion or of your daily commuter's journey, possibly when some trick of the late afternoon light has made the houses, the wharfs, the freight-cars float and swim in a golden dusty haze, you open that Georgic of Virgil that discourses so pedantically on bee-keeping; and after suffering a certain disappointment and almost wishing you had not removed your eyes from the western glow, you suddenly come upon that reverberating cry, "Eurydice! Eurydice!" in the story of Orpheus; it is as though the desperate lamentation down all the ages of such as have lost their one of all ring and ring in those piteous syllables, echoed from the cold lips of that blood-stained, wave-tossed head.

It is at such moments as these that you bless the gods that you had the wit to leave the modern novel and to take the old poet, for at such moments, out of the printed pages of a book, the whole pitiful-terrible history of human life mounts up before you like a beckoning exhalation; and the feelings within you that are yet uncorrupted, that have remained simple and primeval below all your "bowings in the House of Rimmon," rush forth to greet it, spirit encountering spirit.

Any attempt to live a cultured life must imply many such occasions as this one; when, at first, you are vexed with yourself for your priggishness or your pedantry in persistently carrying an old book about with you, when there are so many lively and distracting new ones and when you may so easily grow weary of Virgil and his bees. But in this whole matter of culture it must be remembered that we are deliberately sacrificing certain sprightly, gay and lively pleasures for the sake of a happiness which flows through us like the flowing of a tidal wave.

The great passages in the books which live forever become, when you suddenly reach them, like the opening of the gates of paradise; but you can only learn the magic words that open these gates through ears that have been purged by a long and silent journeying over ways that are often tedious, over rocks that are cold and austere, by shrines that are simple, quaint, homely and common.

CHAPTER XI

CULTURE AND HUMAN RELATIONS

The most difficult adjustment that one's personal culture has to make is between one's own secret, mental growth and the growth of the other human minds with which one comes into contact. Excessive gregariousness is certainly a great hindrance to any deep intellectual or imaginative life; and though, when one considers the innate sociability of certain exquisitely mellow natures, like Goldsmith or Sterne or Lamb, or even Anatole France, one hesitates to claim for the congenital recluse all the desired advantages, it surely needs an inordinate originality, some diverting twist of character that no frivolities can smooth away and no superficialities side-track, to enable us to retain the innate flavour of our reactions to life under the impact of social pressure.

It is hard enough to find leisure for one's personal intellectual existence when one is earning one's living in any kind of daily drudgery. But if all the free moments of one's life are to be spent in pleasant social chatter; spent in the amusing discussion of totally unimportant things, what margin is left to us for anything else?

The enjoyment of what is called having a good time is often a far more serious hindrance to an intelligent consciousness of the subtleties of life than the most monotonous drudgery. During such drudgery, whether physical or mental, the mind has many solitary and free moments in which to think and feel and dream; but the warm, gross impact of other personalities, as we enjoy ourselves in an atmosphere of maudlin and indiscriminate camaraderie, stultifies all the finer edges of our vision.

From every human being there emanates a psychic force which is nine-tenths just common animal vitality and one-tenth the projection of something original and unique; and it is this one-tenth, because of its more delicate attenuation, that tends to be completely swamped on these occasions. The art of conversation consists in the fostering and nourishing of certain psychic emanations of unique feeling. From these emanations every one in any harmonious circle gains something; adding here a fragment, there a fragment, of fresh mind-stuff, exciting, illuminating, disturbing, full of new vistas and unexpected *aperçus,* to what he has stored up already.

But to be provocative of these stimuli the circle must be a small one—doubtless even that famous Athenian circle which was the background of Plato's "Symposium" was too large. One grows faintly aware that it was too large from the length of the individual speeches and the absence of any tentative fumbling, so to speak, in the air, as all these lovely ideas are caught and held. Two minds get more out of their conversation than three can; and three get more than four. One of the greatest destroyers of real conversation is argument. Argument is the silliest of all methods of passing the time; and by far the most sterile. In argument people discuss in order to shine, to make others look fools, to make a show of their own originality, or cleverness, or learning.

There are few who discuss in order really to influence or really to convert anyone else; and yet this passionate earnestness of mind leads to much more interesting conversation than the itch to score people off. As a rule no one joins in an argumentative discussion, before a group of listeners, without being betrayed into a gross desire to astonish, to make a hit, to cut an imposing figure. All this is totally alien from real culture; for in real culture what one is after is some new angle of vision, some new organ of research, some new mirror of reflection. It is nothing to real culture who wins in a casual argument or who shows off most brilliantly before a casual crowd.

A cultured nature is far too egocentric to bother about shining before other minds or even about watching the picturesque displays of others. What it seeks is some new avenue of approach, some unexplored secret of sensation, some fresh magnet of sensitivity, that will help it to explore like a liberated tide certain hitherto untouched promontories.

It is when two people who are very fond of each other are together—two lovers or two friends—that the most illuminating vistas of perception unfold themselves and the rarest-winged moths of life's wavering margins are caught upon the wing. What renders the least flicker of an argument so profitless, so sterilizing, is that the minds of both the disputants are turned towards something quite different from either's authentic inner truth. All argument is based upon the illusion that there exists in space-time or behind space-time some static objective system of relations and values, some arrangement of forms, colours, laws of Nature, laws of human nature, processes of magnetism, chemistry, electricity, workings of psychology, methods of evolution, which taken together constitute the truth. There is no such thing. What we call Nature or the universe is a congeries of mysterious units of energy, each with a material side and a psychic side, which are perpetually, by an ultimate and absolute movement of their essences, creating new worlds.

Thus there are as many separate truths or illusions as there are units of apprehension or bubbles of transitory being. What, therefore, every one's innate culture derives from contact with other people's cultures is confined to a narrow margin of wavering exploration. But, since one's culture is a live thing and a growing thing, this margin, though of necessity greatly limited by the fatality of one's temperament, is of the utmost importance in our life. Here, upon this tremulous and quivering borderland, all the most sensitive antennae and tendrils of our natures are feeling their way to an enlarged awareness.

At the first moment when our temperament encounters another temperament all these delicate feelers retreat and curl up, drawing inwards and curving back like the feelers of sea-anemones. If the Nature we are encountering be unsympathetic, all that we shall present to the intrusion of the stranger's approach will be a shapeless jelly-like substance; but if this other mind turns out to be akin to our own or possessed of something in common with our own, then, by slow degrees, these spiritual antennae of our secret being will reappear, and will begin to expand and shimmer in the wave and the sun of that other's comprehension.

It is much wiser for any young man or young woman who is earnestly and passionately aiming at a deeper and more subtle vision of life to close up tightly, just as the sea-anemone does, at this first impact with an alien mind. Let such a one then proceed to be as civil and polite as he can with the surface of his closed up mind, while he sounds by well-timed questions the nature of the other. But when the moment arrives wherein he perceives that the new-comer is of a human type sympathetic to himself, then let him be as frank and open as he pleases, caring nothing about conventional dignity or worldly reticence. Let him pour forth all the likings and dislikings of his inmost being. Let him describe the various mental tricks and devices by means of which he has come to cope with this difficult world. Let him try to articulate with the utmost precision his inmost personal philosphy; and, as he does so, interrupt himself again and again to catch, as it were, upon the very wind, the nuances of his new friend's agreements and disagreements. If all he desires to do is to express what he really does feel; and if all the other one desires to do is to express what *he* feels, the culture of each of them is bound to be enlarged, if not by some considerable vista, at least by some small mole-run or tiny worm-hole of new apprehension.

Very early in the life of every youth there will be presented the most teasing of troublesome dilemmas, the question, namely, of how far he ought to sell his soul for the sake of his life. Let him clearly recognize at the very start that no one can live for one single day in this world without selling his soul to some extent. Compromise is so profoundly of the inmost essence of life, that it might be called life's basic and fundamental law. The opposite of selling one's soul is suicide. The alternative to compromise is death. Selling one's soul, however, is something that ought to be done quite frankly and quite honestly when it is done. Nothing that one does honestly,—that is to say, with a child-like attempt to brazen out what one is ashamed of— hurts one's culture in the way that whitewashing or idealizing one's meanness hurts it.

The really cultured man is preoccupied all the while in an unwearied and persistent struggle to reduce the margin of soul-selling that is necessary for his life upon earth. And it is with regard to this margin that youth were wise to take heed. The great thing is never to let yourself reach the point of taking your soul-selling for granted. The more you dislike it, the more conscious you are of it and ashamed of it, the less likely is it to become one of those worldly compromises that you gloss over with unctuous and conventional clap-trap. It is, in fact, often quite possible to sell your soul for your life without selling it for the "worldly" life. It is this worldly life that is the deadly enemy to everything subtle, gentle, beautiful, and simple; and one will do well to guard one's culture with the most ferocious care from the least tincture of this accursed thing. Sell, O youth, just frankly and honestly as much or as little, of your soul as you have to sell, to live at all; and then fortify yourself against the conventionalities and brutalities of the world with every tool and every weapon at your disposal!

The occasion for this innocent Machiavellianism may easily arise in a young man's life when in the stress of his career he has to propitiate various people, who are in a position to help him. So much is done at the beginning of a youth's career by personal influence that in this particular "bowing down in the House of Rimmon" it is advisable to sell at least a few wafers of the sacred substance of your soul. But let it be done consciously and without any pretence. When, however, it comes to be a matter of propitiating people by "going into society," there, if you value your culture at all, it is necessary to be as cautious as a fox approaching the kennels of a hunting-pack. Of course if you have some vein of peculiar genius, driving you on, as Henry

James or Proust were driven on, to analyse these people and collect them, as entomologists collect butterflies, it is another thing. If you have a Watteau-like love of beautiful backgrounds or a mania for that particular form of airy evasive wit that touches one subject after another and exhausts none, it is also another thing. But these cases are rare—most young men and women "go into society" for very different reasons from these; and the whole proceeding is like a subtle acid in the veins of their culture, or like one of those insidious wood-worms that eat out the heart of a tree. All these social entertainments have a tendency to make a person expressive rather than subtle or deep. A certain nimble wit and superficial cleverness is in demand; and although there are some delicate humourists who swim like fish in such waters, the general psychological effect of society upon a young mind is to force it to adopt some premature and striking pose; some pose wherein it begins, half-unconsciously perhaps, to betray its integrity by exaggerating whatever dramatic and picturesque originality it may have, such as lends itself to dinner-tables and drawing-rooms.

It is one thing to sell one's soul, fragment by fragment, grudgingly and grimly, for one's very life. It is another thing to dance it up and down, like a Punch-puppet or a Judy-puppet on fantastic wires in order to tickle the curiosity of a group of well meaning people, nice and intelligent, but neither particularly interesting nor particularly pathetic. What a boy or girl really should aim at acquiring, in this difficult art of adjusting one's culture to human relationships, is a Lord Chesterfield-like courtesy. This is the kind of courtesy so beautifully defined as the essential aristocratic quality, in Proust's analysis of the De Guermantes;

and just as Swann acquired it by a mental tour-de-force and the young Marcel acquired it by an imaginative saturation, so, by using one's intelligent will over a certain length of time, one may acquire it as one learns to swim. What it really amounts to is an elaborate imitation of the great mediaeval virtue of humility by a mind that is in reality both proud and rebellious. However mistaken Behaviourism may be as a philosophy, it can lead us to a certain suggestive idea as to our method of conduct; the idea, namely, that if we deliberately assume the tones, gestures, actions, and expressions of polite courtesy our inner mood will by degrees correspond to this admirable masquerade,—correspond to it, I mean, not in any genial self-deception as to the nature of the persons we are propitiating, but in an ironic recognition of the tragic fatality of all human temperaments, born to so many inherited limitations, obtusenesses, weaknesses, without their having had the least power of choice to determine what manner of person they would select to be.

There are, indeed, two stages in the very beginning of this difficult art of adjusting your culture to human relationships. The first stage is to behave with people, in tone and gesture and action, as if you sympathized with them far more profoundly than it is possible for you to do. The second stage is to acquire an inner mental attitude towards them, which, if not exactly sympathetic or tender, is an intellectual substitute for these stronger emotions. It is in fact possible to concentrate your will on people's behalf in a very definite, concrete, psychic manner, without being able to feel any real love. It is possible to identify yourself with them in a link of imaginative understanding while your emotional reaction to them is neutral and colourless and your nervous reaction positively hostile. The cold-blooded imaginative understanding to which I have alluded—and this is the third stage in our psychic technique—can be converted by slow degrees into something much tenderer by a concentrated habit of thinking. It can, in fact, be converted into pity. Pity arises of itself from the very coldest heart when certain trains of thinking have led to mental recognition of the basic terms of human life, realized in their most stark and unblurred austerity. The reason why so many warm-hearted people are less considerate and aware of the tragic human figures that they encounter than cold-hearted people who have more imagination is that the former see everything in a rosy, glamorous, subjective light. But when certain lines of thinking have led anyone to recognize the part played by the destiny of temperament in every one's existence, there must often rise up of necessity, in the coldest heart alive, a wave of pity for the annoying, teasing and repulsive types among such a fate-driven flock. But this inevitable pity is not even yet the final stage of what the will can do for the mind in this direction, if the will is steadily orientated and the mind is kept moderately alert.

What culture has to do today in these human adjustments—and that is what makes it all so difficult—is to find some substitute for religion. What we have reached so far is a combination of Chesterfield-like politeness and Anatole France-like pity. One has only to name these two cults, however, to experience an intense revolt against them. But are the only alternatives to these things either a Buddhistic resignation or a Pauline charity based upon a living faith in Christ? If it is so, our attempt to reach some substitute for religion in these developments of what culture contains has certainly failed completely.

But there is an alternative and it is to be looked for in the intellectual imagination of the great poets and artists. Consider Shakespeare and Cervantes, consider Albert Dürer and Rembrandt. Not one of these four men but managed to acquire his own particular attitude to human beings, which, while influenced by Catholic Christianity as well as by the Classical civilizations, became in each case something quite new in the world. And, moreover, when you consider these four men, and saturate yourself with their diverse reactions to the human crowd that jostled round them, it gradually dawns upon you that there is something in common among them which is precisely what our culture requires if it is to establish some habitual mood in relation to the impact upon us of the human stream.

And what is this something? Our Chesterfield civility, our Anatole France pity is thickened out now into an awareness, full of an earth-bound rooted humility, of a certain equality of all souls. Our culture, as we return to "King Lear" and "Don Quixote" or reproduce in our minds the pictures of Dürer and Rembrandt, begins to gather such a basic sense of the tragic poetry of normal human life that by degrees a feeling of stark, terrible, poignant beauty comes over us, and all human beings shape themselves in the mirror of our vision as something infinitely helpless, touching, vulnerable and frail.

This attitude to the tide of humanity does not necessarily imply a loving heart any more than it implies a Pauline "Agapé" or a Buddhistic "Peace to all Beings!". It is, as a matter of fact, not an emotional attitude at all, nor a philosophical one—it is an imaginatively rational one. We come to look at human beings with the same feeling for their pathetic turbulent vitality and the sad brevity of their days as we have when we look at animals or plants or birds. The worst of the idealistic education that most of us have had under Christian authority is that it makes us so ashamed of our real feelings towards human beings that we indulge in a constant process of self-deception. This kind of deception is by far the worst. Perhaps it is the only kind that is intrinsically bad.

A cultured mind need make no hopeless effort to think pretty thoughts of its fellow-wrestlers in the stark arena of life. It can very often allow itself to think monstrous and hideous thoughts, repulsive and obscene thoughts. It is in fact a very wholesome and very restorative process, this thinking in wild, fantastic, bizarre images of the people that surround us. There is nothing to be ashamed of in this process. It is an indication of some deep atavistic craving for solitude; a craving for solitude so intense that every human figure that interrupts it tends to assume hideous proportions and to bulk, large and gross, like a Rabelaisian nightmare.

This indeed is a magical trick of a cultured mind, to push real life back, so to speak, a few removes; and to allow the imagination and even the fancy to play with it to a desperate tune. If a young man, or a young woman, feels a longing to indulge in savage mental caricatures of the people in whose company life has to be passed, why not indulge it, why not give way to it? It is by such mental indulgence in huge titanic ribaldry that we can become tolerant, gentle, amiable, to the harmless people of our life. There is a deep restorative comfort in these blasphemous impieties that makes it far more easy to feel patient and indulgent. We cannot go too far in allowing our fantastic images of our friends' behaviour to mount up into these mental Saturnalias or demonic malice-dances. When we have thoroughly sated ourselves by visioning our companions in such monstrous Witches' Sabbaths, we can settle down to regarding them again with quiet courtesy, watching their faces with tenderness and relief.

Here indeed we touch a secret method wherein our culture, in its inmost growth and self-protection, can exploit both the atavistic savagery in our Nature and the most delicate Christian refinement. Our culture has not acquired its full awareness until we cease to take for granted the impact of other people, until we cease to accept their presence as an ordinary thing, in a crude superficial way. Just as culture implies an intensified awareness of works of genius and of the forces of Nature, so it implies an intensified awareness of these troubling and disturbing miracles, these mysterious alien personalities. Not a day should be allowed to pass without our having made some appreciable advance in the complicated art of dealing with these thrilling and shocking *eidola,* these alluring and repulsive apparitions upon our mental horizon!

Nature herself seems to teach us a thousand nuances of behaviour in our relation with any one with whom we are in love; but, even here, of what gross misunderstandings, of what clumsy stupidities, of what ungovernable outbursts are we often guilty! It is long before we learn the simple secret that between men and women it is as if they belonged to two different species of creatures. A latent irritation is always ready to rise to the surface due purely to this—man is an irritating animal to a woman—a woman is an irritating animal to a man—the cruder the level of culture in any society, the more will men tend to herd with men, and women with women. It is the supreme test of a highly sophisticated culture to be able to enjoy to the extreme limits the companionship of the opposite sex.

What modern writers delight to call "sex-war" and "love-hate" is the most rudimentary and primeval of sexual relations. Where sex-love is liable at any moment to turn into sex-hate, the true Eros, the real emotion of love between the two has not been born at all. The abrupt and violent changes of sex-partners which is the fashion of the present hour is simply an indication of the fact that true love is a rare and delicate birth and requires the most concentrated and conscious attention; an attention that a generation divorced from leisure, simplicity, and routine has no desire to give. Whether you are in love with the companion or with the companions of your life, or whether these beings are merely affectionate friends or friendly acquaintances, the whole essence of culture in its relation to them consists in self-control. Not to possess absolute self-control is either to be always an uncultivated barbarian or to be, at moments, simply a madman or a madwoman.

Culture and self-control are synonymous terms—no refining of one's taste in aesthetics or in literature can palliate the enormity of being guilty of ungovernable anger.

What culture ought to do for us is to enable us to find somehow or other a mental substitute for the traditional restraints of morality and religion. This mental substitute has nothing to do with either selfishness or unselfishness. It is a matter of simple wisdom and can be used to satisfy both unselfish impulses and profoundly selfish ones. It is the application of intelligence to the difficult imbroglio of not being able to live alone upon the earth. One's secret imaginative life, one's secret sensational life is subject to the most miserable disturbance until we gain an absolute control over the expression of our feelings of pique, vanity, anger and irritation. This is no counsel of perfection —to feel really sympathetic, to feel really tender to others is something beyond all this and requires a much nobler nature than most of us possess; though even this can be attained by the meanest and the basest if such a one desires it with sufficient intensity. But assuming that one's emotions are hopelessly egocentric and one's heart naturally cold, the attainment of self-control should be the object of our cult and this is well within every one's power.

The great thing to do is divide into rigid, separate, water-tight compartments our secret thoughts and the expression of our thoughts. Jesus, that divine psychologist, spoke truly when He taught that the state of a person's soul is tested by inward thoughts rather than by any overt actions. He offered, in His divine inspiration, one cure, and one alone, for the purgation of these inward thoughts; the magical attraction, namely, of His new idea of love. But since in this matter of the meaning of culture we have no right to assume that any reader has reached the point, either on mystical grounds or on traditional grounds, of accepting the teaching of Jesus, it is inevitable that we should go to work in a more roundabout and less drastic manner; the end, in either case, is the same—namely the attainment of a vital art of life. Granting, then, that the impact of alien personalities upon our own is a menace to the peace of our minds and the quiet growth of our secret culture, and granting that the form this menace usually takes is a series of violent shocks to our deepest life-illusion, it seems unavoidable that our private thoughts about people should be corroded with wounded pride and poisoned by mental and physical repulsions. But even if we lack the grace or the insight to accept the new idea of love so mysteriously discovered by Jesus, there is an incredible gain immediately within our grasp, namely to acquire a self-control that shall build up an impassable barrier between what goes on in our minds and what we express in words and gestures. If, as I have already hinted, we indulge ourselves to the full in the maddest and wildest envisioning of our friends' characteristics, exaggerated to a point of fantastic excess, there will speedily flow over us a redeeming flood of friendly reaction towards them, and it will be out of this reaction that our words and gestures will then spontaneously spring; while before we indulged ourselves in this furtive "malice-dance," they were dictated rather by habitual courtesy than by any sympathetic feeling.

In one's contact with the human beings that surround one it is barbarous to reveal every secret emotion that they excite—it will only be after long spiritual training that we acquire the art of feeling towards them as we wish to feel; but our culture is gravely at fault if we cannot habitually reassure them. We know well enough how wounding to our own pride certain brusque rebuffs and certain insensitive blunderings are; and it reveals us as lacking in the very rudiments of culture if we cannot at least speak and act with courtesy and consideration.

Such invariable and unwearied courtesy is in an especial sense due from us to all servants, and to all queer, retiring, nervous and unsuccessful people. No one can be regarded as cultured who does not treat every human being, without a single exception, as of deep and startling interest. To be treated with courtesy of this habitual sort is the unquestioned right of every person belonging to the race of Homo Sapiens; for every one of us is a world by himself, mysterious and unique.

Our philosophy, if it be worthy of its name, must have already taught us something of this insight. Our aesthetic sense, if it be worthy of its rôle, must have given us the trick of catching the magical pathos of life flickering across the countenance even of the most uninteresting. And the same habitual courtesy which a true culture extends to human beings, simply because they *are* human beings, it will extend to all sentient earth-born lives. Since the whole essence of such a cult is a heightened awareness of the mysteriousness of the universe, one will gradually acquire, if one concentrates one's attention on this, an automatic gesture of psychic reverence in the presence of every living thing. What indeed is culture if not an elaborate substitute for that spontaneous outpouring of love for all beings, whether human or sub-human, which so many of the mystics and saints and artists seem to receive as a gift from Nature? Such a spontaneous flow of love cannot be acquired by taking thought; but something corresponding to it can be acquired if certain almost ritualistic movements of consciousness are deliberately repeated again and again. What we must assume as our starting-point, so as to keep our cultural doctrine well within the reach of all, is a natural temperament rather below than above the average degree of intelligence.

With such a temperament to work with, the one thing needful is a desire to make something worth while of one's personal life, something worth while independently of success or failure, of poverty or wealth, independently of any sort of overt achievement. Nothing except such a desire is required; such a desire extended over a long space of time. Given this desire, the most poorly and meanly equipped person, as far as natural endowments are concerned, can go almost any distance.

In this respect real culture resembles religion and love, well known to be no respecters of persons. More profoundly than in any other aspect of its relation to life, culture must consciously seek to rival religion and love in their most sensitive attitudes towards the personalities of others. And in this delicate art culture has a certain advantage over both these formidable forces, in that it is free from those dark fanatical passions which are the inverse side of these world-shaping impulses. Culture in fact is interested in the people it encounters just exactly as it is interested in the animals or birds or butterflies or plants it encounters, and it has within it the power of proving that this interest—a purely imaginative, sensuous, and intellectual interest—can be less harmful to the objects of its attention than bigoted religion or jealous love.

When once a certain detachment from possessive vice and objective ambition has occurred in the mind, one starts free and fresh in this complicated art of dealing adequately with alien personalities. Vice and ambition are such absorbing motives that under their influence one grows completely oblivious of the rarer qualities of others. It is as though one were passing through a field full of the rarest flowers and grasses with one's head so insanely obsessed by some amorous design or some business encounter that one might as well be plodding through arid sand. The average or the sub-average Nature we must assume as our material, for this premeditated cult will of course contain many tendencies to just such absorbing vices and ambitions;

and it would be demanding the impossible to require their eradication. They need not be eradicated! All that is necessary is that there should be some intervals, some conscious "holidays," wherein vice and ambition let us off for a breathing-space. If we set ourselves resolutely to make the utmost of these oases in the desert, the very thrill we shall derive from our liberation from such servitudes, the lovely relief that will come pouring into us, will of a certainty lead to a gradual prolongation of our moments of freedom. Leisure of some sort we must snatch. Out of the economic slavery of each day we must steal, by hook or by crook, enough margin of unburdened consciousness to keep our souls alive. If one is very poor and finds one's moments of freedom wickedly curtailed, there is at least this consolation; that the rich and leisured who could have so many moments of magical delight waste them and despoil them in every kind of fatuous distraction. There can be no doubt that for most of us who have preoccupied ourselves for some while with the sort of culture I am defining, our happiest moments will be when we are quite alone, or alone with our very dearest companions.

To display a preference for living with a large group of people or for going about with a large group of people seems a sign of a very rudimentary stage of human development. In the presence of such a group one can only assert oneself grossly, crudely, ineffectively, and if one is of a retiring disposition one can only be trailed about after the rest. The lovely and magical influences which in every moment of silence flow forth from Nature, influences which hover like tutelary spirits round every plant, tree, and hillside, are disturbed and with sighing sent away by the uproar of any crowd. To escape among such calm influences and to be alone with them is the chief secret desire of every cultured mind, and how often is it frustrated!

What culture must learn to do, when the insolent impact of noisy people has spoilt moment after moment of precious, unreturning felicity, is to use its memory. How intensely and tenaciously one must drink up every drop of mystic-sensuous pleasure from these calm magical scenes, notice everything, miss not the curve of a leaf, or the bend of a grass blade, or the stirring of a feather! Only by letting each least detail of the earth's life sink into your mind when you are alone can you store up a sufficient number of memories to protect you from those arid and sterile moments when you find yourself forced to live in a group of people.

A great imaginative man-lover, like Shakespeare or Sterne or Lamb or Dickens, has the power of deriving the same profound satisfaction from the agitated countenances, so grotesque, so rapturous, so troubled, of our battered humanity, that another type of mind derives from Nature; but for most of us this thing is beyond our reach. For most of us the more intensely and obstinately we build up our inner life of sensations and ideas, the more difficult does it become to bear the impact of other personalities. The great thing is, as I have tried to suggest, to practise a Lord Chesterfield-like courtesy towards everybody one encounters, especially towards those who are poorer, weaker, less lucky than oneself. This practise, this habitual ritual of consideration, is entirely within the power of the mind; whereas to feel love or tenderness, or even pity, implies a temper of spirit that one perhaps can never reach, or only reach after long practice of the outward gestures. Any philosophic contemplation of the injustice of social differences, any philosophic recognition of the pressure of fate upon us all, making one person healthy and another person unhealthy, giving one person a well-balanced temperament and another a self-lacerating temperament, any philosophic awareness of the fact that no ego selects its heredity and environment, ought to be enough to throw some degree of sympathy, however cold and detached, into these automatic and habitual gestures of universal courtesy.

The race is not always to the swift. Time and chance wait for all men. The luck that is yours today may be another's tomorrow. The misery that is yours today may be past like a summer shower next month or next year. Not only the fatality of one's temperament, not only the destiny of one's heredity and environment, but pure accident plays an overpowering and dominant part in one's days. One may well be awed and hushed when one thinks what a part, for example, pure chance plays, chance the greatest of all the gods, in those accidental encounters with this personality or with that personality such as absolutely change the whole course and current of one's life.

Destiny and chance taken together give one in fact all the people of one's life—these, and just a residual element of choice, if we have had the wit to keep alert and watchful as we went through the market-places of the world. When, however, a certain pessimistic type of temperament concentrates upon this fate and upon this chance, and refuses to allow any place at all for that energetic, interior, resistant power of the whole personality that used to be isolated from the rest and named "the will," one ought to reassure oneself in the simplest of all practical ways, namely, by the exertion of this will. It will be found, and this is what experience itself, not any extravagant faith, teaches, that every time you gather up the forces of your personality to deal with some hostile or indifferent human being, such forces prove more available and more formidable than before. It is a grievous pity that the finest culture, instead of fortifying this interior gathering together of one's forces, very often weakens and disintegrates it. The less culture people have, the more resolute seems to be this interior resistant energy. The less intelligence, the more will-power, seems to have to become a sort of natural law.

It is a shocking thing to see delicate, refined, imaginative natures living under the stupid despotism of some gross, unenlightened animal-will. Yet how often do we see exactly this. It is almost invariably the weaker in will who set about to struggle to win the secret of culture. It is, in fact, because they are the weaker in these more primitive forces that they are led to think about culture at all. People whose natures tend to what is called "force of character" are generally people whose energy is directed upon the toughening of the fibres of their personality rather than upon the refining of their sensitiveness to the subtleties of things. This toughness, this sturdiness and massiveness of character, is a much more valuable asset in the struggle of life than it is in the struggle to gain culture. In fact it often may be noted that the more competent a person grows in his handling of practical life, the more blunt, opaque, and impenetrable he grows in regard to the imponderable influences of the intellect and the senses. Thus while no youth or maid who loves culture need be for one instant depressed by aspersions upon weakness of character, it is nevertheless a wise thing to develop the will. It is a wise thing because, just as in the case of a certain necessary self-confidence and a certain necessary dissimulation, one has often to fight the world with its own weapons. If you are not a saint, and sometimes even if you are, it is necessary to deceive one's fellow-creatures in many important matters. What, of course, one longs for is that power shall fall into the hands of the intelligent, the non-moral, the considerate, the gentle; and to this desirable end it is important that all weak, sensitive, and nervous people should deliberately gather together the forces of their natures so as to revolt against the dominion of the stupid.

One must always do what one can to assist this subterranean conspiracy of the sensitively weak against the insensitively strong. This invisible psychic contest, occurring wherever two or three are gathered together, is like the contest between light and darkness; and there are few such encounters when an opportunity does not arise to throw whatever weight one has into the mêlée.

To sum up the whole matter; what an imaginative culture must do in dealing with others is to acquire the habit of regarding everyone except oneself as under the absolute domination of fate in all their ways and words and feelings, while at the same time one recognizes that all one's own ways and words and feelings are under the control of one's free will. It is the assumption that people could be different if they liked that is so dangerous to our temper and our patience. We must assume that they cannot be different and never had the chance of choosing to be different. It is we ourselves who have to use our will to change, to re-create the reactions of our consciousness to life. To leave other people alone is the wisest and kindest thing; but if an obvious appeal, conscious or unconscious, is made to us to intervene, the best way of influencing others towards what we ourselves regard as the true way of life is to let them see that we already assume that they are what we would have them be. If in your opinion people are behaving basely and you desire to change them, it is always to their imagination that you should appeal, rather than to their will. Upbraid them not for being what they are; but on the contrary let them grow aware that you take it for granted that they already are the very thing into which you seek to change them.

There are, however, few things more dangerous than to go about spreading any philosophic disbelief in the power of the will. In your general attitude to mankind it is best to regard all men as absolutely bound by the fatality of their temperament, while you alone are responsible and free; but in any statement of your philosophic opinion it is imperative to confess your secret knowledge, based upon your inmost experience that there is no limit to the power of the human will. In contact with others what one is forever confronted by are the startling varieties of religious and moral dogmas. One were wise to keep in mind the antiquity of the earth and to note the immense divergences between the various systems wherewith men have mitigated the frightfulness of suffering and the gaping ambiguity of death.

There is something impertinent and arrogant in an attitude of condescension towards any religious belief or any moral scruple. The earth is so old and the generations of men recede so far into the abyss of time that one should take it for granted that there is some measure of earth-wisdom clinging to every vestige of superstition.

In regard to one's attitude to this startling variety of religious and moral opinion, it seems as if it were advisable to do reverence to all of them and regard them all as of equal value and weight, while with proud humility one obstinately follows one's own individual path. To consider one's path not the noblest or the wisest but simply as one's own seems the best way; as the path upon which one's own private and quite personal experience of life has inevitably thrust one. Consider the contrast which is always presenting itself in these modern days between the old-fashioned attitude to life and the new-fashioned enlightened attitude. Consider the contrast between a rigid sex-morality and a fanatical faith in free-love. No one can live in any modern community without overhearing fierce and violent discussions of all these things. A person who is what I have been trying to define as cultured will slip out of such discussions and refuse to commit himself. He will know that there is much good to be got out of every single heart-felt way of life; only perhaps more good where the thing is very old.

He will know that some human beings ruin and blight themselves by old-fashioned sex-suppression while others ruin and blight themselves by new-fashioned sex-excess. He will know that if religion and sex-morality are destined to perish, they will perish slowly—over the space of many years—and not without several intense, passionate re-births. He will know that as far as other human beings are concerned it is always best to leave people mentally and morally alone while you lavish whatever generous impulses you may have in making their bodies comfortable. The more money you give to people the better; and the less advice.

No man really enters into the sorrows of another or knows what hurts his heart; but every man can see the difference between a person who "puts himself out" and one who goes bluntly and tactlessly on, and is aware of nothing. In dealing with human beings there is no need that your secret life, your secret mythology, should be interfered with by your impulses to unselfishness. What people want is money; and after that, attention. They do not want to be interfered with any more than you do yourself. Give and pass on. Listen and pass on. It is incredible what a difference it makes to one's feelings towards the whole human race when one is treated with politeness and kindness in buses, trains, trams, subways, ferries, stores, shops and streets.

And knowing what one feels oneself, it seems simply barbarous to act curtly, brutally, indifferently to others. It need not be a matter of Christian feeling—Christians have very often the worst manners in the world. It need not be a matter of goodness of heart or of unselfishness. It is simply a case of natural earth-wisdom. If you are morbidly sensitive yourself, it is certain that the general atmosphere of sensitiveness in the world will be palpably and appreciably increased by your own civility.

There is no great culture needed to make one behave with courtesy and lively attention to the rich, the beautiful, the famous. Where our true sophisticated culture shows itself is in our attitude to the unimportant, the negligible, the weak, the mean-spirited, the pig-headed. The weaker and sillier a person is, the more intense should be the concentration with which one listens to his words and gives his fumbling spirit one's full attention; for it always requires more effort to get interesting reactions from a simple fool than from some clever devil who delights in showing off.

Deep should be our philosophic awareness of the extraordinary drama in which we are all involved; this life of which not one day is a replica of the last, these encounters whose crucial and terrible importance may never be recognized, or only recognized long afterwards when it is all too late. It is a monstrous thing, the way we all drift and jostle and barge against one another without any method or any awareness of what is going on between us. Skeletons, clothed in flesh, clothed in coverings stolen from other animals, we talk, jest, and scold. But the look from the eyes of a living being is a strange and terrible look, not easy to be discounted. What is it that gazes forth, so grim, so furtive, from the eye of a man? None knoweth! There may be yet some deep, undiscovered power in human personality that will one day crack the complacent walls of this tough world and plant the crazy gonfalon of its impious importunity in some plane of existence altogether beyond the mathematical fourth dimensions. Meanwhile, involved as we all are in the same tragic imbroglio, our feelings, our minds, our nerves all vibrating to old totems and old taboos, encrusted with old, dark, perilous superstitions, nourished by old, deep, bitter-sweet earth-wisdom, it is an impertinence for any among us to separate ourselves from the rest and patronize the rest.

Educated people can take sides fiercely and violently in the controversy between Catholics and Protestants, between moralists and non-moralists, between Liberals and Communists. Cultured people find it hard to do this. They may lean to one side or the other; they may even belong to one side or the other; they cannot bring themselves to denounce the antagonist of their side as just an ill-bred, dissolute and wicked ass. They cannot bring themselves to patronize such antagonists or to behave superciliously towards them with an airy, snobbish condescension. In relation to one's fellows, culture implies an earth-deep humility. Like that charity defined by St. Paul it is not puffed up. Culture does not show itself among men as something ponderous, majestic, pompous, imposing. It does not "show" itself at all! Like the *Tao,* so subtly described by the philosopher Kwang Tze three hundred years before Christ, it flows through the air, swims in the water, burrows in the earth, moves imperceptibly from mind to mind, and "by doing nothing does everything." It draws out others rather than asserts itself; it is a listener rather than a dogmatist, a peace-maker rather than a disputant. It has as much respect for the peculiar intelligence of women as for the peculiar intelligence of men. It uses the woman's mind as well as the man's mind in its perceptions of truth.

And as for the truth which it pursues through all situations and through all obstacles with the flexible sinuosity of a serpent, it finds it forever in two places—in everything and everyone; and in nothing and no one.

CHAPTER XII

CULTURE AND DESTINY

Since the aim of culture is to nourish within us a sturdy yet sensitive organism that shall be able to deal with the eternal recurrences of life and death, it is clear that there must be many occasions when we have to come to terms in some sort of way with the moral, social and political systems in the midst of which it is our destiny to live. What then are the moral implications which culture—by the mere fact that it is what it is, a definite orientation of the mind and the will—contains within itself as the laws of its very being? What, in plain words, is the morality of culture, in its contact with the current morality of the society around it?

In the first place it preserves below all earthly contacts some kind of instinctive communion with the hypothetical first cause. This communion implies neither piety nor superstition. It implies nothing but an alternation between gratitude and defiance.

In the second place the unspoken creed of culture implies an obstinate determination to be happy at all costs; and even where happiness is impossible, to assume what might be called the mental gesture of happiness until the wheel of chance shall turn.

In the third place the morality of culture implies a *laissez faire* attitude towards others. This means that cruelty of every sort, righteous or unrighteous, sadistic or disciplinarian, mental or physical, is a thing to be abhorred. Other people are not to be meddled with.

In the fourth place, whenever other people meddle with us; and either by exciting our pity, or by making overt appeals to us for help, for comfort, for influence, for love, impinge on our solitude; culture, let us hope, will not be lacking in the two great virtues of imaginative compassion and self-controlled courtesy. These two impulses will generally be found to drive us to certain actions of practical charity: but what we give to humanity in return for its gifts to us is not our love, nor our meddling, but our patience and our work.

In the fifth place, the fluctuating and malleable creed of culture will imply a constant refining upon our powers of imaginative analysis, in regard to the Protean truth of things, and a constant refining upon our powers of perception, in regard to the mysterious beauty of things. Thus in a large measure one's notion of true culture follows the great Goethean doctrine, "live in the Whole, in the Good, in the Beautiful," while we must still allow ourselves to remain very fluid and sceptical as to what this whole may be, or this good, or this beautiful.

Of the three Goethean Absolutes it would seem, if our interpretation of culture is not grievously in error, that the good is the most unmistakable. No tricky sophistication, no parodoxical aesthetic theorizing, can spoil our simple, direct recognition of the good. The good is the spontaneous, instinctive attitude of goodness in the human heart. It is the possession of a sweet-natured, considerate, courteous and compassionate disposition—a disposition which may often co-exist with the most rudimentary education and with the most unenlightened ignorance. It is this courteous and compassionate goodness which culture, if it is to follow its destiny without remorse, must, by hook or by crook, develop; and if it cannot develop it, all in a moment, it must perform the gesture of such feelings, until the feelings themselves and their outward practise become an inward impulse.

From what precedes it will easily appear that the cultured person, as long as tolerance of cruelty is not concerned, will take an extremely free and sceptical attitude towards the various sex-taboos of the community into which his destiny may have flung him. Against cruelty of whatever kind—perhaps most especially when the impulse behind it is a perverted and corrupt morality—he will protest, "to the fire exclusively" and sometimes into the fire! But short of cruelty he will be wise enough to hold his tongue. Ironic submission will be his cue. Such submission, wary and sly, weary and patient, humble and proud, grave and ironical, has been from time immemorial the retort of culture to the uncultured. Culture is not everything. Life will go on somehow; Nature will right herself somehow. Culture must steal something of that abysmal humility of spirit which, along with its grand discovery of what might be called the equality of all souls, is the gift of Christianity to the training of the human mind.

Here indeed lies a secret. Culture learns from the greatest of all psychologists, the speaker of those sublime sayings in the Gospels, that until, in a very curious and peculiar sense, it acquires the art of forgetting itself it does not attain its subtlest illuminations.

But although life will go on somehow, and the great mysterious movements of the world proceed, whether culture flourish or perish, it remains that in the decline of religious faith and the collapse of moral custom some new orientation of the human spirit is above all things necessary.

In regard, then, to the attitude of culture to the morality of the community wherein its destiny has plunged it, it must be remembered that its basic creed contains no conception of what is called sin, except when such sin takes the form of cruelty. The one grand commandment of culture is, "Thou shalt not be cruel." On all other points what true culture does is to suspend its judgment, retain its self-control, govern its own actions according to its secret cult of silent happiness and its secret hostility to noisy, violent pleasures, and leave other people alone. A cultured man or woman is a stoic-epicurean in a community of greed and piety; but if he is wise, no one will know what he is. There will be however, as with the early Christians, a secret free-masonry between cultured people, drawing them together in an intense communion of intellect and binding them, in an invisible company, with the spirits of all similar lonely ones in the past.

Culture is not all honey. Stark and austere are many of the moods by means of which it has to defend itself. On all sides are its enemies; enemies of tolerance, enemies of light, enemies of pity, enemies of imagination.

Its greatest hindrance, its most troublesome stumbling block, will be the ugliness of the objects around it and the bustling ineptitude of the unenlightened crowd. These obstacles to its life will be much worse in any town than in any countryside. In the country Nature will always have her secret ways of restoring a human spirit that has been bruised by the brutalities of the world. But in a town such brutalities echo from wall to wall and ricochet from pavement to pavement; for they have only the obscure coping of the sky to absorb them and the hot dusty airs to swallow them up.

Granting that the wiles of ironic submission have enabled us to deal with personal contacts, how are we to adjust our minds to all this external hideousness? How are we to stiffen ourselves against these poisonous effluviae, this brazen clamour? We have already hinted at the only wise resource. We must acquire the art of forgetting. The art of forgetting is indeed culture, her very self, practising her own peculiar magic. The grand device is to see these horrors without seeing them, to hear them without hearing them, to smell them without smelling them, to taste them without tasting them.

The same method applies to the human crowd. One has a perfect right to feel altogether differently towards crowds from the way one feels towards individuals. The best way to deal with a crowd that is pressing hard upon you and jostling you, is to repeat over and over again in your heart the Buddhist formula "Peace to all Beings!" If this formula fails of its effect you may know that the maliciousness in your nature is stronger than the humility; and the best thing to do then is immediately to reduce the whole crowd before you to invisibility; which can be done by thinking it away. To every other unit in the crowd you are yourself, of course, part of the crowd; and while you reduce them to invisibility you must submit to the hope that they in their turn will have the wit to practise this same delicate magic upon you.

Just as you reduce to a shifting vapour a lively crowd in a street, so it is often wise in any group of people so

completely to sink into your own thoughts that all material substances—including human bodies—disappear from
consciousness. But the destiny of our days often compels
us to listen to people's conversation, or even, if they are
of a dogmatic turn, to their teaching. This misfortune can
be avoided by acquiring the harmless little art—a very
easy thing—of displaying intense interest in what people
are saying while you are thinking out some problem of your
own or dreaming some dream of your own totally uncon-
nected with them.

And as with human beings, so with buildings. It is very
unlikely that your destiny will have placed you in a beautiful city. The chances are that you will have to encounter,
day after day, shops, office-buildings, chapels, churches,
hotels, municipal buildings, bank-buildings, theatres and
picture-houses, not to speak of those surprising freak-
erections called "residential sections" that make human architecture a wanton jest—buildings in short which cause no
reaction of any kind in the mind except a numb, weary
patience with the whole trend of modern civilization. All
around you, above, below, and in the air, hum and buzz
and drum and scream and snort the various mechanical inventions of our western world. Here destiny has placed
you, here in the midst of all this, and if your culture is
worth anything it must enable you to deal with it. And it
can, it can! It can enable you to be as completely indifferent to these things as if they were of less importance
than the soap you use, than the brush with which you brush
your hair, than the polish you put upon your shoes, than
the enamelled walls of your wash-room.

Culture does not fail her idolaters. One has only to
watch the ecstatic absorption of any boy or girl reading a

book in the midst of the city's traffic; one has only to watch a group of people staring in sublime, world-forgetting rapture at some Shakespearean gesture of Charlie Chaplin; one has only to watch the entranced expressions on the faces of the devotees of some great musician as they lean forward in their balcony and forget everything that awaits them when it is over, forget even what continent or planet they inhabit; to become aware that culture has the power of enabling us to be happy in the only way wherein most human beings can be happy—in complete defiance of their surroundings.

Outworn, misused, misapplied for so long, the aristocratic ideal is now quite dead. There is no escape from machinery and modern inventions; no escape from city-vulgarity and money-power, no escape from the dictatorship of the uncultured. All over the western world rules that fatal star which the crazy interpreter of the Apocalyse in "The Idiot" calls "the Star Wormwood."

If culture were everything, lamentable indeed would be the outlook. But culture is not everything. It is much that the poor should have bread. It is much that women should be liberated by the power of machinery from the servitude of the old time. It is much that people's nerves should be attuned to the sufferings of others. It is much that education and electricity should be brought into the homes of the masses. All honour to social progress, to social emancipation, even though paid for by so terrific a price. But the price is heavy—universal education means a press, a pulpit, all pandering to that universal taste which is the opposite of all taste. Ideas may be proletarian ideas, Fascist ideas, capitalistic ideas, imperialistic ideas; but they must, above all, be ideas that can appeal to public opinion. At the steering wheel of the great industrial machine sits, not wisdom, but efficiency.

These are days when the very word culture has become a term of contempt. And all attempts to stem the tide have a certain shame-faced air of self-conscious affectation. The great standardized torrent of megalopolitan pleasures, megalopolitan sports, megalopolitan values, sweeps round us and over us uttering a raucous monotone of irresistible triumph.

What then, in the name of all the high traditions of our race, is culture to do? One thing it can do and one thing alone; and it is the purpose of this work to point steadily to this one thing. It can save the individual.

There is no reason why, in this age of scientific invention and mass production, the individual consciousness should not find its own interior happiness, its own interior peace, in those thoughts and feelings that have inspired and sustained humanity for unnumbered ages. Although science can change the outward customs of the world we live in, it cannot despoil the winds of heaven of their power, or take the poetry out of the seasons, or strip the morning and the evening of their solemnity, or make the sun and the moon to be of small account, or turn the ocean into a little thing. Birth and death, the mystery of love and the mystery of the passing of love, the wonder of the oblivion of sleep and of the refreshment of sleep, the marvel of the heroic affections of men and women looking beyond loss and separation and the bitterness of the grave—these are the things upon which that deliberate simplification of the imagination, that unwearied training of the feelings, which we have come to name culture, must continue to concentrate their obstinate attention.

In the old days, as has been so often proved of late, the lives of human beings were bound closely together in those traditional and imaginative cults which were at once political, mystical and aesthetic. With the appearance of scientific industrialism and democratic imperialism all this has come to an end. Money and machines between them dominate the civilized world. Where these are checked to some extent by a certain public spirit, as in England, or by a certain semi-religious despotism, as in Russia and Italy, or where they produce widespread prosperity, as in America, their practical efficiency forces us to condone their abuse. But, between them, the power of money and the power of the machine have distracted the minds of our western nations from those eternal aspects of life and nature the contemplation of which engenders all noble and subtle thoughts.

What therefore it behoves culture to do is to save the individual in the midst of this industrial hubbub and endow him with enough peace of mind to breathe, to look round, to look forward and backward, to take stock of his emotional and intellectual resources and to see where a calm happiness can still be found. One thing we know: such happiness will not be found between the dilemma-horns of pleasure and ennui. Rapid movement and nervous exhaustion are the alternating poles of our disorganized life. Stoical enjoyment of the little, simple things which alone bring permanent contentment has become the unenvied fatality of those who gain a precarious living on the land or at sea. The rest of the world looks at these primitive lives with uneasy wonder; or makes hapless, spasmodic attempts to snatch at their advantages without paying the price.

It is culture alone that can relieve this emotional and im-

aginative sterility; and it can do so only by its appeal to
the individual. For the individual who depends for his
happiness purely upon the motions of his own mind has
become independent of his material surroundings. He can
live in the most crowded city and yet solace himself with
the night and the day, with the look of clouds and the feel
of air and rain, with the dark-blue light that comes on
clear evenings and stretches itself, like the great concave
transparent wing of some titanic archangel, over the lighted
city-roofs, with the patches of grass and with the smell of
the salt sea or a solitary sea-gull's passage over the highest
tower, and above all with his called-up images of country
days, vaguely remembered in his blood and bones. And
such an individual man or woman, carrying to a comfort-
less job through clanging streets the cheapest of old school-
editions of some immortal book, can mount the stairs of
his secret psychic watch-tower and think the whole ant-
heap into invisibility. This is what religion and love can
do for the uncultured and it is what the cultured—if their
fate is to be without love and without religion—can do
for themselves. Out of the pages of a book can spring
forth a whole terraqueous landscape; seas, shores, pastures,
orchards, fields of barley and of rye, Arabian gardens
and Gothic roofs. Vague, delicious memories, obscurely
recovered sensations from our remote past, aye! even from
the past of our people, can buttress us—if we let a wisely-
dreaming imagination play upon them—against all the
iron-shafts, all the evil smells and brazen clatter, all the
litter and the dust, of the worst city in the world.

Our destiny is something that has gathered about us like
a great sea, drawing its tributaries from many inland
rivers and many far-off hills. On its heaving tide fluctuates

the mirage of the material moment, with its edifices of money and industry, the apartment-houses and the paved roads. Up and down, upon its rocking phantom-waves, tremble and topple the walls of our material surrender; but wrestling with destiny, all but free of destiny, the mind that nourishes itself upon the imaginative traditions of our race preserves the integrity of its being. Such a mind is aware of the great inviolable constellations that follow their unchanging orbits, high up above the surf, in the calm heavens. These majestic watchers are untouched by fashion; indifferent to invention; but they are fecund of healing and prolific of peace; and for the voyager who detaches himself from the hurly-burly and drinks the grey rain of silence upon the roof of the world they are the glow-worms of pure thought.

Among other aspects of our destiny in this modern regime, the rumour of politics makes itself only too audible. Is our man of culture implicitly committed to any cause, to any party, to any reaction, to any revolution? It does not seem so. Common sense alone would indicate that there can be good men, religious men, heroic men, absolutely disinterested men, under any gonfalon. So also there can be cultured men under any. It is the heart, where the mischief lies. It is the heart that turns a capitalist into a boa-constrictor, a communist into an inquisitioner, a Fascist into an assassin, an Englishman into a double-dyed hypocrite.

Culture demands that you should be good and humble and free from the burden of possessions. Such humility, such goodness, such freedom from possession, are necessary mediums of psychic clairvoyance. Conceit seals up the exploring antennae of your free sensibility. Malice and hate distract you and waste your life-energy. Possessions make you a fussy super-cargo. Three men lack the porous skin through which the magic of the world can flow: the conceited man, the vindictive man, the rich man. There is a kind of literary vagabondage that is as conceited as an alderman on Sunday. A tramp—though it is scarcely for the lucky ones of the world to blame him— can ruin his casual moments of happiness by his natural fury against society. A king's son can detach himself from an empire's privy purse. It is all in the mind.

What the cultured person finally comes to assume is that—short of hideous physical pain or the loss of the only one he really loves—his mind can do anything he decides it *shall* do. We refer, of course to whether such a mind decides to be happy or decides to be unhappy. It cannot make itself clever or learned or humorous at will. But happy or unhappy it can make itself, though not by any fixed rules. Towards a steady, obstinate determination to be happy—to endure happily or to escape—a thousand little things, "feathers in doorways, straws upon winds," gravitate by an inherent necessity. If mystics can, by an effort of their spirit, unite themselves with whatever mysterious power it may be that they regard as their deity, why cannot an ordinary cultured person, who doubts perhaps the very existence of the *anima mundi* itself, will, in conscious premeditation, his own happiness? Like that lovely spirit of divine charity which Christian mystics teach can be acquired by the meanest of men if they want it enough, a certain stoical happiness can be won by the cultivation of the imagination and the will—if one wants it enough. Day after day one has to practise the sublime art of forgetting. There are horrors in life that must not be thought on, for that way madness lies. At first it is so hard to forget certain horrors that one feels it is a fantastic undertaking even to try. But when one begins to believe, lo! in the wink of an eyelid the miracle has been half-accomplished. Practise, and a certain stubborn fierce, fighting resilience in one's nature will do the rest. Culture is the bed-rock, the final wall, upon which one leans one's back in a god-forsaken chaos.

But what a silly mistake it is to take for granted that the human mind necessarily wills its happiness! There is a great, black, horned devil in it that wills unhappiness. One has to grow very wise or very simple before one recognizes the fact that each solitary human mind is its own creative god and its own destructive devil. The mind is a portion of the absolute; and if it can draw upon all the absolute's celestial armoury, it can also draw upon all the absolute's infernal engines. In the absolute both good and evil descend to fathomless depths; and both can be tapped at will by the conscious mind; for the back of the conscious mind is a strange No Man's Land, whereof all the borders melt into the absolute.

There must be certain works of art in every intelligent person's life, in whose presence he has had the luck to surrender himself where the hour and the place cohered, which must remain forever in his mind as symbols of his deepest wrestling with destiny. Such, for one man, no doubt, would be the Ninth Symphony of Beethoven; for another, the Moses of Michaelangelo, for a third the Pentecost of El Greco, for a fourth the enthroned Demeter in the British Museum. A cultured man must have of necessity something of the polytheist in his blood; and there will be for him in all probability more than one of these god-like symbols of his secret life. At the bitter moments when things are hard with him, he will revert to these "huge cloudy symbols" of the heroic wrestlings of man with fate, and will gather comfort and strength. A person who has stared at the Pantheon, or who has climbed alone on some still evening when the crowds of the city were *en fête* in another direction, the high Acropolis hill, has something in his memory that he can plant, like an inviolable monolith, firm and sure, in the swampy ground of the evil moment.

When one travels among uncongenial people and has to listen to tedious talk and "the loud laugh that speaks the vacant mind," how salutary a device it were if one carried in one's pocket a small Greek or Roman coin, so that without making any sign one could secretly, with the tips of one's fingers, trace the outlines of some cold, unapproachable, god-like profile. The mere touch of such a thing would restore one's feeling of the dignity of the human race, and wipe out the outrage done to it by this warm, sticky, perspiring atmosphere of boisterous goodfellowship with its undertone of insensitive brutality.

It would seem that what is really covered by the great classic word "destiny" is first of all one's inherited tendencies and then one's environment. Something else more intimate than either of these, however, seems to have become attached to it, connecting one's inherited fatality of temperament and one's external circumstances with a certain direction of movement which springs from some subconscious element in one's own unique character; something intimately peculiar to oneself, neither "made," as the creed says, nor begotten, but proceeding.

Our premeditated and personally built-up culture can

have, of course, no effect at all upon our inherited disposition. This portion of destiny is altogether outside its control. And it is only if one is of a very competent, drastic, reckless and bold character, that one can do much to alter the outward circumstances of one's life. In desperate straits even the weakest worms will turn, and even the least practical among men and women will assert themselves and shuffle the cards of their outward fate. But if one takes as one's stoical motto the oracular words "endure happily or escape," it will be generally the enduring rather than the escaping that will be our lot.

But it is over this strange, residual element of destiny, this queer bubbling up of destiny-quicksilver which seems to spring from something in us which is larger, wider, and more magical than our conscious self, that culture can exercise its rational power. Over this sublunary, magnetic force, drawing its magnetism, it might almost seem, from some secret mine-shaft in our being, our rational culture does come to win a most significant control. It is indeed one of the subtlest of all the secrets of culture, this trick of bringing one's conscious reason into harmony with the strange power in oneself, the power which seems in touch with something outside the fatal streams of both heredity and environment.

To alter the main direction, as one moves through the world, of this formidable *daimon* or tutelary pilot of one's inner life, is as difficult as it would be unwise. This power within us—this portion of our destiny which belongs neither to heredity nor environment—is wiser than our conscious being, wiser than the rational processes of our culture. It drives us by some mysterious impulse into many actions and many changes that well might seem rash, mis-

taken, foolish and ill-advised. But as time goes on
these actions, these changes, will be found strangely
justified. They will turn out to have been after all not
debouchings from our true path, but bridle-paths rather,
by which we attain, where we least looked to find it, the
King's High-road of our fate.

Though it were unwise, and perhaps impossible, to
alter the main occult direction of this portion of our destiny
which is our very own, it is legitimate, and indeed absolutely necesary, to steer it, guide it, govern it, in all matters
of detail. Here we find ourselves, our inmost selves, face
to face with our most vivid self-consciousness, and like a
rider mounted upon an immortal horse, the conscious self
commands its mysterious companion. This commanding of
our inmost destiny by our conscious mind is one of the most
important engines of our course through the world; and it
is here that all the acquired tastes, refinements, insights,
illuminations, that we have with difficulty made our own,
find their purpose and their orientation fulfilled.

What seems, at least to the present writer, to render
books and the choice of books so much more important an
aspect of our culture than music or painting or architecture
can ever be, is the fact that unless we are born with some
strong bias in favour of any of these great arts, they are
so much harder to get into touch with in their highest
forms than literature is. Second-rate music, or first-rate
music inadequately rendered, is around us all the while.
Fifth-rate paintings, or great paintings inadequately re-
produced, hang upon all our walls. Unless it is our luck to
live in an old country, where the anonymous work of many
generations, mellowed by time, insensibly heightens the
whole background of our days, we shall be constantly con-

fronted by fifth-rate houses, offices, theatres, city-halls, shops, factories, warehouses, schools, tenements, residential sections, among which it will be only now and then that something noteworthy emerges. This inferior music, these wretched reproductions of paintings, this uninspiring architecture, is around us all the while. Few children of men are so favored by the gods as to escape from them.

But second-rate books one can entirely escape! No one can force you to read books—unless you are at school or at college—which you know to be inferior to the best. Wherever you may be now, reader, at this very second, while you are reading these simple words, if you are in a house or in a city or a town, "stop, look and listen," and you will be aware of architecture, of furniture, of pictures, of bric-à-brac, of musical noises, of carvings, of mouldings, of fabrics, of scents, of tastes, and above all of an aura, that will contain something—not a great deal perhaps, but certainly something—that is so repulsive to you, so poisonous to your nature, so contrary to all your ideas of what beauty is, and what truth is, and what noble simplicity is, that it will scarcely bear thinking on. To try not to taste it, smell it, feel it, hear it, see it, or catch the invisible vibration of it, will be your only refuge; in other words you will find yourself instinctively practising the nice art of forgetting, the art of using a certain subtle magic that can reduce these things to invisibility, to inaudibility, and even into temporary non-existence.

One's normal days in any large city, and in most small ones, are continually spent amid architecture that is no architecture, pictures that are no pictures, music that is no music, and sights, smells and vibrations that are just the very things to loathe and abhor which the culture of half your lifetime has been sensitizing you and refining you.

Literature alone is something that conceals itself; for no one can force you to read advertisements or literary supplements; and withdraws itself, hiding in shelves and libraries and bookshops, until the exact moment arrives, propitious, auspicious, and under the right astrological influences, when you need just that particular book and no other. The outward destiny which places you near a good library is one of the redeeming aspects of a big town or a big university; but the nucleus of your culture will never abide in such a library, no! not even if it be the very Bodleian itself. It will abide in your own mental fortress. Your mind will be its own little round tower of Montaigne the Essayist. And as for collections of books, how independent of outward destiny is the man whose great library of Alexandria is contained in one small, portable shelf! Small enough that shelf can be to stand at your bed's head or even on the ground of your nomad's tent or beneath your charts in your ship's cabin.

Every cultured man, every cultured woman will have his own secret *ecclesia* of precious books. The present writer's would be the "Iliad" and the "Odyssey" the texts of the Chinese "Tao" in James Legge's translation, the Psalms of David, the four great novels of Dostoievsky, Goethe's "Faust," Shakespeare's Plays, Wordsworth's Poems, Pater's "Marius" ànd as many of the volumes of Proust as such a tiny shelf had room for. It is, as we have hinted, a matter of your outward destiny what music, what drama, what sculpture, what paintings, what architecture, what delicate bric-à-brac your wanderings may have enabled you to light upon. But it is a matter of your inward destiny

—beyond heredity and beyond environment—what books your mysterious *daimon,* upheaving from out the eternal through the phenomena of the temporal, has given you the grace to select.

Here, in the depths of your being, the real cultural struggle goes on. Your culture is the rational guidance, by all the intellectual consciousness you can bring to bear, of this instinctive, impulsive, sub-conscious choice; and in this deep underworld of your nature you are at once a creative god and a destructive devil. Heaven forbid that we should underrate the life-creating effect upon this inward destiny of ours of the great music, drama, sculpture, architecture, painting, that we have the luck to encounter.

Certain things once heard, once seen, may have the effect of changing the "timbre" of one's whole life. The huge series of Wagner's "Ring," a single Symphony of Beethoven, the Cathedral at Chartres, the Ruins of Glastonbury, Titian's Bacchus and Ariadne in the National Gallery, Leonardo's Virgin of the Rocks in the same place, The Three Fates in the British Museum, the Aphrodite of Melos in the Louvre, these are things that might easily launch a person, whether of a romantic or of a classical nature, upon a long quest.

Culture, heaven knows, is a very indulgent and sometimes a very eccentric mother. Precious and never-to-be-despised is a naive, idealistic, half-conventional adoration of the world-famous objects of art, objects that, like the Louvre Aphrodite, or Raphael's Madonna at Dresden, or the Hermes of Praxiteles, or the Elgin Marbles, or the Gothic Cathedrals, have obsessed the imagination of our race for so long. To regard with supercilious contempt such simple reverence, however innocently expressed, however ignorantly conventionalized, is to insult that noble hero-worship in the heart of man by which the generations lift themselves up. But it cannot, all the same, be denied that the more cultured a person is the more daringly will he follow some curious bias in his own secret nature in regard to music and art. The age of sublime, heroic objectivity in these high matters seems to have been destroyed forever by the terrible cosmopolitanism of modern inventions.

Behold individualism, rampant, shameless, romantic, realistic, angelic, devilish, proud, humble, childish, senile, gay, pessimistic, mad, marches conquering across the whole terraqueous globe! With cosmopolitan industry, cosmopolitan commerce, cosmopolitan finance dominating the world, in the wake of cosmopolitan science, what can local, aesthetic traditions do against such a tide? Still they hold on, fierce, stubborn, reluctant, earth-rooted, these heroic racial traditions, each with its own mysterious, sub-conscious destiny.

But rapid transportation erases their boundaries day by day. Day by day the wireless neutralizes them, aeroplanes drop spiritual poisons upon them; the press, the movies, cheap translations, vulgarized tourist-facilities, corrode and corrupt them. Their hidden earth-bound destinies, drawing sap and pith from their immemorial local legends, are caught up, are swept away, on one tangential wind after another; and, as they waver, fluctuate, diverge, take alien colours, alien shapes, their old, revengeful, exclusive, local divinities forfeit their faithful obedience.

What then is left? Spengler in his great book suggests that the day will come when grass will grow in the streets of Berlin, London, Paris, New York, Chicago; when the inspiration of inventors will cease; when nomadic fellaheen tribesmen and rustic heathen peasantries will bow themselves in passive helplessness under warring Caesars and despotic Tamburlanes. These new rulers of men will have dispossessed of their transitory authority both capitalists and communists, both cosmopolitan financiers and cosmopolitan proletariats; and the high destiny of our race will sink back and sink down into some long epoch of history-less chaos, out of which, once more, in its orbic cycle, in its great new "Platonic year," the creative energy will emerge and enter upon some totally unforeseen, unpredicted avatar.

But confronted as we are by so much vigorous, youthful, violent activity, by so much savage science, it is hard to visualize our present industrialism, whether capitalistic as in America, or communistic as in Russia, as something old, world-weary, "civilized," and in the autumn of its days. Who can tell? Science and machinery may, for all we know, get into quite other hands than those of new predatory conquerors. There may arise some grand, irresistible, devoted free-masonry of men of good will and of wise wits all the world over. If there were enough individual men and women in every country who had acquired in place of an angular nation-spirit a well rounded earth-spirit, who can predict what might not be done?

As things are now, it seems wiser to gather together one's own personal life-forces, one's intelligence, one's instincts, one's imagination, one's will, and make something of the only democracy, the only kingdom one has control of—namely, oneself. It seems wiser to do this than to engage in the already lost cause of re-establishing on wavering and quaking foundations the old local cults.

Any real, beautiful, noble culture is founded upon

dreams. Without long, lovely moments spent in day-dreams life becomes an iron-ribbed, sterile puffing engine. And that is what our rulers and moralists of today want to make it and keep it: a moralized machine. But how cunningly must we guard our leisure to dream and with what divine unscrupulousness must we steal it! Any boy, any girl, who has spent an hour in happy dreaming has already fulfilled the purpose of creation. Out of His dreams God created the world; and shall not His creation imitate Him?

It is against this new-fangled, commercialized motto of "Service" that culture must lift up her beautiful thousand-years-old snake's head. Contemplation, not activity of any sort, is the purpose of the universe—or at any rate of that universe which all mystics and artists and lovers and sensualists and saints have substituted for the sterile mirage of objective truth. And every day-dream, begotten of pleasant leisure, by well-side or fire-side or window-sill, is a sort of "chewing of the cud" of immortal and god-like contemplation, and is worthy of a high place in the order of a good life.

Happy are those persons whose outward destiny leaves them at least one solitary, independent room to retire to at night. It is a pitiful and a wicked shame when young girls have to go on for years and years living at home. It is easy for young men to retain their individuality and live a life of culture in their parents' dwelling: it is almost impossible for a girl to do so. There is something about the parental "aura"—however kind and unselfish her parents may be—that is deadly to a girl's nature; and as cruel to her culture as the most insidious drops of poison. Her parents indeed may be fussing anxiously about her chastity while they themselves are all the while murdering her noblest culture more wickedly and effectively than could the most treacherous of lovers!

One learns indeed from the subtle stories of Dorothy Richardson what exactly it is that a mother's influence does to a daughter's life. Every woman is a creator, in the sense of creating a kind of spiritual *ménage* round her, wherever she is. She does this as instinctively as a silk-worm spins its cocoon. But by a terrible and cruel law of Nature there cannot be two *ménages* under one ceiling; so when a girl lives with her mother the deep creative instinct within her, that instinct which is her inward destiny, that instinct which is the very material of her culture, is teased, suppressed, tantalized, unsatisfied.

Even so—for "old maids" under certain conditions can be the most cultured persons of all—an unmarried woman living with her mother can, by sheer intellectual and imaginative power, liberate herself while she is still enslaved. But she must fight tooth and nail for a room entirely her own—never entered by her mother—and for the right to retire to this room as often as she pleases. It is in the direction of cultural solitariness, not in the direction of rowdy parties, that young people's liberty, of both sexes, should be gained.

True culture demands a certain degree of sensuality, of sensual ecstasy even; but this sensuality need not be *gregarious*. Culture, in fact, desires for a young person just the very opposite of what most employers, preachers and moralists desire. These desire for the youth of both sexes, when not hard at work, an exhausting round of lively, gregarious, wholesome, athletic distraction. Culture, on the contrary, desires for the youth of both sexes, long, silent, solitary hours full of mystical, poetical and metaphysical thought.

The outward destiny of all of us is of course most fatally influenced by public opinion. Except where public opinion is opposed to cruelty—and this, alas, is rare—public opinion is always wrong. Thus in the great struggle between culture and destiny, which resembles those austere contests in classic drama between the hero and fate, culture will be found constantly at war with public opinion. Public opinion is always trying to democratize culture—in other words to prostitute it and change it. Public opinion—led by affected rhetoricians—is always seeking to encourage the latest fashions and obsessions in art, the latest fashions and obsessions in thought, religion and taste. Against all this, culture stands firm; grounding itself upon the eternal elements of Nature and human nature.

The world is very old and the human race is very old. All these problems of human life are difficult and obscure. No ready-made solution can deal with them—not even the best of modern theories about education. What has been suggested in this book is a view of culture, by no means the only possible one, wherein education plays a much smaller part than does a certain secret, mental and imaginative effort of one's own, continued day by day, and year by year, until it becomes a permanent habit belonging to that psyche or inner nucleus of personality, which used to be called the soul. But theories of this kind have been offered to the world for more than ten thousand years. Again and again have they been offered; far more nobly expressed and far more subtly and clearly thought out than in this tentative and hesitant work. But the real deep thoughts of the individual human being are left very much as they were ten thousand years ago. Dubiously, fluctuatingly, they alternate —these ultimate human thoughts—between gratitude to the unknown and indignant stoical defiance. Philosophers have repeated again and again their smooth rational pronouncement that it is foolish to be afraid of the gods. But in spite of philosophy—and doubtless because of our stupid and cruel offences against one another—"conscience doth make cowards of us all." Culture, as some of us have come to understand it, does not take up any dogmatic attitude with regard to the existence, or the non-existence, of God or of the gods. It recognizes irrational hopes and fears. It takes account of many rumours caught on passing winds, of many voices heard in solitary places, of many reef-bells over strange waters. It allows for queer second-thoughts and for startling, mysterious intimations that escape all logical capture. In its patient, slow, dreamy methods of waiting upon the motions of the spirit, culture comes to recognize that there are levels in human feeling that apparently belong to dimensions of existence beyond the chemistry, beyond the electric magnetism, of the whole stellar system.

Remembering these feelings in its calmer and more rational activities culture is loath to commit itself to any final word. In the midst of the turbulence of modern life it offers a calm refuge, a patient, sceptical but not cynical standing-ground, from which we can survey the track of our journey through the years without too much self-abasement and without too many regrets.

For culture has at least this—that it reconciles us to the two destinies, both the inward and the outward, and resigns

us to that final shock of death which brings these two incomprehensible things together; brings them together on
the brink of a third thing, more incomprehensible still, the
great Perhaps of silence.

THE END